Nightmares of an East Prussian Childhood

Nightmares of an East Prussian Childhood

A Memoir of the Russian Occupation

ILSE STRITZKE
with BERNIE STRITZKE

McFarland & Company, Inc., Publishers
Jefferson, North Carolina, and London

LIBRARY OF CONGRESS CATALOGUING-IN-PUBLICATION DATA

Stritzke, Ilse, 1934–
     Nightmares of an East Prussian childhood : a memoir of the
Russian occupation / Ilse Stritzke with Bernie Stritzke.
          p.   cm.
     Includes bibliographical references and index.

     ISBN 978-0-7864-7354-0
     softcover : acid free paper ♾

     1. Stritzke, Ilse, 1934– —Childhood and youth.   2. Stritzke,
Ilse, 1934– —Family.   3. World War, 1939–1945—Personal
narratives, German.   4. Germans—Prussia, East (Poland and
Russia)—Biography.   5. Prussia, East (Poland and Russia)—
Biography.   6. World War, 1939–1945—Prussia, East (Poland
and Russia)   7. World War, 1939–1945—Refugees.   8. World
War, 1939–1945—Occupied territories.   9. Russians—Prussia,
East (Poland and Russia)—History—20th century.   I. Stritzke,
Bernie.   II. Title.
D811.5.S877 2013
947'.240842092—dc23
[B]   2013004784

BRITISH LIBRARY CATALOGUING DATA ARE AVAILABLE

On the cover: Ilse wearing the sweater Tante Friedel knitted
(picture taken in Berlin in 1947); sparrow (Ingram Publishing/
Thinkstock)

Manufactured in the United States of America

McFarland & Company, Inc., Publishers
Box 611, Jefferson, North Carolina 28640
www.mcfarlandpub.com

Table of Contents

Acknowledgments by Bernie Stritzke — vii

Preface by Bernie Stritzke — 1

Preface by Ilse Stritzke (née Glaus) — 3

Introduction by Bernie Stritzke — 5

1. A Mother's Regret — 7

2. The Evacuation — 15

3. Back to Palmnicken — 30

4. The Second Evacuation — 41

5. Omi's Sacrifice — 54

6. Desperate Times — 60

7. The Commandant's Assault — 65

8. The Statue — 74

9. Attempted Kidnap — 80

10. The White Horse — 89

11. The First Winter — 94

12. Off to Goldbach — 100

13. Then, Five Women — 110

14. Three Dead Soldiers — 115

15. A Stolen Potato — 118

16. A Sparrow Falls — 126

Table of Contents

17. An End in Sight 131

18. The Expulsion 138

19. In Germany 144

20. Mutti's Meltdown 151

21. Gerd 160

22. The Engagement 164

23. The Voyage 172

24. Chicago 178

Appendix: Maps and a Brief History of the Region 183

Chapter Notes 187

Index 191

Acknowledgments

by BERNIE STRITZKE

I would like to thank my mother, Ilse, for her patience in sitting through recorded interviews and a litany of questions. Her vivid recollection of events, attention to details, recall of dates, and captivating enthusiasm during the interviews made her experiences easy to recount. I also want to thank my wife, Debby, for her encouraging support and for putting up with countless requests to critique the manuscript. I would be remiss if I didn't thank the wonderful group of friends at AllWriters in Waukesha, Wisconsin. Their constructive criticism was a tremendous help in making this book a reality.

Preface

by BERNIE STRITZKE

This book is a memoir of my mother, Ilse Stritzke, *née* Glaus, and her childhood in East Prussia. As a child, I was captivated by her recollection of the tragic events of the 1940s. She always said that she wanted to write a book about them, but never got around to it. I started interviewing her, capturing the events in writing. Her memory of the events and dates is remarkable. This work is true to the best of my ability to write it through her eyes and memory. Ilse also kept a diary for the last year and a half of her time under Russian occupation, which helped with the timeline.

The reader should understand that conversations and minor details are impossible to chronicle exactly as they occurred seventy years ago. I have researched historical events that happened when my mother experienced them, but minor irregularities in dates may exist. In some cases, in the interest of protecting individuals' privacy, names have been changed, or new names created.

Preface

by ILSE STRITZKE (*NÉE* GLAUS)

My childhood in Palmnicken, East Prussia, went from the most wonderful time a child could hope for to a time of suffering and tragedy because of Hitler's war. Over the years, I told parts of my story to many people, including my children. I always wanted to write a book about my life, but never did. When my son, Bernard, got older, he expressed more of an interest in my background and one day surprised me with a short story based upon my memories, "A Sparrow Falls," which became one of the chapters of this book. From there he interviewed me and tape recorded my recollections. Fortunately, I kept a diary of the last eighteen months under the Russians which helped very much with recalling dates and events.

Then, he surprised me, on my birthday, with the entire memoir. I was so overwhelmed and felt sometimes like I was actually reliving my past as I read it; he so precisely expressed my feelings and emotions. I was amazed at how accurately he recorded the events of my past. Everything he put down is exactly truthful, and he described so lovingly my wonderful childhood, he even was able to express my feelings which I had then. Writing my story was the greatest gift anyone could have given to me. What moved me the most was how he put my thoughts into words, how I felt about things, how he really felt my emotions when I told him of my experiences.

Deep in my heart I had no hatred toward the Russian people; they were like you and me, most of the time involved in the war unwillingly like we were. The Russian soldiers were pushed into hatred. Their civilians were uprooted from their own dear homeland to occupy our beloved homestead. What I found so interesting was that there was no animosity between us and the Russian civilians. In fact, after the U.S.S.R. was dismantled, Palmnicken remained under Russian rule. But former Palmnicken people who were finally able to revisit befriended the Russian people who continue to live there. I myself returned when I was 70. Sadly, it was not my home anymore. So much had changed, only the beautiful Baltic Sea had stayed the same. But the Russian people welcomed us lovingly and my house was the most beautifully well-kept in the whole village. It made my heart glad that the people who lived in my beloved home cherished it as much as I did.

Through all the difficulties, I still thank God that I felt His guidance throughout my life and He led me to my dear Gerd. Together we then came to our beloved America, the most wonderful country in the world.

In conclusion, war is horrible! That is why it is important for people to understand and learn from these written experiences which gave me a better understanding of how important it is to spread love and compassion, because only that can help us to live peacefully and be happy with each other. It's a lesson I hope all can learn from this book.

Introduction

by BERNIE STRITZKE

Ilse Glaus was born in 1934, in Palmnicken, East Prussia, the same year Adolf Hitler became Führer of Germany. East Prussia was then a part of Germany, a stronghold that the Russians were never able to overpower in World War I. Palmnicken, a small coastal village on the Baltic Sea, offered a year-round playground, and was the envy of any child. Ilse's wonderful and caring family owned enough land to raise livestock and vegetables and even have an orchard. It was everything a young girl could want.

In 1944, Ilse, then ten years old, began to realize that her little sanctuary in East Prussia was about to change. The effects of the war were being felt throughout Germany. Shortages in goods, conflicting reports and demands from the Nazi government, and a sense of desperation by local and national governments all signaled the war was not going as planned.

For Ilse and her older sisters, Anneliese and Irmi, life was confusing. Their older brother Günter was fighting in the war for the Nazis and their other brother Hans, a newborn, had a rough road ahead of him. Refugees from the East were coming in droves to avoid the advancing Red army, a clear indication that the Nazi army was in retreat.

As the front lines drew nearer, Ilse's maternal grandparents (Omi and Opa) moved in with Ilse's family because their house was, by law, given up for refugees. Also, Ilse's aunt, Tante Friedel, moved from her home in heavily bombed Königsberg to live with them. Tante Friedel's husband, Ernst, was the brother of Ilse's mother (Mutti) and was fighting for the Nazi army.

The end of the war was inevitable. All the signs pointed toward a Nazi defeat, but what was Ilse's family to do? The atrocities of the advancing and occupying Russians were readily discussed by the displaced refugees. The Russians vented their anger against the Nazis onto the German civilians.

Many families fled to the West, to neutral Denmark, or to western Germany where the war wasn't going well either, but it was also well-publicized

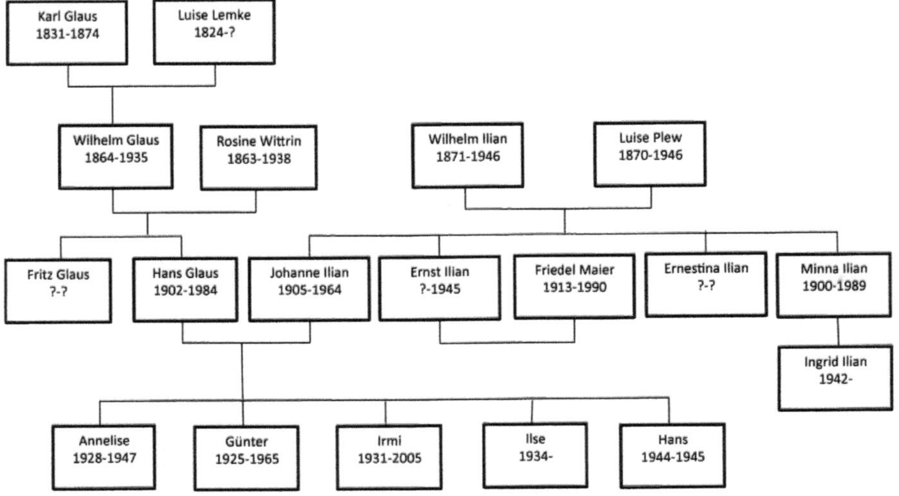

Ilse's family tree.

that the Americans and British at least treated civilians respectably. Ilse's family, like many others, was confronted with a life-changing decision: to give up their roots and flee, or to stay and take their chances with the advancing Russians.

1

A Mother's Regret

April 13, 1945, Papa came home early. He burst into our house with eyes wide open and a look of purpose.

"The Russians are a few days away from reaching our village," he said quickly. I had never seen Papa afraid of anything, but today, he had fear in his eyes. My knees weakened and my throat dried. "All of the soldiers from the base already left, except Karl and me." He looked around the room at all of us and said, "There is one airplane left, and Karl will fly out tomorrow morning to the west. There is room for five more passengers and a baby, and he told me to get my family ready quickly. So start packing whatever you can carry and we'll fly to safety first thing in the morning."

My two older sisters and I were elated about the opportunity and jumped for joy in anticipation of our first flight. I think we were more excited about an airplane ride than the escape from the advancing Russians. What wonderful news. I looked at Irmi and squealed, "A plane ride—oh my goodness!"

Irmi looked at me wide-eyed. "We're going on a plane ride. I can't wait!"

"What should we bring with us?" I asked.

Anneliese showed a little more restraint and said, "We can't bring much. There's not much room and weight is an issue on a plane—only your most important things."

"Papa," I said, to my father. "Can I bring—"

"Hans," my mother interrupted. "We can't leave. What about my parents, and Friedel, and the baby? I need a baby carriage, and—"

"Hanna!" Papa shouted at my mother. "The Russians are two days away. We can't stay here. The baby will be fine. You can hold him on your lap on the plane. We'll be going to a refugee camp in the west and they will have baby carriages."

"Go, Hanna," my grandmother encouraged. "We will watch the house. Don't worry about us. We're too old to go on a plane. Come back when it's safe."

Tante Friedel, Mutti's sister-in-law, chimed in, "Yes, Hanna, don't worry about us. Please, take your family to safety. You should go now."

My sisters and I couldn't contain ourselves and pleaded with my mother, "Mutti, let's go. We all want to go, please, please?"

Our excitement came to an abrupt halt when Mutti quickly stood up. She walked toward Papa, but didn't look him in the eyes. She looked past him toward the wall behind him and shouted, "*Nein*, we're not going!" She trembled as she spoke. She motioned her hand forward as if to accent a statement, but she couldn't speak. She retracted her hand and tried again and this time, in a fragmented voice, she shouted, "This is crazy. I'm not leaving my parents, and—and I'm not getting on a plane with our baby. Besides, it won't be so bad. How do we know? The Russians may not be so bad. They're human, too."

Papa became more enraged. "Don't be foolish. This is a war. You heard what the refugees said will happen. The Russians will rape and—Hanna, you don't want to put our family through that, do you? How can you defend your decision when every refugee corroborates the same story?" He pointed to the refugee couple who was staying with us and said, "Ask them. Are they making it up? The Russians are looking for revenge and will take out their frustrations on the German people." He took a breath and tried to sound more reasonable. "Hanna, we talked about this. We need to flee to the west. We can fly to Denmark which is neutral ground, or if we must, we can fly to western Germany. In western Germany, the British and Americans won't harm us like the Russians will. Now come on and get your things and—"

Mutti interrupted him and screamed like I never heard before. "*Nein*, I'm not going and that's final."

Papa walked up close to Mutti, the blood flushed from his face. He had fire in his eyes as he raised his hand. Papa never hit Mutti, but in his rage, I thought this might be a first. He clenched his hand into a fist and lowered it right in front of her face. I was frightened; I had never seen Papa this angry. He pointed his finger right in front of her nose. The afternoon sun cast a beam of light through the window which highlighted Papa's face. Against a dark background, the light shimmered on the spit flying from his lips as he shouted, "Hanna, this will be the biggest mistake you ever made in your life!" He put his hand down and waited a few seconds to see if she would reconsider. I anticipated her response. I think my lips even moved to say; *Okay, Hans, we'll go*, but she offered no rebuttal. Realizing she had made her decision, he abruptly turned around, went out and slammed the door so hard that the picture next to the door fell to the floor.

Tears blurred my vision. I wasn't sure what emotion overcame me. Was it anger or fear? Was Papa coming back? Did he abandon us? Why didn't he take just us children and flee to the west? Would I never see Papa again? I loved Papa more than anything in the world. I'd never known him to be wrong. I couldn't help but think that he was right and that Mutti made the biggest mistake of our lives. I suspected that I wasn't alone in this belief.

No one spoke a word. Mutti just stood, gazing out of the window for hours. I went to my room, hid under the covers, and cried. I skipped dinner, which I had never done before. I expected Mutti to call me to the dinner table, but stifled with emotion, she never said anything.

After dinner, Irmi, three years my senior, at fourteen, came and sat on the edge of my bed. I removed the covers from my head. Her head was down and her hands were held together tightly between her thighs.

"What's going to happen?" I asked.

Irmi lifted her head and stared at the wall in front of her. She shook her head. "I don't know ... I don't know, but I'm scared."

Irmi was my tough older sister and to see her afraid added to my angst. "What does Anneliese think?" I asked. Anneliese was the oldest sister at seventeen and Irmi and I always looked to her for advice.

Irmi turned and looked at me. "She says things will be okay."

"Do you think she means it?"

"*Ja*, she believes Mutti is right ... that it won't be so bad," Irmi replied.

Hitler's war was a part of my life for as long as I could remember. Yet as much as the war engulfed our lives, it had not, until now, reached our remote coastal village of Palmnicken, East Prussia, a province of Germany. The Russian soldiers were near, just as Papa predicted, based on the reports from his forbidden short-wave radio. In his bedroom hung a map of East Prussia. He meticulously monitored reports and tracked the advancing army with red-flagged pins. The pins were only approximately five kilometers to the east of Palmnicken, our home. The map showed the majority of East Prussia covered with red pins concentrated around the larger cities such as Königsberg and Tapiau. The Russian soldiers were penetrating the German front with little resistance, although Nazi radio broadcasts would have us believe we were winning the battles and pushing the Russians back. The relentless evening bombings of Königsberg, the capital city about forty kilometers away, hinted at the weakened resistance of the Nazi army. The deep thunderous booms were felt in my chest even at that distance. A constant flash of explosions lit the southeast evening skies as if sunlight loomed just beyond the horizon.

We all knew that the Allies would eventually exact their revenge on our tyrant dictator. Over the last few weeks, refugees from the east—Germans, Poles, Lithuanians, and even Russians—streamed through our village trying to escape the Russian soldiers. It was German law that if a house had more than two bedrooms, refugees must be accommodated. That's why we had a refugee couple living with us.

The day after Papa left brought long faces and a solemn atmosphere. Mutti hardly said a word. She spent most of the day sitting in a chair by the window, staring out as if Papa was going to return. I imagined the thoughts going through her mind. She was second-guessing her decision. For the life of me, I couldn't understand her stubbornness. My grandparents didn't even want to go on the plane and Hans, an infant, could easily travel on a plane.

Glaus family 1935. Top row, from left: Ilse, Mutti, Papa. Bottom row: Irmi, Günter, Anneliese.

The stories we heard from the refugees about the vengeful Russian soldiers would cause any logical person to flee.

This all didn't make any sense to me. Papa was probably not coming back, and our fate was now in the hands of the Russian soldiers. Gunfire outside was getting louder. Chaotic activity surrounded us as German soldiers and equipment scattered in every direction. It was clear that the German soldiers were in retreat. I started to shiver in fear, yet Mutti remained expressionless. *What happened to her?*

Papa never returned that day. Did he board the airplane to safety, or wait at the airport for his imminent capture by the Russians? Why didn't he come back and save us? That night, I had little sleep. Between the gunfire all night, worrying about Papa and our fate, fear outpaced my need for sleep. It wasn't like there was anything that I could do, but to not worry was impossible.

The next morning, I was startled by the sound of gunfire next to our house and heavy trucks driving down our street. There was an unfamiliar sweet diesel fuel smell in the air, unlike the smell of German trucks. The trucks also made a loud, harsh exhaust sound that captured my attention. I looked out of the window and saw several military trucks. They weren't the familiar German vehicles. They were shaped differently and were lighter in color. *The Russians are here.* I ran out of my room and saw Mutti, Tante Friedel and the refugee couple staring out of the window.

"Mutti, is it the Russians?" I asked.

She let the curtain fall back over the window and looked at me and said, "Yes, the Russians are here. Don't worry." Her words cast no comfort my way and my upper body started shaking uncontrollably. Soon, my sisters came out of their bedroom, asking the same question. Trucks drove by for about twenty minutes. Russian soldiers started running through the streets. Occasionally, we heard gunfire which sounded as if it were right on our street. As the gunfire ensued, Mutti told us all to get away from the windows.

The front door opened. In walked an unescorted Russian soldier. His left chest and right arm were decorated with medals and stripes. The soldier's grey pants had a sharply starched crease and his light grey wool jacket fit him perfectly. The bottom of the jacket came down to the beginning of his legs, covering his hips. Around his waist was a wide, deep red, almost maroon, belt. He was a very tall, good-looking man. There was no dust or dirt on him and his shoes were spotless with a mirror finish. He was obviously not in direct combat—perhaps an officer. A pistol was the only weapon he carried and it was secured in a holster attached to his red belt. The soldier's stately appearance commanded respect, yet I was not entirely afraid of him, perhaps because he came to the house by himself and entered without a weapon in his hand. He was obviously confident and showed no fear. For all he knew, we might have had German soldiers hiding in our house.

His light-green eyes searched the room, and in a soft voice and broken German, he said, "Don't be afraid, no one will harm you." He paused as if searching for the correct German words. He looked directly at my grandfather and demanded, "Are there any German soldiers here?"

Immediately, my Opa responded, "No, no soldiers." His facial expression and quick response were convincing enough to the Russian. He slowly walked toward us. We all backed away, bumping into each other as we provided him wide berth. I was relieved to discover he was simply heading for the bedroom behind us. It was my parents' bedroom. The entrance to the room was a right-turn, so after he entered, I couldn't see what he was doing. I heard the footsteps of his hard-soled shoes on the wooden floor; about six steps, a shuffle, then silence. Fifteen seconds later I heard a thump on the wall and the sound of paper shredding.

My baby brother was sleeping in his crib in my parents' room. The long silence, not knowing what the stranger was doing in the room alone with the baby, was too much for Mutti to bear. She walked into the room. Now we were all scared. Anneliese and I took a step in the direction of the room to get a view of the soldier. As Mutti entered, she looked at him holding a ripped map in one hand, and the other hand resting on the crib railing. He was leaning over the crib, looking at my baby brother admiringly. He looked up at Mutti and said, "I have a baby at home." Mutti forced a smile. He then walked past her into the kitchen. He slammed Papa's map onto the table and quickly pieced the ripped sections together and exclaimed in a stern voice, "This map is all wrong." He moved what colored pins were left on the map further west into our village. "This is where we are!"

The Russian then marched into another bedroom. I heard some shuffling noises and he quickly returned with Uncle Ernst's full-length leather coat draped over his left arm. Uncle Ernst was Mutti's brother—Tante Friedel's husband—who was away fighting as a German soldier in the war. Without giving anyone so much as a glance, the Russian briskly walked out the door with coat in hand.

We stood and looked at each other, not knowing what to say. Then Mutti spoke, "See, they're not so bad. We will all be okay." I wanted desperately to believe her. We even laughed a little about him taking the leather coat.

Then five minutes later, two more Russian soldiers entered our house. Each soldier was carrying a machine gun held with both hands waist-high. They were young, clean cut and very handsome men. Their shoes were dusty; their uniforms worn and plain, lacking the ornaments of the first Russian.

I froze. Immediately, I sensed these men were up to no good. *Were they going to kill us, or just take everything we had?* I was flushed with fear. I felt tingling in my hands and arms as the blood rushed from my extremities. They stood just inside the door and looked at all of us. One leaned over to the other and said something in Russian while pointing in our direction with a head movement. The other snickered and responded with a sinister smile on his face, and pointed out my oldest sister with his gun. They both nodded with a smile, and then walked over to us. One stood in front of Tante Friedel, and the other in front of Anneliese.

The soldier in front of Anneliese pointed his gun at her and said, "Frau," in a strong accent as if it were the only German word he knew, and then motioned with his gun and his head for her to go upstairs.

Immediately, my Opa approached the soldier and screamed, "No, please!" The soldier quickly responded aggressively by pointing the gun at him and backing him to the wall. The other Russian stepped back and waved his gun back and forth at the rest of us. Fear forced my heart to race and I couldn't breathe. My vision became cloudy at the edges. I felt faint until I finally took a breath. Opa raised his hands and kept yelling, "No—no." There was nothing he could do. He crumbled to the floor still saying, "No." At this point, Mutti was hysterical, screaming words no one could understand.

The soldiers came back to my aunt and sister and pointed the guns at them and then to the stairway. The women were both crying and had a look of terror on their faces. They didn't move. The soldier in front of Tante Friedel placed the tip of his gun in her side and pushed her in the direction of the stairs. The other soldier did the same to Anneliese. Tante Friedel and Anneliese quickly went up the stairs, sobbing profusely, with the soldiers close behind speaking Russian to each other.

My eyes welled with tears. I wasn't even sure why I was crying, but being led away at gun point could only result in something bad. I knew that the soldiers were going to do terrible things to my aunt and sister. I wasn't exactly sure what, but I only wished that they weren't going to kill them. Judging from the adults' hysteria, they knew exactly what the soldiers had in mind, but they didn't share it with me.

Sounds of struggle emanated from the second floor: muffled screams, slapping or hitting, yelling by the Russians, and furniture shuffling. I looked around and all of the adults were wailing and had their heads in their hands.

Ten to fifteen minutes later, I heard the sound of footsteps on the stairway. It was Tante Friedel. I couldn't really see her face because she was looking down, but I saw enough to know that she was crying. When she got down the stairs, she walked into the kitchen. She reached into the flour jar and sprinkled flour in her hair and grabbed a large handkerchief and draped it over her head, leaving the now-white hair exposed at her forehead. She tied two ends of the handkerchief under her chin and sat down. I was confused by the flour and handkerchief. I must admit, she looked like an old lady; it was an excellent disguise, if that's what she had in mind. *Why would she want to look like an old lady?* I thought. My grandmother sat down beside her and put her hand on Tante Friedel's arm. Tante Friedel didn't move. I was at least comforted to know that she was still alive and didn't seem to be harmed.

Next down the stairs was Anneliese. I hardly recognized her. She slowly shuffled one foot to the end of the step and basically flopped to the next step, then followed with the other foot. Her shoulders were slouched forward and her arms dangled loosely in front of her. Her head was down and her hair a mess. Most of all, her pasty-white, almost ghostlike complexion revealed a look of horror. I had never seen anyone look so frightened and distraught. It was as if she witnessed the devil himself. I think she was too afraid to cry. It wasn't until Mutti went to comfort her that she cried uncontrollably. Mutti reached for her at the bottom of the stairs and hugged her to her chest. She held the back of her head, pressing the side of her face under her chin. Anneliese continued crying, catching deep breaths between whimpers. Mutti walked her to the kitchen table and sat her down, still holding her tightly.

I started to puzzle the pieces together and it became clear to me what happened. No one had ever explained to me what rape meant, but it was mentioned by just about every refugee who came through our village. I didn't know much about sex, I was only eleven years old, and my parents never explained anything about it to me, but I understood the difference between boys and girls. I envisioned how sex worked, but never in my wildest dreams did I think it could also be an act of evil brutality performed by a man to degrade and humiliate a woman.

Down the stairs came the two soldiers, laughing and carrying on in Russian, paying no attention to any of us, as if we didn't exist. In fact, neither of them looked at any of us as they walked across the room and out the door.

They had their way with Anneliese and Tante Friedel, and for them, it was over and on to the next. This is what we had to look forward to. We were victims of the Russian army's revenge.

The war was not over, but for us, it sure seemed like it was. No one came to our rescue; no one tried to protect us. The enemy was in our home and German soldiers were nowhere to be found. In one day, our lives turned upside-down. Germany was run by a ruthless dictator, and now it was being overrun by his equal. The gates of Hell were open for business and we were its welcomed guests.

I had a sick feeling in my stomach and felt a thickness in my throat. For the first time in my life, my family was completely defenseless. I felt awful for Anneliese. There was nothing anyone could say that would make this go away. In a world of lawlessness, the ones with the guns ruled. The Russians could do to us as they pleased and Papa wasn't there to protect us. Still, perhaps it was good that he wasn't with us. He probably would have been killed, attempting to stop the soldiers.

I looked at Mutti, sitting at the table, her arms around Anneliese, a look of utter desolation on their faces. And in the back of my mind, I could still hear Papa saying, "Hanna, this will be the biggest mistake you ever made in your life!"

2

The Evacuation

We sat in the kitchen in disbelief. This couldn't really be happening. How long would this go on? Was I too young to be raped? What will happen to us? What will the Russians do with us? We sat helpless; defeated and in shock and no one uttered a word. I wanted to understand what happened, but couldn't make myself ask.

Within a half-hour of the soldiers' departure, two more Russians entered our house. I anticipated that their intentions were similar to the last two. I felt my heartbeat in my throat. However, it was quickly apparent their only motive was to evict us from our home. The two soldiers approached us with machine guns drawn and pointed at us. In broken German, they shouted, "*Raus, raus*, we need this house."

We only had minutes to gather whatever we could and were forced out of the house. Fortunately, Mutti had packed rucksacks and small bags for all of us in anticipation of this day. This brought another puzzling question to mind: why did she pack ahead of time? She must have known that we were going to be forced out of our house. If we were going to be evacuated, why didn't she listen to Papa? At least we could have evacuated to safety.

She stuffed the baby carriage full with barely enough room for the baby. She hurriedly grabbed things and handed them to us and hung the rucksacks on us. Meanwhile, all the other adults were frantically gathering together our food, blankets and a few family heirlooms we could easily carry. Every minute or so, the soldiers came back in with guns drawn, shouting at us to get out. After about the fourth time back, it was clear their patience had run out. They pushed the barrels of their guns in our sides and forced us out of our house. Our street was a line of civilians as far as I could see, all carrying their possessions in anything that had a handle, or in bundles strapped on their backs. My grandfather fortunately had a bicycle and we hung as much as we could onto it. We were forced into the line by the Russian soldiers and were headed north.

Before we made the first bend in the road, I looked back at our beautiful home, the house that Papa poured his heart into. I forced myself to remember as much as I could about the way it looked, before it was out of eyesight. I thought to myself, *I may never see my house again.* I loved that house with its beautiful garden where we played and had so much joy, and now we were forced to leave. Soldiers were already walking in the front door. It was difficult to see someone else take ownership where I had always lived. This was our home, what right did they have to take it away from us?

"Papa, where are they taking us?" Mutti said.

My Opa hesitated, "I don't know ... we're heading north." He looked around. "My guess, the Russians just took over our village, along with villages along their path and they're evacuating all of the civilians... I bet they will take us to a camp until the war is over."

"A camp," a refugee lady said. "What kind of a camp? Are they going to put us in a forced labor camp?"

"Come on," Opa pleaded. "Let's not jump to conclusions."

"Maybe Siberia," Tante Friedel said. "Or, what if they just want to take us somewhere to kill us?"

"Friedel," Opa argued. "If they wanted to kill us, don't you think they would have done that already? Look," he motioned his arms in the direction of the long line of civilians. "Would they waste their time marching us along a road, if they wanted to kill us?"

I sensed Mutti's nervousness from her expressions. She frantically looked in every direction, as if to find an escape. "We need to get out of here," she said. "In between guards, can we run?"

"Hanna, are you crazy," my grandmother cautioned. "You have a baby carriage. Are you going to run through the woods with a baby carriage ... and then what ... run to where? We're staying right in line. It's our only option."

"Ja," Opa added. "Do you hear those gunshots? Those could be for people who step out of line and try to run."

This conversation went on for a long time, with no logical conclusion. The only thing we knew is that we were headed somewhere against our will. I was so confused and scared. Nothing seemed certain. Adults, who always had answers, in this were clueless.

Some Russian soldiers walked with us while others stood every few hundred meters to make sure that we kept moving and stayed in line. It was an orderly march, three to four people wide, no pushing or shoving, except for the occasional butt end of a gun, from one of the soldiers. I saw a few civilians run out of line and vanish into a patch of woods. Mutti whispered, "See they are fleeing... I wonder where they will go." They escaped detection by the Russian soldiers. Maybe Mutti was right and we should have run.

Opa was next to me with both hands on the bicycle, steering it as he walked alongside of it. He had his head down. I had never seen him like this before. He was always smiling, always happy, and never let things worry him. He was the only man with us in our family and I think he felt ashamed—

almost useless—because he could not protect us from the Russians. I felt bad for him because there really was nothing that he could do. I grabbed his belt loop and tried to keep step with him.

As we walked, the horrible reality of war was apparent. We saw homes burning, their flames reflecting off the shattered windshields of demolished vehicles that were abandoned in the roadway. In every direction lay the injured, the dying and the dead. Farmers tried to bring along livestock; cattle, horses and chickens. What were they thinking? How would they take care of them?

It was apparent that this trail of displaced civilians started several villages ago and who knows how long they were walking. Many animals were dead on the road; either killed from stray gunshot, or starved to death. The stench of rotten flesh burned my nostrils and made me sick to my stomach.

We came across a German soldier, lying in a ditch with his head resting on a large rock. He was bleeding from his chest. Struggling to speak, he said, "*Wasser.*" The civilians in line in front of us were too afraid to stop and help him. But Mutti and the refugee lady walked up to him. The rest of our group stepped out of line and waited. I was closest and could hear the conversation.

"He is barely alive," the refugee lady said. His face was like marble. Life had left his eyes—he was staring at nothing. I don't think he could see us. Mutti reached for her canteen and gave him some water.

"He must have been caught up in gunfire last night," said Mutti.

A Russian soldier saw us giving aid to the soldier and approached us.

"*Weiter, weiter,*" he said. Mutti ignored him. I looked at the Russian soldier and thought that he was going to shoot us. Instead, surprisingly, he just stood by us and watched the civilians walking by. The German soldier whispered something, but we couldn't hear what he said. The refugee lady leaned over to him. The soldier's lips moved slowly as he struggled to speak. She quickly searched through her bags to find something to write with, and started writing.

"*Weiter, weiter!*" the soldier shouted as he pushed the tip of his gun into the refugee's side. We quickly got up and ran to the line. As I ran, I looked back for one last glimpse. The soldier's eyes were closed. He had a look of peace on his face. As we walked, the picture of the wounded soldier haunted me. For months, I heard the gunshots and explosions, but until then, I had not witnessed anyone dying; I had never seen firsthand the gruesome nature of war. I said a silent prayer for the soldier and asked God to not let him suffer.

"He said, 'Please contact Mutti,'" the refugee lady whispered. "I wrote down his name and promised to contact her."

We continued north for a few hours until we were at the coast, and then started heading east. By the late afternoon, we arrived at Gross Kuhren, a small town on the northern edge of East Prussia, on the coast of the Baltic Sea. We had walked about fifteen kilometers since leaving Palmnicken. We hadn't seen a Russian soldier for roughly the last half-hour.

"It's getting dark," Mutti said. "What are we going to do for the night? We just passed a large hotel. Should we try to sleep in there?"

"*Nein,*" Opa barked. "Russian soldiers could be in there—way too dangerous."

"But we haven't seen any in a while," Mutti replied.

"Doesn't matter, let's keep going." Just down the road was a large field. Many civilians were already laying blankets down on the ground and preparing to spend the night there. Fortunately, it was an unseasonably warm spring day, so we decided to prepare a spot in the field as well. As much as I wished that I was back at home safe in my bed, I childishly thought it would be an adventure to camp outside. One refugee family that was walking with us decided to continue walking to see if they could make it to their home in Lithuania.

There was no peace for us that night. Russian soldiers with lanterns scanned the field in search of victims. Women were screaming in the darkness. It was horrible, the sound of evil that engulfed us. We had no escape. They were like wolves preying on fenced-in sheep. My grandfather placed Irmi and I under his knees beneath a blanket to shield us from their sight. There we stayed all night, shivering in fear. Not only did the Russian soldiers do terrible things to the women, they also stole what few possessions we civilians had. I heard the voices of soldiers demanding, "*Uhren … Ringe.*" It was apparent that most of the soldiers were peasants who coveted our watches and rings. We had more than they did.

God protected us that night. None of the women in our group were harmed, at least as far as I could tell from under the covers. The next morning brought another warm day. Everyone packed their belongings, yet there were no Russian soldiers directing our whereabouts. It was clear that the Russians didn't know what to do with us either. Apparently, they had no directive from their commanders. As a result, they let us go where we wanted. We heard many people say that they were heading back to Palmnicken, while others said they would continue walking toward Lithuania.

"Hey, what about that large hotel?" said Tante Friedel, "We can at least go investigate."

Opa clenched his lips and formed a grimace on one side of his mouth. "Let's go see, but be extra cautious."

"If it's safe, we can stay there for a few nights and then head back to Palmnicken once things settle down," Mutti said. "We can't stay out in the field again. What if it rains, or gets colder?"

We found it odd that, all of a sudden, there were few soldiers around and we were left to our own devices. Soon it became clear why the soldiers had left. Military police arrived in special army vehicles to instill order. We saw them chase a few soldiers away from the civilians. Although we didn't trust the military police completely because they, too, were Russian, at least we saw some evidence that they reprimanded the soldiers for abusing us.

We arrived at the hotel and I was dazzled by the opulence, ornate crystal lighting, polished wood paneling and luxurious woven carpeting over inlaid wood floors. To our astonishment, there were only a handful of civilians inside. Behind the entrance was a large room—perhaps a banquet hall—where people had laid out sleeping areas in rows. Mutti asked someone why they didn't go upstairs to a hotel room. She was told that Russians might be staying upstairs. We quickly got settled in and laid out eight sleeping spots of our own. In one row were Opa, my grandmother "Omi," Tante Friedel, then Anneliese. In the adjacent row were two refugees traveling with us, Mutti, and lastly one of our neighbors from Palmnicken. Even though there was a presence of military police, my grandparents decided not to take a chance, so they made it look as if there were only eight people.

"Ilse and Irmi," Opa said as he laid out the blankets. "You two will hide under my legs again." He leaned over to us. "We can't take any chances and have you be seen, all right?" He made it sound more like a game so we wouldn't be afraid.

After setting up our sleeping arrangements, it was still afternoon, so we ate some dried meat and drank some water from our canteens. My grandfather said, "At least the military police seem to be getting things in order. Maybe this will all be over soon. Tonight, we will sleep in peace."

"I wonder if they will let us go back to Palmnicken," said Tante Friedel. "I have to believe that the war will be over soon and we will be allowed to go back home. What good is it to keep moving us around?"

Opa responded, "I wish they would at least tell us what they intend to do with us. Come to think of it, I don't think they know what to do with us."

Mutti chimed in uncharacteristically and said, "These Russians are too stupid to know what to do with us. They don't seem to know what they're doing."

Regardless, they controlled us now. Stupid or not, they could do with us as they wished.

Darkness arrived and we all hoped that tonight we would be left alone. But after a few hours of darkness, we suddenly noticed a few lanterns casting light among the civilians, and screaming quickly ensued.

"The soldiers are back!" Tante Friedel said as she quickly hid under the blankets.

"Oh no," Opa said. "Irmi—Ilse, under the covers—quickly!"

For the moment, the only sound I heard was the beating of my heart, then screaming again.

Irmi sternly whispered to me, "Ilse, stop shaking, the Russians will know that we're here." I tried, but couldn't stop. My grandfather lifted his leg a little higher to keep the covers from shaking.

Nearby, I could hear two Russians talking and saw the beam of light through our blankets. I was terrified and Irmi now was shaking as badly as I was. I heard a footstep between us and the row where Mutti and Tante Friedel lay. One soldier snickered something in Russian, then I heard something fall to the floor. Suddenly, I heard screaming that was ear-piercing. In between the screams, I heard "Stop," and "No," and it went on incessantly. By her voice, I could tell it was the refugee lady.

Angered by the screaming, the soldier shouted something and I heard a slap, but the screaming kept on. I don't know what provoked me, but I stuck my head out from under the covers to see what was happening. Across from me were two soldiers, one lying on top of the refugee lady and the other on top of Mutti. Their pants were pulled down to their ankles and they were thrusting themselves onto the refugee lady and Mutti. Mutti still had my baby brother in her arms.

Mutti didn't make a sound. I think she didn't want Irmi and me to know what was happening. As tears rolled down my cheeks, I couldn't help but softly cry out, "Mutti."

Omi realized that I poked my head out. She quickly covered my mouth with her hand and whispered, "*Shh*."

Mutti turned her head toward me and quietly said, "Yes, Ilsechen."[1] She then looked at my grandmother who quickly tucked me under the covers. This was painful for me to see, but now I understood what had happened to Anneliese and Tante Friedel, and why the women were screaming. The soldiers left, but the sobbing remained. A while later, the refugee lady started screaming again. I didn't dare stick my head out this time.

I don't think Irmi saw what happened and she didn't ask. After a few hours, it was silent. I tried to sleep, but I couldn't get the picture out of my mind. I prayed for God's protection, but I couldn't understand why he would let something like this happen.

In my sleepless state, my mind reached back to a time before the Russians invaded our home. *My body chilled as I recalled one of the refugee families that passed through in January. Refugees came and went, but this particular family's warning struck a chord with me. It was a single woman with her parents and three small children. They were from an area near Tilsit.*

She started explaining what happened to them. I recalled her voice as if she were right in front of me. In an excited tone, she warned us to escape to the west. "We didn't pay attention to the warnings from the refugees." She looked right at Mutti, "Like we are now warning you. We stayed and waited thinking it will not be so bad. One day four Russian soldiers appeared in our house. At gun-point, they..." She started to break down. She covered her mouth with the back of her hand. Sobbing, she continued, "they gang-raped Mutti and I right in front of our family." It was difficult for her to tell this story, and it was difficult to listen. She was reluctant because of us children, but she obviously wanted to warn us so we didn't fall prey to the same horror. She continued: "They took my husband to a work camp; who knows, perhaps in Siberia." I heard this word rape from other refugees and other adults. No one ever cared to tell me what it meant, although I could sense the context of discussion concerning rape was always met with fear and repulsion.

Our family often discussed the prospects of going to the west for safety. I'll admit, I wasn't excited about leaving my little sanctuary, but given the circumstances, staying here was fruitless. "Hanna," Papa pleaded, "Be reasonable. This war will soon be over and Germany will lose. The writing is on the wall. The question is: do you want to be captured by the Americans and British ... or the Russians?" His voice raised and had a sarcastic tone as he emphasized the latter. "The Americans and British are a civilized folk. They have no axe to grind with us; they want Hitler. The Russians, well you hear every day what they do to civilians. Is that what you want?"

"I have to take care of my parents. Your parents are no longer here, so it's easy for you to say," was the familiar response from Mutti. "And I have a baby to take care of. How can I travel with an infant?" I never heard my parents argue about anything until this topic erupted, and always ended without resolution.

Morning came, and as I awoke, the adults were gathering our belongings. Irmi and I got up to help. I kept looking at Mutti, but didn't know what to say. She sensed my confusion and came to me and hugged me. She then said, "It's all right, Ilsechen. I'm all right and all of this will be over soon." I was comforted by her words.

Opa said to some of the other older men, "It is not safe here. Let's take a look upstairs and see if we can stay in one of the hotel rooms. Maybe there are no Russians up there. At least then we can lock the doors."

Three men, along with my grandfather, cautiously went upstairs. In a few minutes, they came back down and excitedly told us all to go upstairs, there were no Russians there. We quickly gathered our belongings. The stairway was brightened by sunlight shining through a tiny window on the landing, the warm light bringing out the hues of an elegant carpet runner I lightly grazed my hand along the railing as we walked up the stairs. The railing was very smooth and cool, and my hand left a path in the dust that covered it as we walked up to the second floor.

The upper floor was less ornate. The walls were white. Tall wooden baseboards flanked the wide wooden floor planks that were laid in the direction of the long hall. These planks creaked as we walked, and there was no carpet in the hall, so every noise seemed to resonate. There were no windows in the hall, and the end of the hall was dark. Some people were already getting situated in the first rooms, so we took the third room from the stairway. Rooms were only situated on the right-hand side.

Others followed and soon all of the rooms were filled. Our room was long and narrow, just wide enough to lay two rows toe-to-toe with about twenty people. There were no beds in any of the rooms. There was only one piece of furniture in our room, a large dresser. The men moved the dresser near the door, so that at night, it could be used to barricade the opening.

It was about noon, and Russian soldiers came into the hotel and told us we all had to get out. Now that we finally felt safe, were they moving us somewhere else? The soldiers never explained anything to us. They just pointed their guns at us and said, "*Raus.*" This time, they had a different mood about them. They weren't quite as demanding. Believing that we were being moved again, we started gathering our things.

"*Nein*," one of the soldiers said. "*Raus*," and he pointed his gun at us. Of course we vacated. We moved reluctantly, always looking back, expecting them to steal our things, but the soldiers simply followed us. We arrived outside and there were already many people standing in the courtyard of the hotel, surrounded by soldiers. We stood outside for a few hours, wondering what they were going to do to us. Periodically, small groups of civilians led by Russian soldiers arrived from other areas in the town.

Eventually, a few personnel carrier trucks arrived. We heard them coming from a long distance. The Russian trucks were very loud. The beds of the trucks were tarp-covered with seats along either side of the bed. One of the officers announced, "Men must go to work, all men into the trucks." There really were not too many men. Most were too old, or too young to serve in the German army. Opa started walking toward the trucks.

Suddenly, Mutti grabbed his arm and said, "You are not going. We need you here."

"But they told me I have to go in the truck."

"No, you stay here." Mutti pushed him behind her and Tante Friedel came and stood next to her. Fortunately, Opa was very short. The soldiers didn't notice him. They filled the trucks with men and didn't really look around to see if all of the men were loaded.

The trucks left in a cloud of black smoke. An officer said, "Food," and he pointed to a building down the road. The soldiers all walked away, most in the direction of the building that he pointed out.

There we stood, not knowing exactly what had just happened. I looked around and Opa was the only man left, other than a few very young boys.

"We were lucky they didn't see you," Mutti said. "Think about it, they don't want any men here—they're a threat ... I'm sure they're on their way to some labor camp ... probably in Russia."

Our group decided to go upstairs and make sure the soldiers didn't steal anything. Some civilians headed to the building that the officer said had food. We got back to our room and, to our surprise, nothing was taken. Opa said, "Well, that's good that nothing was stolen. Why don't you all go get some food and I'll wait here and watch our things." I think Opa was afraid to go because he thought they would capture him and send him to a work camp.

The rest of us walked to the house that was supposed to have food. A military police truck was parked in front, so we felt a little safer. We stood at the door and heard soldiers inside, talking and carrying on. I watched Mutti's hand hesitantly reach for the door. She grabbed the door handle and turned it quietly. She stopped and turned her head toward Tante Friedel, who stood motionless and expressionless, offering Mutti no signal to stop or go. She pushed the door open slowly as she leaned her head in the door opening. She continued and walked through the doorway. We hesitantly followed.

In this makeshift cookhouse were several wood burning stoves. The stove chimneys were crudely vented through the roof. I could see daylight between the chimneys and the ceiling.

Atop two stoves were large pots, perhaps forty liters each. There were tables and chairs set up in what would have been the living room. Russian soldiers sat at the tables, eating something. Some soldiers stood with a bowl in one hand and a spoon in the other. Few soldiers made eye contact with us. For the most part, they didn't care that we were there. Some civilians were already in the house, sitting and eating at one of the tables unoccupied by soldiers.

A short young man stood behind the stoves. He wore a uniform, but didn't look like a fighter. He wore smudgy glasses with tarnished frames that hung crookedly on his nose, topping a big smile with large gaps between his teeth. He noticed us walking in and waved us toward him.

"Kasha," he said as he dropped his ladle into the mix to give it a stir. As we approached, he pointed to a stacked pile of steel bowls. We all waited in line to be served by the friendly young man. A soldier came to get a second helping. The young man serving us immediately dropped the ladle, and went to the other kettle and filled the soldier's bowl. As the soldier passed, I peeked in his bowl at a thick pasty stew. My mouth watered.

Our portions were watered down, compared to the soldiers.' Instead of a hearty stew, ours was more of a soup.

"Mmm," said Anneliese. "This is good."

"*Ja*, I think it's barley," Omi surmised. "With some oil to add flavor."

We were so hungry, it seemed a feast. The soldiers that were eating when we arrived quickly left, so we sat at the tables to eat. There wasn't enough room for all of us to sit, so some of us ate standing up, while others went outside.

One of the civilians went back for a second helping as some soldiers had. Our server barked, "*Nein*," as he held up his hand with his index finger extended, signifying just one serving. We quickly realized our standing in the food chain.

We finished our kasha and left. It was very awkward. Here, our supposed enemy was serving us food. We certainly appreciated it, but were glad to leave.

"Are they going to feed us every day?" I asked Mutti as we walked back to the hotel.

"I think they will, how else will we survive? They have to feed us."

I wasn't impressed with the confidence in her tone. I sensed it was more wishful thinking than factual. Questions ran through my head. Why should

Irmi and Ilse at Palmnicken house 1936 (school is seen in the background).

they feed us? They took over our country. We meant nothing to them. We were only a problem to them. I'm sure I wasn't alone in thinking that the free meals may not last.

We arrived at the hotel. My grandfather was sitting on the front porch with his feet on the first step and his elbows leaning on his lap. He was smoking his pipe, probably his last bit of tobacco.

Irmi couldn't contain herself and said, "Opa, they fed us soup—kasha, they called it, and it was good. You should come with us tomorrow." He smiled as she sat on his lap.

He took the pipe out of his mouth and said, "Good, I'm glad you liked it." He looked at Mutti and said, "Was it safe? Should I go?"

Mutti tilted her head and replied confidently, "Yes, of course you should come with us. You are safe going there. They won't bother you."

He turned toward Irmi, and said, "Okay, tomorrow, I will go with you. Now let's go upstairs and get things ready for tonight."

We arrived at our room.

Omi pointed to a bucket full of water. "Is there running water in the hotel?"

"No, Gross Kuhren has electricity—at least to the hotel, but it's not working, so no running water. I found a hand pump in town and filled this bucket. We can get drinking water tomorrow and fill our canteens. Oh, there's a toilet at the end of the hall. It doesn't flush, but we should use it anyway." He pointed to the bucket. "If anyone needs water for drinking take it now, because it will be used for washing up."

I walked around our little room and looked out the window. It was a dormer, so I could see the main roofline right under the window and there lie Opa's bike on the roof tied with strings to the window.

"Opa," I said. "What is your bike doing on the roof?" Anneliese and Irmi quickly pushed their way to the window.

Opa laughed, "I hung it out there to get it out of our way. And I can't keep it where the Russians will steal it. There on the roof, they won't see it and won't be able to get to it."

My Opa, what a smart man. How did he think of that?

It took us a while to get cleaned up and situated. My grandfather said to one of the young boys, "Tonight, after everyone is in and done using the toilet, we close and lock the door and move this dresser in front of the doorway so that the Russian soldiers cannot come in." The young boy nodded his head in a formal acknowledgement. He appeared to be honored that Opa asked him. Manhood was to come early for this young boy, whether he liked it or not.

As we waited for nightfall, conversations broke out regarding our condition. Omi said, "This war will be over shortly, if it's not already. God punished us for what Hitler did. He was a bad man and we are all suffering because of it."

"I just don't understand why they need to be so wicked and cruel," one woman said that was in our room. "What have we done to them?"

"What have we done?" another in their group responded. "We, as in us here ... nothing, but we, as in Germany, that's another story. Our friend Franz, he understands Russian and heard the soldiers shouting, 'take that for killing our people, you Nazi,' as they beat a German man." He was really agitated. I never heard a German speaking like this. "That Third Bellorussian Front, the first wave of the invasion, they were told to take out their revenge on the Germans; payback for Hitler's aggression on the Russians." It was a sobering diatribe.

Tante Friedel later commented, "Well, I think the war is already over, they are just not telling us. I just want it to be over ... I hope Ernst is all right." She dipped her head down, obviously thinking the worst.

"The sooner this war is over, the better his chances," responded Omi. "With any luck, things will get back to normal once Hitler surrenders. Then perhaps we can go back home." The conversations went on until nightfall, with all of us hoping an end would soon come to the suffering.

Opa stood up and asked if anyone needed to use the toilet before bedtime. No one responded. He looked at the young boy and said, "Let's move this dresser." The boy eagerly got up and helped my grandfather barricade the door. We finally felt safe and so retired for the night.

Our room soon succumbed to darkness. The moon cast a dim shadow across several mounds of huddled blankets and bodies, making the floor of our room look frighteningly like burial plots in a cemetery. A few hours later, we were awakened by a ruckus in the hall. A stampede of footsteps rushed from room to room as we heard Russians shouting and pounding doors. My grandfather got up and leaned against the dresser in case they tried to break into our room. The doorknob to our room clicked back and forth, then again at a faster pace. Angry Russian conversation erupted out in the hall. Outside one of the nearby rooms, shouting intensified. The Russians were clearly angry. The shouting and pounding on a door down the hall continued and then gunfire erupted. I heard three shots followed by hysterical screaming and crying inside the room.

The pounding on the door increased. I thought the next sound would be the door hitting the floor. Louder screaming ensued. Fear paralyzed me. The screaming rang in my ears and drowned my thoughts. I couldn't tell if the soldiers were able to get into the room. Within a few minutes, I heard vehicles arrive at the hotel. Then more footsteps upstairs and more angered Russians shouting.

Opa inched the dresser back enough to open the door a crack to peek into the hall.

"Papa," Mutti whispered a shout. "What are you doing? Close the door. You'll get us all killed." Opa ignored her. Soon, we heard a large object crashing down the stairs and more shouting in Russian. We all wanted to know what happened.

Opa whispered, "The Russian soldiers are drunk and wanted to get to the women in one of the rooms. Military police came and literally threw a soldier down the stairs and hauled him away. Thank God. It's now over and the police are here. We should be safe."

There was still a commotion down the hall, but it appeared things had calmed down. I closed my eyes as I lay down to sleep, still feeling my heart pounding in my chest. I was amazed that the police treated the soldier with such force. I was impressed. Was this a turning point? I was glad the soldier was taken away. I prayed that the police would now bring order.

The next morning, we went to the room where all of the disorder occurred. My grandparents, Tante Friedel, and a few other civilians went inside. It was clear that tragedy had occurred last night. People in the room were still crying and talking hysterically. I glanced into the room and saw a woman sitting on the floor, cradling a lifeless boy. I overheard them talking and understood that the boy was shot through the door by the Russian soldier whom the police kicked down the stairs.

Mutti, standing in the hall, looked at him in disbelief with her hands over her mouth. "They killed a young boy! Oh, my God!"

My heart sank in my chest. The mother was rocking back and forth, sobbing and clinging onto her son, consumed with grief. People tried to console her, but to no avail. That morning, everyone who stayed in the hotel came together to help bury the boy—he was only ten years old. We had no shovels, but the Russian soldiers lent us a few. Omi had her Bible at the grave site and recited some Psalms in the modest funeral ceremony.

We continued to stay at the hotel because we really didn't know where else to go. Bombings and gunfire continued in the distance, so we knew the war was still ongoing. As the bombings became more distant each day, we knew the Russians were penetrating further into Germany.

There wasn't much to do during the day. We had no house to clean, no chores, none of the adults worked; so most of the time, we sat around idly. Irmi was certainly short of patience and needed to exercise her creativity so she decided to go exploring. Naturally, wherever Irmi went, I could be found right behind her. Mutti knew that Irmi was full of mischief, but she, for the most part, trusted her to be safe.

Irmi announced that she was going outside to play. I quickly got up to follow her. Mutti said, "Stay clear of any Russian soldiers. Don't go anywhere near them ... and don't you dare stray too far away!" Irmi gave her one of those—what, do you think I'm stupid—looks as she walked out the door. I didn't say anything and just followed her. "And you especially," Mutti added. I wasn't quite as bold as Irmi, although I wanted to be.

I just looked up at Mutti and said, "Yes, Mutti." As I closed the door, Irmi was already down the hall and marching down the stairs. I ran down the hall, saying, "Irmi, wait for me." I don't know why I always said that, because she never acknowledged me, and never waited. I think it was to let her know that I was there. But that was Irmi; independent minded and mission oriented. I finally caught up to her outside. "What are we going to do?" I said as if we were a team.

"I want to look for stuff in the village." She would always say I after I addressed our team as we. She always wanted to make sure that she was the leader.

"The village," I questioned. "We can't go that far. Mutti said—,"

"*Ach*," Irmi grunted. "We'll be fine. Just keep your eyes open for soldiers or any trucks."

"I don't know," I said hesitantly. "This isn't safe. What if the Russians catch us?"

Irmi looked at me like I had three eyes. She kept walking, "They're not going to catch us. We're too smart."

As confident as Irmi was, I was still very nervous. If the Russians didn't kill us, Mutti would, if she found out what we were doing.

Once we arrived at the village, she picked a road that looked deserted. As we walked down the street, Irmi constantly scanned the terrain, looking for warning signs. The houses we approached were eerily silent and appeared vacant. We did hear machinery a few blocks away, so we knew soldiers were still in the village. "Okay, this street looks safe." Irmi headed toward the first house. Mutti would have our hides if she knew we were going into houses in the village. The front door was half-open. Irmi peeked her head through and quietly walked in; I was right behind her. Our little covert mission was underway. This was exciting and I knew Irmi was too clever to get caught; which meant I wouldn't get caught either. There was enough light cast through the windows to see inside. The house was a disaster. Empty boxes and cans were lying on the floor in the kitchen. All of the cupboards were half-open and barren. It didn't look promising. We searched every corner of the house and found nothing of value.

Irmi stood in the middle of the kitchen with her hands on her hips and said, "Nothing in this house. The Russians sure cleared this one out. Let's go." The next two homes yielded the same results. In the fourth house, we found only some candles and matches in a drawer. We gave up searching indoors and walked outside. Set into the rough stone foundation were two big wooden cellar doors that were almost horizontal. Irmi and I had to open the doors together—she pushed and I pulled. After we managed to get the doors vertical, we pushed them over and they came crashing to the ground. A crude cellar stairway awaited our entrance.

The cellar had that familiar musty smell of moist dark enclosure. Irmi fearlessly went down the steps first. Soon, she was engulfed in darkness. I got on my hands and knees with my hands at the edge of the opening and lowered my head down into the opening to try to see Irmi. I couldn't see anything, and I was too afraid to follow her down into the darkness. In a timid voice, I said, "Irmi." There was no response. I breathed in to call to her louder, when I saw a spark. Irmi lit a match. Soon, she had a candle glowing, dimly lighting the cellar.

She looked up at me and said, "What are you waiting for?" I jumped up and rushed down to meet her. I held onto the back of her blouse as she slowly moved around the cellar, careful not to trip over debris or let the candle go out. There were tools and opened boxes scattered everywhere from others who searched the room previously. We looked throughout the cellar, but didn't find anything useful. Then Irmi said, "What's that? It looks like a shelf." It was a step in the concrete right under the floor joists. Irmi and I moved a dresser under the shelf. Irmi handed me the candle, jumped on top of the dresser, and reached onto the shelf. She pulled out a glass jar. "I wonder what this is. Ilse, take this outside in the light and see what it is." I grabbed the jar and ran up the stairs, outside.

I tilted my head down the opening and yelled, "Canned fruit. Looks like peaches. Get them all." I placed the jar on the ground outside and went back in to help Irmi get the rest. All in all, we discovered eight jars of canned peaches. We found two burlap sacks and split the load in two, so Irmi had one bag and I the other. We carried the sacks over our shoulders and walked slowly and carefully, to avoid breaking the precious jars.

On the way home, I excitedly thought about our discovery. There was a great deal of satisfaction in our accomplishment, our risk having paid out in much-needed sustenance for our family. As we walked quietly side by side, I cracked a smile, looked up at Irmi and said, "That was fun."

Our family was delighted at our find. I was afraid Mutti was going to interrogate us on how we found the peaches. Instead, Irmi just said that we found them in *a* house—no further questions were asked. The Russians were providing one serving of kasha per person each day, which was not enough to sustain us. Mutti was especially worried because my baby brother was not eating and wouldn't take breast milk. He developed terrible diarrhea and was getting weaker by the day. The peaches were a godsend. He couldn't get enough of them. He smiled as he gulped down the peaches. It was good to see him smile.

We stayed in the hotel for about two weeks. Irmi and I kept searching through the abandoned homes, and found little odds and ends, but never to the extent of that first day. The military police had by now instilled order and our nights became safe. We were still very leery of the Russian soldiers, especially if we were alone and away from the safety of the military police. We still heard stories of women and children being attacked.

One morning, Opa was looking out of the window from our room and shouted, "Hey, where did ... who took my bicycle?" He opened the window and poked his head out and looked in every direction. "How did they do this?" He saw a ladder perched against a lower roof tier. "They must have crawled up here at night and carried it along the roof to that ladder. Wow!' He was obviously upset, but almost equally impressed with their apparent acrobatics getting to the bike and carrying it down. A day or two later, we saw a Russian riding Opa's bicycle. No one said anything, we couldn't, and it only added to our anger and frustration.

On the 5th of May, I was awakened by wild gunfire, honking horns and muffled yelling. Looking out the windows, I could see Russian vehicles driving through the streets, filled with soldiers waving Russian flags, holding vodka bottles in the air and shooting into the sky. Several of us ran out of the hotel and gathered in front to watch the makeshift parade, now hearing clearly what the soldiers had been shouting with such glee, "*voyna kaput! Hitler kaput!*"

3

Back to Palmnicken

May, 1945. A part of me applauded the riotous celebrations the Russians were having over the death of Hitler and the end of the war, while at the same time I was uneasy supporting anything the Russians did. Should I be joyous over the defeat of our country? Wasn't that traitorous? And where did that leave us? We were of no value to the Russians who now ruled us. They could care less whether we lived or died. In fact, if we died, life would be easier for them.

"So this is it," Omi said. "The fall of the Nazis." She shook her head in disgust. "They got what they deserved, but us, innocent bystanders ... we didn't believe in them. Why are we being persecuted? Someone should have killed Hitler a long time ago!" She took a deep breath. "Four assassination attempts and all of them failed—even here in East Prussia, in Rastenburg. How could they not have killed him?"

Opa waved his hand's downward to try and calm her down, and looked around, worried that someone may have heard her.

"Who's going to imprison us for talking bad about the Nazi party now," Omi said sarcastically. "Wilhelm," Omi tilted her head toward him. "The Nazis lost and Hitler is dead—we don't need to worry about criticizing the Nazis—we have bigger worries ahead of us." Opa looked down and raised his hands and said, "I guess it's just been pounded into my head to be careful what we say ... it'll take a while to get used to."

"Opa," I interrupted. "Can we now go back home? Will everything be back to normal?"

Opa looked down, "I don't know if normal exists anymore. I've been through this before in the Great War. I hate to say it, but I think the Russians are here to stay."

The celebrations intensified as vodka bottles emptied. I could just imagine the Russians' jubilation—this was a huge victory for them. Years of fighting and killing coming to an end with the death of a power-hungry dictator. The Russians got their revenge and now they were going to cash in on the spoils of war. Military Police came to us and urged all women and children to lock their doors and stay inside. They said the Russian soldiers had lost their senses to vodka and victory, and the police could not protect everyone. By nightfall, there was complete mayhem. Fear along with a cacophony of yelling, singing and fighting, led to yet another sleepless night. Fortunately, we were once again safe.

The next morning, like so many sheep, we awaited instructions from the Russians. How quickly we submitted to our new ruling leaders, although it was clear they did not know much more than we about what was to happen.

Mutti mumbled, "These idiots took over our country? I guess no one figured out what to do when they won." We asked the soldiers in charge what we were to do, but they just shrugged.

One soldier replied with a puzzled look, "Just go home." I found it interesting that our family was apprehensive about going home. *Wasn't that what we wanted?* The adults just stood there, looking at each other wondering, who was going to direct us? *Should we go back home?*

Mutti, disgusted, said, "The Russians are not telling us anything. What is going on here?"

Tante Friedel smirked, "Well what's worse: The Russians telling us nothing, or the Nazis telling us non-stop lies?"

Mutti looked at her like a light was just turned on. "You're right. The Nazis told us too much, and now we're told nothing." One side of her mouth curled into a smile. "Do you remember that *mist* we heard on the radios and in the newspapers—all propaganda."

"To the last days," Tante Friedel replied. "Hitler's army was defeating the Russian's and driving them back. All lies. Did they think we were all that stupid?"

"Well, we were stupid enough to put him in power," Mutti replied.

To that, no one had a comment.

A family of refugees was walking down the street. They were carrying all their possessions, so they were obviously on the move.

"Where are you headed?" Tante Friedel asked.

"We're going home," one of them replied. "Going south ... the Russians don't seem to care."

Finally, Opa said, 'Staying here is pointless. Let's cautiously walk back in the direction of Palmnicken and see if it's safe. If all looks good, we'll continue home." This was welcome news to Mutti. My baby brother was severely malnourished and dehydrated. We were optimistic that the hospital in Palmnicken was still operational. It was our only hope of saving Hans.

We packed our belongings and headed back home. A light misty rain came down that morning. Much of the scenery was the same as on our outward journey. None of the corpses were removed. The smell of rotten flesh stagnated in the moist spring air. It was a putrid aroma that I'll never forget. The remains of war were left in the open for all to see.

There were few signs of Russian soldiers. At first, passing Russian trucks struck fear in us as we thought we might get arrested, or taken to a work camp, but they didn't seem to care that we wandered without escort. Eventually, we felt comfortable about our decision. There was gunfire in the distance. It was unclear if there was still fighting going on. One could imagine, with all of the confusion and communication breakdowns, that some of the soldiers on either side might not know that the war was over. Although hearing combat gunfire was nothing unusual and no longer frightened us, we still had to be watchful. But it was the Russian's treatment of civilians that we most feared.

Anneliese, Irmi and I had a spring in our step that mirrored our buoyant thoughts: *we're going home, it's over and this will all be a distant memory.* Irmi finally broke the silence. She caught up to Mutti who was pushing the baby carriage and grasped the carriage along with her. Irmi leaned over the carriage, so that she could see Mutti's expression. Irmi bounced up and down as she followed alongside: "Mutti, Mutti, we're going home, will everything be the same? Will..."

"Yes, yes, Irmchen," Mutti replied expressionlessly.

"Will Papa be home soon with us?"

"I hope so." Mutti was clearly preoccupied with Hans's well-being. She didn't sound very convincing and Irmi's excitement waned, and her optimism quickly turned to doubt.

Mutti prodded us along. She wanted to get Hans to the hospital as soon as possible. That entire day, he wouldn't eat or drink. Mutti even tried to force-feed him, but he just choked and spit it out. He was severely dehydrated and his condition was critical. We walked at a brisk pace without ever stopping.

I remember my excitement when he was born, August 4, 1944. Oh, to have a baby brother. I was the youngest, until he was born. My goodness, I planned to spoil him. I couldn't wait to help take care of him. I was ten, but the responsibility made me feel more adult. Mutti had some complications with his birth; she was already thirty-nine years old. She managed, though, and we all helped raise him. At the time of his birth and thereafter, food and medicine were already scarce. I remember Mutti saying, "The odds are stacked against Hans, so we need to pray for him and give him as much nourishment as we can to get him strong as soon as possible."

We rationed our food and ate stale bread and dried meat while we walked. We had water and I drank plenty of it, but a full belly of water only temporarily abated my hunger. I remember Opa and Tante Friedel heading off to villages we passed, to refill our canteens while we marched forward. Because of the rush to get Hans to the hospital, they didn't want to delay our journey and so caught up to us later.

When we finally made it back to Palmnicken, it was almost dusk. Our house was vacant, but a disaster. Most of the contents were tossed into a huge pile in the front yard. Inside, the Russians must have dropped trash on the floor wherever they stood. Empty vodka bottles and discarded food ration cans littered the floor. The only furnishings left in the house were two beds in my grandparents' room and a sofa in the living room. As there were still some soldiers in the area, my grandfather asked one if we were allowed to occupy our home. He looked as puzzled as the rest of the soldiers, shrugged a yes and walked away.

We quickly moved in, but Mutti knew that Hans needed immediate attention. She and Tante Friedel rushed to the hospital. The rest of us started cleaning up the debris. I was hurt to know that this house that I loved so much was treated with such disrespect. This beautiful sanctuary had housed drunken fools. My mind tried to imagine what they said or did while they inhabited our house. In their drunken stupor, I'm sure they bragged to each other about what they did to the German women. A tear started forming in my eye as I carried their trash from my house. I wanted desperately to erase the notion that our house was invaded.

Papa poured his heart into the construction of this home to provide comfort and protection to our family. He built most of the house himself, along with friends and relatives when available. It took him two years to finish. They moved in during the winter of 1933, just a few months before I was born. Unlike surrounding villages, Palmnicken had electricity, a benefit of the amber mine. So our house had electric lights and running water. Papa also installed steam heat, rather than the wood- or coal-burning stoves or tile ovens typical of other homes in the area.

I was so proud of this house and what Papa accomplished. It was a progressive and sturdy home for its time. The Russians, apparently unimpressed by its advancements, thought it nothing more than a place to toss their trash.

It occurred to me that it was good that Papa didn't see his home in such shambles. I didn't want him to see the house like this, so I hurried to help clean it up, in case he came home soon.

Once we put a dent in removing the rubbish, Mutti and Tante Friedel arrived back from the hospital without Hans. It was now dark. The electricity was out and we only had one candle in the middle of the floor. Mutti didn't say anything. Her eyes never looked above the floorboards. Her agony was felt by us all. Tante Friedel told us that the hospital was now run by the Russians, but they had forced many German nurses and even doctors to continue working there. The hospital was filled beyond capacity with critically ill infants and the elderly; even some injured soldiers. Quietly, she let us know the staff wasn't optimistic about saving Hans. I heard her whisper to Opa, "there's too much chaos at the hospital. They didn't let us stay with Hans."

My grandfather suggested it was safer not to occupy the main floor, so we arranged our bedding upstairs and settled in. The night was fairly peaceful, save for a few gunshots and periodic army truck traffic. I finally felt a little safe. It must have been the refuge of our home. But what would prevent the Russians from taking over our house again?

That night I dreamt of Russian soldiers carrying on in our living room. *I was hiding in my parents' bedroom with the door slightly cracked open. I was invisible to the Russians. They were all clearly drunk laughing it up. A bottle was tossed to the floor as another opened.*

Suddenly the front door opened and Papa walked in with a club in-hand. He started yelling, "Get out of my house," and waved the club at the Russians; hitting several of them at their exit. There Papa stood in the front room as victor. Papa always was my hero. This wasn't the first time since the invasion that I dreamt of Papa saving us. The only problem was my hero only arrived at night in my dreams.

The next morning, Mutti and I rushed to the hospital to check on Hans. I don't remember much of what the hospital looked like before the war, but now it was absolutely chaotic, filled to overflowing with the sick and dying, and so few there to attend to them. We frantically searched for someone who could help us find Hans. The workers considered our questions a hindrance; they simply pointed us in a direction or told us to ask someone else.

It was a miserable place that held the smell of death. Everywhere, patients and visitors were moaning and crying, and clearly some of the people in the beds were already dead, but lay there, blank-eyed, uncovered. Soiled bandages and metal pails holding rust-colored water were left scattered about. I was overwhelmed and frightened and I wanted so badly to leave, but I knew we had to find Hans.

We were told to go to the back of the main room; through a plain, windowless solid door. It looked like an exit to the outside. Sure enough, the doorway led us out. We stood outside; Mutti looked around, puzzled, thinking that someone led us the wrong way, when a woman came out of a wooden shed, carrying something small wrapped in a thin sheet. She looked up at us as she walked by. The look of grief in her glassy eyes said it all. If we were directed to the right place, Hans didn't make it through the night.

I remember when my Omi Glaus died, I was not afraid, or even terribly sad, for I knew that she lived a good life, was going to heaven, and that's what happens to us all eventually. But Hans never had a chance to experience what life was all about. It was stolen from him. I loved my baby brother tremendously. I wanted to be his role model, and help him experience what I did growing up in Palmnicken.

After all that Mutti went through in the last few days, how would this tragedy affect her? I knew she didn't want to enter the shed and face the reality, but she was compelled to know. I reached for Mutti's hand. It was warm and sweaty. We entered the shed and there were several babies lying in a row on one bed. A dozen or more were lying on tables set up along the walls. There was no one else in the room. No one attended to these poor children or their grief stricken loved ones. Anyone who entered was left to simply pick up their lifeless child and go.

We viewed the babies one by one, and Mutti stopped at one of the babies on the table and said in a soft, but clear voice, "That's him, that's Hans." I looked at the body, and it did have some resemblance to Hans, but it seemed much too skinny when I could clearly remember Hans' belly was huge from malnutrition. Plus Hans inherited the unmistakable high cheek bones from my mother's side, and this baby didn't seem to have them. The skin on his face was thin and droopy.

I replied to my mother, "Mutti, this is not him. This doesn't look like him." The sunken features of this lifeless baby made him difficult for me to recognize, and maybe I didn't want to face reality, but preferred to believe he was in the main hospital, still alive. Undeterred, Mutti quietly picked him up and cradled him in her arms. Still, I noticed that she looked again at every baby before we left, perhaps not completely convinced herself that she held her son.

There was no formality, no paperwork, no certificate of death. We simply took Hans and walked away. We could have easily had the wrong baby and no one would have known. It was strange and cruel, but what were they to do? There was no one to care for the dead.

I started crying as we made our way home, but when I saw Mutti's stoic face, I bit back my tears and grew quiet. We continued on in silence It wasn't until we entered the house and everyone realized what happened to Hans that Mutti could no longer hold it in. She broke down in a display of sorrow that I wished I would never witness again.

After a time, Opa got up: "I'm going to see if Herr Färber is still here. He can build us a coffin, or I can build one if they give me some wood." Anneliese got up to follow, then Irmi, and of course, I had to follow Irmi. I think everyone just wanted to get out of the house and avoid the depressed atmosphere. Herr Färber was an old man and was our resident carpenter-cabinet maker. His shop was a few blocks in the direction of town.

Opa knocked on the beautiful, hand-crafted shop door, and it was answered by Herr Färber himself. He was a little man with fairly long wavy grey hair. This was unusual for the time. The wrinkles in his face shaped deep grooves at the end of his mouth that traced downward and somehow made it appear like a smile. He always looked happy and was a very kind man, and very talkative. "Willie, good to see you. Is everything okay?" He was clearly happy to see my grandfather. They were close to the same age and had known each other since childhood.

"*Nein*, not exactly, little Hans, Hanna's son, died. We need to bury him. Can I get some wood to build a coffin?" They were talking in East Prussian dialect. I couldn't make out everything they said, but I understood that Herr Färber offered to build the coffin and that the Russians had taken over his wood shop, and made him a worker in his own shop. He had to be careful and not let the Russians know that he was building a coffin. They carried on for quite a while and shared stories of all that happened. I think my grandfather didn't know that we understood as much of the dialect as we did, because he told of the rape, and the killing of the boy at the hotel in Gross Kuhren. From what I understood, Herr Färber said that it wouldn't have been much safer if we stayed here. The same atrocities happened. He, somehow, was able to stay at his home when the Russians came. They carried on for quite a while, sharing accounts and knowledge of friends' whereabouts.

Finally, Herr Färber said, "Willie, I can't get the coffin built today. Is tomorrow good?"

"*Ja*, sure," my grandfather replied. He had a resigned look, like he wanted to bury Hans today, but understood Herr Färber needed to build the coffin in secrecy. They exchanged goodbyes, we children politely said thank you, and then we left.

When we arrived back home, Hans was placed on the floor in a basket. We didn't even have a table to put him on. Wildflowers were not yet in bloom, so various plant cuttings were placed on the ground under his basket. It was as close as we could get to a wake.

My grandfather left again, this time in search of a shovel to dig a grave, "Maybe there is one in the pile of rubbish, or I can ask a soldier if I can borrow one." Even a simple shovel was difficult to get now. A few hours later, he arrived back. "A soldier was kind enough to give me a shovel, he said to leave it at the graveyard for anyone else to use. I dug the hole and tomorrow, we can bury Hans when we pick up the coffin."

The rest of the day we spent rummaging through the pile of things in the front yard and trying to make the inside of the house presentable. It was difficult knowing we suffered our first casualty and we were only a few weeks under Russian rule. Hans' death hit me hard. Suddenly, material things such as toys and pretty dresses didn't matter. Food, shelter and security were now paramount in my mind.

The Russians had tried to burn the rubbish in our yard, albeit unsuccessfully. It must have been wet from the rain and never really ignited. The pile reeked with the sour smells of mildew and smoke. I searched through the pile, hoping to salvage clothes that we had left behind and thought we wouldn't need. Knowing that we might be without any new clothes for a while, any fabric was valuable. Old clothing could be cut and sewn into something new, or the fabric could be torn apart and the thread used for repairs.

I pulled on a rag which was stuck on something solid. It looked like a wooden box. I managed to dig around it and discovered that it was my dollhouse. A few years ago, Papa built a dollhouse and presented it to me for Christmas. It was a beautiful and exact replica of our house. I loved it and played with it often. Now it was only suitable for kindling. The toy no longer had any use for me.

These past few weeks, I had grown up faster than any young girl should.

Kids on the beach in 1937. From left: Anneliese, Günter, Ilse, Irmi.

Toys and fun no longer mattered. Survival became our priority. Sad, but stricken with reality, I tossed the dollhouse into a small fire that we started, to get rid of waste. This *was* the end of my childhood.

Tante Friedel came and helped me. I managed to find a few chairs. I held one upside down and said, "Tante Friedel, What do you make of this?"

She took the chair and analyzed it. "Somebody used a saw to cut off the bottom of the legs," she replied.

"What on earth ... why would they do that?" I asked.

She looked up. "I found some wooden pieces ... I wonder if they belong to the chair. Let's go see." We walked to a small pile in front of a chair, one that had its legs still intact. "Look," she said. "There, in front of the chair are a few sawn off legs."

I bent down to look. Now, it was just a matter of curiosity than anything. "*Ja,* those came from the chairs, and there are leather strings, thick thread and ... *shoe soles?*"

Tante Friedel smiled, "One of the soldiers staying here must have been a cobbler. He repaired shoes in his spare time. But what's with the cut off legs?" She shook her head and tried to fit the leg onto the shoe sole. "I don't know much about making shoes, but he must have needed some wooden piece inside the shoe to sew the sole in place ... interesting!" We never did quite figure it out, all we knew was that we were going to have some short chairs.

From the side of the house, we heard Opa cheering, "Hey, I found it! Look here." He came walking toward us with two black bottles, one in each hand. Black soot was up to his elbows. "I buried some peppermint schnapps in the coal pile before the Russians came." He had a grin that was a delight to see. It was nice to see someone happy and smiling for a change. "Those dummies didn't find it." Opa was not a big drinker, but enjoyed a shot of peppermint schnapps every night after dinner. I was glad for him; a small victory.

His finding a hidden treasure reminded me of Papa's secret compartment under the floorboards in a corner of the house. I figured I better go inside and assess the floorboards and see if they were tampered with. I picked up a few items that I thought could be of some use to us and walked into the house. "What do you think of..." Anneliese, Irmi and Omi were in a conversation, analyzing the wall in the living room and not paying attention to me.

"They didn't shoot it because it would have gone through the house," Anneliese said in contrast to what apparently was said by Omi before I arrived.

"This doesn't make any sense. What purpose could this have," Omi said with a bewildered look. "Could they have used this to hang their coats?" There were about a half-dozen small holes pounded into the plaster walls about the size of a coin; all pretty much identical in size. Anneliese and Omi had their fingers in some holes and their face right up to them to look for clues. Irmi was too short to reach, but attentively listened, always eager to solve a puzzle. Anneliese backed off every few seconds, put her hands on her hips, and scanned the immediate surroundings to see if a distant view would offer more clues. This went on for a while.

"Hey, they could have used this to punch holes in the wall." Irmi held up a faucet knob with a short section of pipe still attached. It was on the floor near the holes. Omi grabbed and tried it in one of the holes.

"Yes, it fits. This could have been it, but why?" Omi questioned. Anneliese and Omi both looked at the kitchen sink in tandem. The other faucet handle was torn off as well. "I'll bet they never saw running water. They thought that they could take the faucet handle, put it in the wall and water would come out." Anneliese bent at the hips, did one of her snort-laughs and covered her mouth with her right hand. Everyone burst out in laughter. It was good to laugh. The laughter took our minds off of our problems. "These soldiers were peasants. Maybe that's why they were in the front line—expendable to Stalin."

Anneliese chimed in, "I wonder—that's why all the water around the toilet, and the socks. They washed their clothes in the toilet." Laughter broke out again, this time even louder.

"Phooey," Irmi said, as she tilted her head back with a look of disgust. Granted, at this time, running water in a house was fairly unusual, particularly in rural areas of Germany. Even in the city, many people didn't have running water. But still, even if they didn't have running water, they at least knew or heard of it. We knew that Stalin had taken peasants from the most remote and undeveloped parts of their country to fight. But could it really be possible for these Russians to have slammed a faucet handle into a wall and expected water to come out?

After our fun, I investigated the floorboards of Papa's secret compartment. It appeared to be intact and undetected by the Russians. Hidden in this compartment was Papa's short-wave radio that was strictly forbidden by the Nazi government. If the police had found out that he had the radio, he could have been sent to a prison camp. The short-wave radio allowed citizens to retrieve news and information from other countries. Hitler forbade these radios because he wanted German citizens to only receive his version of news. Papa made each of us swear not to tell anyone, even friends.

I remember Papa carefully removing a few screws and then pulling off a baseboard revealing the edges of the floorboards. One board did not have a tongue-and-groove. Once it was off, he could remove about six boards to reveal a box formed with wooden boards that were nailed to the floor joists. Hidden, along with the radio, he had a few other valuables, most notable to me, was my favorite doll. A few weeks before the Russians came and Papa was putting his radio away, he saw me holding my doll. He asked if I wanted to hide my doll in the secret compartment. I felt proud that he would ask me. None of the other children's toys were allowed in the hiding place.

I stood and stared at the undisturbed floorboards. I wanted badly to get my doll, but even though Papa was not here, I still respected his secret place. I didn't dare open it.

Opa came inside. "Come see," he said. We followed him outside to the open doorway leading to the basement. He walked halfway down the stairway and pointed to the walls along the stairway. "This is burnt. I wonder if they tried to burn the house down, or someone was just careless." We all gazed in disbelief.

"What's wrong with these people?" Anneliese scoffed. "Why would they want to burn this house down?"

This was just another missing piece to the puzzle that made up our unwelcomed guests. They had no respect for anything.

We retired upstairs and again, the night was quiet. The next morning, I awoke with hunger pains and nothing to satisfy them. We had run out of food the night before. At least in Gross Kuhren, there were feeding centers. Here, we desperately needed to find food. Thankfully, at least water was in ample supply. There were water hand-pumps in the village where we filled any container we could get our hands on.

Opa left early in the morning to offer Herr Färber a hand. He said the Russians wouldn't bother him that early—they would still be drunk from the night before. He arrived a few hours later, carrying a small, simple rectangular pine coffin with a handle bolted on each end. The wood was without finish.

Mutti was sitting on the couch in the front room, staring at Hans, still in the basket. Omi, sitting next to her, had her arm around Mutti, trying to comfort her. Omi slowly leaned away from Mutti and asked, "Are you ready?" Mutti just looked at her and nodded. Omi then stood up, walked toward the kitchen and picked up her Bible. "Wilhelm, please put Hans in and let's get started. Friedel, can you help him carry the coffin?"

Opa picked up Hans from the basket while Tante Friedel removed the bedding and placed it in the coffin. Hans was stiff and pale and looked even less like the brother I remembered. Somehow, this made it easier for me to cope—it just didn't look like him. Opa placed him gently on the bedding, and looked down on him a moment before he softly set the lid and began to hammer the nails to seal it. Then, slowly, Opa walked forward with his hands behind him, carrying the front of the coffin, Tante Friedel carrying from behind.

Omi led the procession with her hands clutching her Bible to her chest. The coffin was next, and the rest of us filled in behind. We walked across the street toward the graveyard. Omi started singing a hymn. I don't recall what we sang, but we all chimed in, and the song carried us to the grave site. They placed the coffin in the shallow hole that Opa had dug. Omi read Psalm 23. It was a solemn and surprisingly emotionless funeral. I think we were still in shock and perhaps afraid of what lay ahead—perhaps we thought this was the first of many to come.

The loss of Hans lay heavy on my mind. *Why did this have to happen? The war was over, we were back at home: why weren't things getting better—or back to normal?* I couldn't help but look at Mutti. She was emotionally drained. Did she regret her decision, defying Papa, making us stay in Palmnicken instead of taking that plane to the West? No one ever asked, and she never commented, but everyone wondered.

4

The Second Evacuation

It was becoming painfully clear that the Russians did not intend simply to win the war and displace Hitler; they intended to occupy the region and turn it over to the Soviet Union. So the new questions became: *Were they going to force us to become part of the Soviet Union? Were they going to kick us out? Were we going to become slaves to the Russians?*

Every day, we made progress with clearing our house and the burned piles of trash left behind by the soldiers. It was starting to look like home again and, if Papa happened to come home today, he wouldn't be shocked by the disarray. I wandered through our yard to look for anything left to burn, and opened the chicken coop, now barren of the familiar fluttering activity. The rabbit cages were empty. Scrubbed dirt was all that remained in the pig pens. The fruit trees hand-grafted by Papa were all that was still producing on our little farm. Was our little homestead ever going to be alive again? Memories of our farm as it once looked raced through my mind as I cleaned up the yard. The incredible assortment of apples and pears, Papa's fresh salami, known throughout the region, the fresh vegetables. *Oh Lord, please let us be the way we were and bring Papa home soon.*

One day, our whole family was sitting in the front room. I noticed someone hung a few pictures on the wall. It made everything feel more like a home. I got up and looked at the pictures. One was of our entire family. It reminded me of how much I missed Papa. Also, we hadn't heard anything from my oldest brother, Günter, who was a soldier for the German army. He was now 20, and I hadn't seen him for almost two years.

"What do you think happened to Günter ... is he still alive?" I asked.

No one said anything for a while. Then Omi said, "I don't know. We can only have faith that he was captured—hopefully by the British or Americans, and not the Russians." Again silence, this time for a longer period.

"That stupid Hitler Jugend.[3] It brainwashed Günter," commented Mutti. "His allegiance to the SS could have gotten him killed."

"*Ach*, that Hilter Jugend," added Tante Friedel. "When you think about it though, you have to hand it to that crazy Hitler: he figured out how to

41

brainwash the youth so that the next generation would be eating out of his hand... He started that Hitler Jugend way before he even came into power, right, Papa?"

Opa sucked his upper lip, "Look, forget about it. It's all over."

"*Ja*, Günter was dedicated to the Nazi movement," Anneliese uncharacteristically chimed in. "Do you remember when he would bark back at Papa when Papa talked bad about Hitler? It was scary. I thought Papa would scold him, but he didn't."

"Good thing Papa left him alone," Mutti said. "I can tell you, Papa talked to me about it. He was not happy with the way Günter corrected him, but Papa was also afraid that arguing with Günter could have caused Günter to turn him in. He would be arrested." Mutti looked around at all of us. "You know—you saw parents get arrested because their children talked—and sometimes innocent discussions. How about the Hansel family: you heard how Arnold said something at school and then the next day Herr Hansel was taken away to prison."

"Some of those young Nazis got promoted by turning in so-called anti-Nazi talk," Omi said. "There were many devout Nazis that were eager to please the Nazi authorities by turning in anti-Nazi activity in exchange for political favors."

Mutti snickered, "*Ja*, you would think the higher the rank in the Nazi party, the braver and smarter they were. Ha, the upper ranks were full of slithering kiss-asses. The tattle-tale and the insecure were the ones who got promoted."

In time, we settled into our old home and felt relatively safe. Under strict order by the MP, soldiers were not allowed to enter civilian homes. Unfortunately, hunger was quickly becoming our most pressing need. Although we now knew where the Russian's food centers were in Palmnicken, there was no way of knowing when they would have food. Irmi and I usually were sent several times a day to check and report back. As was typical, civilians were last on their minds. Their focus was on taking over our country, not on what to do with us; this was on-the-job-training for everyone.

One afternoon, Irmi and I were in our yard replacing fallen bricks in our outdoor fireplace. Mutti sometimes cooked outside in the summer, to keep the heat out of the house. I was handing bricks to Irmi who settled them in an overlap pattern. As I handed one brick to her, I held onto it. I wanted to get her attention. She tugged and then looked at me, as if to ask: *what are you doing?*

I tried to be serious, but burst out laughing. "Hey, do you remember when you caught your face on fire here?"

Irmi turned angry. "I didn't catch my face on fire."

"Yes, you did. You were playing with matches at this brick stove and poof, your hair was singed off."

Ilse's first day of school, 1940.

"*Ach*, it wasn't that bad." Irmi shook her head.

"Oh *Ja*, I remember hearing you scream as you raced across the lawn to Mutti. You had no eyebrows or eyelashes left and your hands and arms were black from soot. Your hair was still smoking. *Mensch*, did that stink! Nothing like the smell of burnt hair." We both laughed hysterically. "What happened anyway? I don't remember."

After Irmi finally caught her breath, she said, "*Ja*, it took me weeks to grow my eyelashes back. I tried to start a fire and somehow, the whole box of matches went off all at once." She quickly changed the subject. "Hey, do you remember when we made the candy out here—that melted sugar and nut stuff that we poured out and let cool?"

"Oh *ja*, that was great. How did you know how to make it?"

Irmi kind of tilted her head. "I just knew. I think someone at school told me."

I looked at her from the corner of my eye. "I still can't believe we didn't get caught. Mutti would have chased you with the wooden cook spoon if she knew you were playing with fire again and dragging me into it."

"Probably, but at least it was fun—and the candy even tasted good."

I smiled at her and put my head down and handed her another brick. "*Ja*, that was fun. I had to sneak all the ingredients for you from the kitchen, because Mutti trusted me. You would have been caught."

Irmi chuckled, "*Ja*, somehow she trusts you more than me. I wonder why that is."

"What? You're the one who comes up with all these crazy ideas. I'd never think of that stuff." It was silent for a while. "Irmi, do you think Papa is coming back?"

She looked at me and then down at the brick I handed her. "I don't think so. At least, not for a while."

"Why not? Where do you think he is?"

"Don't know, but my guess is that he is in a prisoner of war camp. Probably in Russia."

"You don't think he took that last plane out and flew to the West—to freedom?"

"No way," Irmi replied. "He wouldn't abandon us! Papa wouldn't do that."

This wasn't the first time we had this conversation about Papa's whereabouts. Irmi was adamant that he didn't take the plane. Anneliese, Irmi and I all believed that he went back to Brüsterort, his army station, and got captured by the Russians. I truly wished he did take the plane—he would be safe, but I too couldn't believe that Papa would abandon us and selfishly board a plane to safety without us.

Memories and unanswered questions ran through my mind as we tried to piece our home back together. Still, our lives lacked security and stability.

We had our home, but where was Papa and Günter? And what about food? What did the Russians have in store for us?

That afternoon, I wandered across the street toward the sea. I walked alone in the field and remembered one day about a year ago. *We three sisters were playing and we saw a German Luftwaffe airplane circling low around us. We were all excited wondering if the plane was going to land in the field. We never saw a plane up close. Sure enough, the plane was coming down for a landing. Our excitement changed. Were we in trouble? All of a sudden we feared what was about to happen.*

The plane made its landing and Anneliese made us keep our distance. Once the plane came to a stop, to our amazement, Papa exited the plane. All of a sudden we rushed to him. How exciting, we thought. Papa is coming during work to visit us. We were screaming and carrying on. The plane was still running and my father quickly corralled us away from the spinning prop. He sensed our excitement, and didn't want to let on that his purpose was not to just see us. He quickly walked to the house with us closely behind. He entered the house, and Mutti, surprised, questioned: "What are you doing here? Is something wrong?"

"No, I forgot my gun this morning. Karl flew me back so I don't get in trouble." Even though Papa was a mechanic, he was primarily a soldier. Soldiers were to have their guns with them at all times during war-time in case they got an immediate call to combat. He could have been court-martialed for not having his weapon. He grabbed his gun and we followed him back to the plane. As they left we ran alongside and cheered as the plane went to flight.

I continued my walk. The coast was waiting for me. I stood at the edge of the cliff overlooking the majestic coast line. The wind was rushing in my face. Its force almost pushed me back off my feet. The crashing of the waves vibrated something inside of me. Just like always, the humid sea-air made it hard for me to breath. The smell of the salt water was unmistakable. I just stood there for a half-hour. My sea was unaffected by the turmoil of this land. Its waves pounded the same as before the war. In the distance, I noticed some low hanging clouds developing along the shore and it reminded me of a fond memory here.

One Sunday morning in the early-fall of 1944, Mutti announced to all the children to get up and get ready for church. I was wise to this warning and knew that after this first attempt, I really had about 15 minutes to enjoy my sleep. I loved to sleep late. I think it was because when I slept late I had what I called a half-sleep, awake enough to remember my dreams. I was a dreamer. It was my little fantasy world. Dreams seemed so real to me that I often sat up in bed in the morning wondering if the events in my dream really happened.

Today, I was entranced in one of my dreams when I heard that familiar deep-toned, bwoowoo, in the distance. I quickly got out of bed, put on whatever clothes were near, and ran toward the door. As I stepped outside, I heard Mutti say "Ilsechen, we only have a few minutes before breakfast." I think Mutti knew that I was infat-

uated with fog, because she didn't get mad that I wanted to go outside this morning before church.

I ran in the direction of the sea, but knew that I didn't have enough time to make it to the coast. I got to the field across the street and stopped in the middle, and said to myself, yes, perfect! It was a crisp fall morning with absolutely no wind: at the coast, this was highly unusual. The fog was especially thick and since there was no wind, there was a definite line of separation about a meter from the ground, so my head was above the fog and I could squat down and put my head under the fog. I've never seen the fog like this before. I could smell the humidity in the air.

It couldn't have been any more perfect. The field was blanketed with a thin layer of fog. I couldn't see my feet. It appeared as if I was suspended in the clouds. I stretched out my arms like a bird. I walked through the field dipping in and out of the clouds like a bird. As I came out of the clouds the sun hit my face and I immediately dipped back in. My shoes and legs were soaked from the heavy dew on the grass, but I didn't care. Again, the fog horn bellowed, bwoowoo.

I didn't want to leave, but I knew that I had to get ready for church. I flew back toward home. At the edge of the field, I turned around to once again capture the magnificence of this day. I may never see fog like this again, I whispered. I came into the house out of breath and took off my dew-drenched shoes. I heard Mutti in the kitchen inquiring, "Did you enjoy your fog."

Out of breath I said, "Yes, it was perfect." She looked at me and smiled. I knew she understood.

About a week passed since we moved back and even though no military combat remained, there was still plenty of activity by the Russians. Construction crews started arriving to fix the roads and rail system. They pounded poles into the ground, apparently to build a fence. Along with them arrived a new regiment. The next day, five or six soldiers knocked on our door: "*Raus, raus, alle, raus!*"

Oh no, not again! They kicked us out of our house once more. At least this time, they didn't point guns at us. This was thankfully a less vicious regimen. We had ten minutes to gather our things. Evacuations were becoming a much too familiar routine. We packed all of our clothes that we had, plus whatever additional fabrics and supplies we could carry. Mutti muttered something under her breath as we packed. Opa quickly shouted in a whisper, "*Shh, they can hear us.*"

I thought for sure this time, we were going to a work camp. We stood outside and noticed others were being evacuated as well. They were targeting only a small region for evacuation, and as always, we were never told what was happening. We asked where we were going and the only response was, "*Weiter, weiter.*" The soldiers marched us and a few other families toward town. After about ten minutes, we crossed the row of poles that the construction crews pounded into the ground. It was a tall fence that they were erecting. Now their intentions were clearer, but were they fencing us in or fencing us out?

We all stopped at the row of poles. One soldier, knowing almost no German, faced the town and raised both hands and waved them toward the town. "*Geh!*" He then raised his arms up and down in line with poles, faced the direction from where we came and pointed: "*Nein!*" while holding his gun out in front of him. He then turned toward the town again and pointed. "*Geh*" We all looked at each other. "*Geh*," he said louder. We quickly took off in the direction of town.

"Papa," Tante Friedel whispered, leaning toward Opa as we walked, "what do they want us to do? Are they letting us go free?"

"*Nein*," Opa replied with an uncertain tone to his voice, turning his head to give the soldiers one last look as we walked. "We're evacuated again. It's best we find someone in town who will take us in." There were several other families in the same predicament. Was this going to be a race; which family will find a place to stay first?

We spent about an hour knocking on doors, asking if anyone had rooms available, always with the same polite and sympathetic response of, "Sorry, *nein*." It appeared that the soldiers had evacuated all of the rural civilians and crammed them into the village so they could keep track of them. Unfortunately, the Russians didn't consider the lack of housing.

This was getting very disheartening. The people seemed sincere. I believe they really didn't have room and would have taken us in if they had. Opa said disparagingly, "This is not working. I think we need to split up. Maybe we can find room easier if we are a smaller group." It made sense to me, who would have that kind of room?

"*Nein*," Mutti quickly replied. "The last thing we need now is to split up."

"I know, I know, but what are we going to do, sleep outside? Listen, we should split up anyway, that will increase our chances of finding something. We'll ask if they have room for three-to-seven."

Mutti just looked up, searching for an answer. Tante Friedel answered for her: "That's a good idea. Even if we have to split up for a night or two, eventually, we'll find a place for all of us."

Tante Friedel and my grandparents formed one group and Mutti and we children formed another. We walked street by street, one group on each side. We were familiar with these homes and who used to live in them, and we were surprised to find that they were inhabited by people we did not know. This went on for roughly another hour. I was getting very tired. We hadn't eaten all day and only had one serving of kasha yesterday. We stopped several times to drink water. That helped fill my stomach, but didn't last long. It looked like we were going to retire under the stars tonight.

We all met at the end of a street. "Any luck?" Omi asked, out of breath.

"*Nein*, this is maddering," Mutti replied. "We may have to sleep outside." We were all very discouraged. Then Anneliese excitedly shouted, "What about

Herr Färber? When we visited him, it looked like he had some room in that storage area in the back."

Opa gazed off down the street we just walked, shook his head and then turned to her. "*Ja*, that's a great idea. Let's go ask." Herr Färber lived toward the middle of town, just at the edge of the merchant center. We had spent all day knocking at the homes of amber mine workers and homes in the neighboring streets. Maybe we overlooked the obvious: the town center.

We arrived at Herr Färber's shop. He lived in a small building next to his shop. We knocked on his ornate door and it took him a while to answer. He looked tired and worn out, too. "Hello, hello, come in." We walked in, single file and stood in his front room. He turned to Opa. "Willie, is something wrong?"

"*Nein*, um, well."

Herr Färber turned to Mutti, remembering that he built a casket for Hans. "Hanna, I'm very sorry to hear about your son. What was his name?" He was speaking high-German instead of the East Prussian dialect. It wasn't polite to speak a dialect if everyone didn't understand it.

"Oh, *Danke. Ja*, it was tragic. His name was Hans, after his father." She forced a smile, but her eyes still revealed grief.

"*Ja*, of course." He paused uncomfortably. "The war has taken its toll. Now that it's over, I hope we can get back to normal."

"*Ja*, I hope as well. Oh, and thank you for Hans' coffin, you did a beautiful job."

"Oh, it was the least that I could do."

By now, his wife came to see what the commotion was all about. "Hello, welcome." She sounded excited to see visitors. She turned to Mutti. "Hanna—right?

"*Ja*."

"Oh, Herbert told me about your son. I'm so sorry." She then hugged Mutti. Herr Färber backed up a little to get a look at all of us, perhaps wondering what we were doing here.

Opa cleared his throat. "Um, Herbert, the Russians kicked us out of our house again," emphasizing 'again.' "They are building a tall fence outside of town and told us to just get out. We've searched all day and found nowhere to stay. Do you have any room to spare?"

Herr Färber placed his thumb on his jaw and rubbed his chin with his forefinger. "Well, we don't have much room." He put his hand down, then held his arm out toward the back of the shop. "Um, we..."

"*Ja*, the room in the back," Frau Färber shouted with excitement. "Our grandchildren stayed there often. They all left with their parents months ago, before the Russians came." She slowed down her speech. "We all should have done that," she said quietly. "But anyway," she switched gears quickly. "You can have the room. It will be tight, but it's all we have. There are others staying in other rooms as well. We'll be full, but it will be cozy."

"It's still full of stuff; mainly wood, but we can move it out. Let the Russians figure out where to put it. It's their shop now." Herr Färber responded bitterly.

I was relieved. We finally found something. It took us another hour to clear out all of the wood and find a spot in the shop. The room was tiny, but fortunately, we had two bunk beds, and a single bed, and the Färbers added a couch. With all this furniture, there wasn't enough room for two people to pass each other, to get from one side of the room to the other, without one crawling on a bed to let the other pass. Mutti slept on the couch, my grandparents on the single bed—although my grandfather slept on the floor most of the time—and the rest of us in the bunk beds. I had a top bunk and Irmi the other. They were miserably small quarters for the seven of us, but I had my little perch where I could oversee everything. I lay on my bed on my stomach, knees bent with my feet in the air and my chin in my hands. I liked this vantage point. I never slept in a bunk bed before and I had fun with it.

This was an unusual building, long and narrow, with basically three living quarters. The Färbers stayed in the front, a family of three in the middle, and we were at the end. We had our own door that opened onto a small back street. This way, we could come and go and not bother anyone. There was a toilet and sink in the Färbers' quarters. What a luxury! However, since the invasion, the electricity was still off. Herr Färber said, "I'm sure in a few days, the electricity will be turned back on. In the meantime, there is a well a few homes down and we bring buckets of water for cleaning and drinking. I also have one bucket by the toilet to pour in for a flush. Flush only when you make the big business."

We introduced ourselves to the family in the middle, Frau Bach and her two daughters, Manuela, Irmi's age and Sigrid, who I guessed at five. I noticed Irmi and Manuela bonded and I could tell they would become friends. I was jealous and feared that Irmi would spend more time with Manuela than me. Frau Bach explained that her husband died in the war and that she struggled caring for her daughters, but she understood that we haven't eaten all day and offered us two pieces of bread. "It's not much, but it's all we have," she said as she handed us the bread. We thanked her and headed back to our room. Frau Färber followed us and once we got situated, she said, "There is a feeding center here in town, but we have to work for the food. They pay us in food for our labor. They normally don't take the elderly or children. I can show you where to sign up tomorrow."

"What do we have to do?" Tante Friedel asked.

"Mainly laundry, cleaning and cooking; it depends," replied Frau Färber. "For a day's work, you usually get two slices of bread, a small cup of sugar, and some butter—it's really more like lard. Sometimes, they have kasha or watery soup. We need to get there by eight, or no work all day." She looked around. "Let's bring everyone except the two small ones tomorrow and see if they take you. I'll wake you up. Goodnight then."

Omi split the two slices of bread into six equal portions and handed them out to each of us. "Mutti," my mother said, what about you?"

"Oh, I'm not so hungry. You go ahead and eat." I found it odd that she wasn't hungry. We haven't eaten all day. How can she not be hungry? It was only a bite full, but better than eating air.

We didn't get everything cleaned up and moved, but we figured we would have time in the morning. I felt safe here. We were among other German families and in town, where the soldiers would leave us alone.

The next morning, Frau Färber came and woke us up. She looked at the adults and Anneliese, "Ready to go?"

With a smile, Omi said, "*Ja*, we're ready ... what about Frau Bach, isn't she coming?"

Frau Färber looked up through lowered eyebrows at Omi and hesitated. "She doesn't work," she finally responded. Omi turned and looked at Mutti and Tante Friedel for clues, but drew a blank.

"Come on let's go," Frau Färber said. Something didn't sit right with her regarding Frau Bach. *Why did they have bread if Frau Bach didn't work?* I thought. On their way out, Mutti turned and said to Irmi and me, "It's best if you two stay inside the first day. Let's see how safe it is, before you go wandering off." They took off and Irmi and I went back to sleep.

In about an hour, Opa came back and walked into our room, looking dejected. "Opa, what happened," I said.

He sat down on the couch and muttered, "They didn't take me. They said I was too old. I think they don't want any men working for them." Irmi and I looked at each other and didn't know what to say. With him not working, there would be one less ration and one more mouth to feed. He looked up at us and continued, "Well, at least they took the others. We'll just have to find some food elsewhere, right?" Irmi and I just nodded. But where were we going to find food?

We filled our canteens with water and the three of us decided to scope out the area. We felt safe with Opa. I noticed the Bach family was home and Frau Färber was right, Frau Bach didn't work. We walked down our block toward the make-shift army headquarters comprised of a group of houses at the end of the street. Opa showed us where they all went to get work and where the line for food was supposed to be.

We walked to the end of town. Opa looked around carefully. "Let's walk along the edge of this farm and get farther out of sight. I suspect this is off-limits, so be careful—don't be seen. Let's walk in the tree-line until we get further out." We nonchalantly walked down the road until we got to the trees, then we crouched down and vanished into the tree-line. I felt my heart beating fast as the excitement came upon me—*hey, this is fun!* We stayed out of sight until we were about three-quarters down the field, then we walked along the perimeter of the field. Fortunately, there was a slight crown in the field, so we couldn't be seen from the road. Irmi and I were following close behind Opa when he stopped and bent down to look at something just at the overgrown edge. "I think this is—it looks like asparagus!" he said, all excited. "I can't believe it's ripe already. Irmi, Ilse, here, take a look." All excited, we got down on our knees to get a closer look. He bent the tall grasses and weeds out of the way to show a few tall strands of a plant. "This is an asparagus plant. It has these triangle-shaped short leaves on its tall stem, and a little crown on top. There will be usually a few clumped together. When you see these," he paused in his speech as he broke the stem, "you break them off right under the last leaf. The plant should grow back in a week or so, ready to pick again." He looked around. "If you see any more, pick them. These are either growing wild or this was an asparagus field years ago."

Irmi and I quickly led the way, looking eagerly for more stalks. Soon Irmi shouted, "Hey, here's another one."

"*Shh*," my grandfather warned. "Not so loud. They'll hear us."

Irmi knelt down to pick a stalk, then said, "There's some more."

"Let me pick. I want to try," I broke in. I was excited to help. We continued to search, but didn't find many more. It seemed like they were just congregated in a small section. Nevertheless, Irmi and I each had a fist-full.

"Now remember where they were; they will resprout and we can pick again," Opa spoke as if he were educating us. "Now that we're out of sight, the real reason I came out here was to see the potatoes." He walked a few steps into the field, knelt down and grabbed one of the plants gently with his left hand and started digging around the root with his right. Soon, he pulled up a few small root balls. "These are potatoes. They need another two months or so to be fully grown. We'll come out here and pick some before the Russians start harvesting them."

We walked back along the same path we came in, being careful not to be seen coming from the field. Once on the road, we hid the asparagus in our pockets and walked quickly toward town. "Now let's find some dandelion leaves," my grandfather exclaimed as we walked. Once near town where there were people we felt safe. My grandfather showed us again what to look for. Along the edge of the road were many dandelion plants. We picked the leaves for about a half-hour and filled every one of our pockets. Some soldiers saw us, but left us alone. We weren't bothering anyone or stealing anything.

We went home. I was excited about our adventure. I gained a new appreciation for what Opa knew about finding edible plants. My grandfather got a small pot and placed all of our dandelions in it, poured in some water and rinsed them. "We'll eat these, and then go out and pick some more. Leave the asparagus for when everyone comes home and we'll share." We ate the dandelion leaves like a salad. It wasn't great, but it felt good to finally get something in my stomach. Once we were done eating, we went back out to get more, but this time, with a basket.

Winter at home with the family, 1940.

That afternoon, when our four workers arrived home, they were each greeted with a heaping plate full of dandelion salad. My grandmother was first to respond, "Hey, how wonderful. This looks good and we're hungry!"

"Irmi and Ilse picked them for you," Opa boasted. He wanted to give us the credit. They soon started eating while continuing to praise us. Irmi and I stood with sheepish grins, pleased that we made them happy. Eager to hear how their first day at work went, Opa gave them a chance to start eating, and then asked, "So how did your day go? Was it hard work?"

Tante Friedel lifted her head, hurrying her chewing, and then answered, "They put us to work doing laundry today. Mutti and Hanna sorted the dirty clothes, I was washing and Anneliese was folding and sorting the clean clothes. There were a lot of women working with us. In fact, they were all women—no men." My grandfather lowered his head, perhaps realizing the Russians would never put him to work.

Mutti followed with: "Each group—sort, wash, and fold—needs to make a quota—it was piles. If we don't make it by the end of the day, we get nothing. Can you imagine? You work all day, then find out you get nothing for it? Fortunately, we all made our quota; it wasn't easy, but we did it. So, each of us got two slices of bread, a scoop of lard and a little sugar."

"We also have asparagus," I cried out, unable to contain myself.

"Ilsechen, how did you get that?" Mutti replied excitedly.

"Opa showed us how to find and pick it by the potato field."

"What!" Mutti's tone went from excited to angry. "You shouldn't go there. That's very dangerous. The Russians will get you."

"I took them," Opa confessed. Mutti looked a little relieved, but still annoyed. "Don't worry, we were very careful, right, girls?" He looked at Irmi and me, awaiting an acknowledgement.

"*Ja, oh—ja,*" Irmi responded, a little uncomfortable being on the spot. "We snuck in along the tree-line. No one saw us and we didn't go out to the field until we passed the hill—out of sight from the street. We found the asparagus at the edge of the field, growing wild."

Mutti apprehensively gave us that look that said she wasn't entirely convinced with our story. "Well, thank you for the asparagus. Please," she emphasized, "Be careful. You can't be too cautious." She changed the subject. "Let's prepare our dinner." Everything was split up evenly. The asparagus was boiled and served separately. We had a tiny wood-burning stove in our room. Once we started it up, we needed to open all of the windows, because it got too hot. The lard was spread on the bread and the sugar on top. The bread was very moist and heavy. It was whole grain and dense. The combination was actually quite good and filling. Poor Omi had only one tooth which was on the left side of her upper jaw. So she would angle a piece of bread in her mouth, lift her lip, clamp down and tear off a piece. It was amazing how she could manipulate food. She took the one bite and then split the rest in two equal pieces and gave it to Irmi and me.

"Mutti, what are you doing?" my mother questioned.

"Oh, I'm not so hungry. Besides, I don't need so much food. The children need more because they are growing."

Opa followed up, "You have to eat."

"No, no, no, really, I'm good." Omi walked away. Opa just shook his head. We took it somewhat reluctantly, but she always framed it in the context that older people don't need as much food, and it made sense.

The events went pretty much unchanged for about a week. Every day, Opa went diligently with the others to see if the Russians would take him for work, but every day, he ended up back at home, helping us gather our dandelion salads. Each day more and more people joined us picking greens. That's when I began to realize, the Russians may have taken us over, but if we were to endure, we were on our own.

5

Omi's Sacrifice

Irmi and I spent a lot of time together. We felt safe wandering outside as long as we stayed in the town center. Manuela started joining us, and at first I didn't like it, but she was a very nice girl, and although she monopolized Irmi's time, I grew accustomed to having her around.

One afternoon, the three of us were headed to the army base. While we were walking, Irmi asked Manuela, "How do you survive?"

"What do you mean," Manuela replied.

"Well, how do you get enough food... Your mother doesn't work and our begging here at the army base isn't enough?"

Manuela's face turned red, and she lowered her head. She sheepishly responded, "We get food ... it's enough."

"But from where?" Irmi persisted.

Now Manuela was getting perturbed, "Just don't worry about it!"

Irmi recognized that she didn't want to talk about it, so she changed the subject. At the army base, we started getting bolder in our search for food. If we saw a soldier eating something, we very politely asked if he could spare us some food. We had mixed responses. On rare occasions, some got mad and yelled at us and told us to get away. We remembered the unfriendly ones and stayed away from them. We were starting to recognize and remember the Russians, since the current regiment lasted much longer than previous ones. Most soldiers ignored us, but occasionally, they threw us a piece of bread or a chunk of dried meat. Some of them made a joke of us and laughed at our expense amongst their comrades, treating us like dogs. I didn't care. As long as I got some food, I kept begging.

I must say, not all of the soldiers were beasts. Some were very nice. They talked to us and were sincere. Back, before the invasion, when we still had school, I was taught Russian, so I was able to understand some of what they said, and I knew the important words like *please, food* and *bread*. The more I talked and listened, the better my Russian became.

One soldier who spoke some German helped me learn Russian words. He told me his name was Yuri. He gave me a pencil and some paper and most days, he spent fifteen minutes teaching me a few words and phrases. Sometimes Yuri would help interpret for us when we were talking to other soldiers.

Most of the Russians smoked; mainly cigarettes, but some smoked pipes and cigars. I picked up some spent cigarettes that still had tobacco left, and saved them for Opa after I saw him scrounging for cigarette butts to put in his pipe one day. The cigarettes were American. It seemed odd that Russians smoked American cigarettes. We also noticed that many of their cans and food wrappers were labeled or stamped with U.S.A. Why would America send the Russian soldiers food and cigarettes? We eventually learned that the cigarettes and food were from care packages provided by the U.S. for displaced civilians, but which were taken by the Russians for their own use. Already, we were seeing the corruption in the Soviet system.

One day as I was picking up cigarette butts, a soldier looked at me with a puzzled expression. I sensed that he wondering why a child was picking these up to smoke. I quickly responded, "*Nyet, nyet,* Grandfather-pipe." He tilted his head back and made an, *Ah* look, then raised his hand, signaling me to wait. He pulled a bag out of his pocket and grabbed a pinch of tobacco, enough to fill one pipe, and he handed it to me. "*Makhorka,*" he said, with a smile on his face. I thanked him profusely. I was so pleased and couldn't wait until I could surprise Opa.

After dinner that night, I reached into my pocket and pulled out the tobacco and showed it to Opa. "*Makhorka,*" I said.

"*Makhorka?* What is that?"

"It's Russian for tobacco. A soldier saw me gathering cigarette butts and gave me some tobacco."

My grandfather's face lit up. He loved smoking his pipe. "*Danke,* Ilse, that is very kind of you. I haven't had real pipe tobacco for weeks. I'm going to smoke it now." He took the tobacco, placed it in the pipe and lit it. Then he poured a shot of his dwindling supply of peppermint schnapps and puffed away at his pipe as he sipped his schnapps. He sat back on the couch, put his feet on a box, closed his eyes and sighed as he rested his head on the back of the couch. He had a look of utter contentment at these small pleasures he could still enjoy. I was so pleased that I could make him happy.

Early July ushered in warm weather. Irmi and I took Manuela on a few trips to the field in search of late-season asparagus. We also continued to pick dandelions to supplement the worker's rations. One day, as we were looking for greens, we heard gun shots and bullets whistling over our heads. Irmi shouted, "Run for the woods ... the Russians are shooting at us!" We made it to the shelter of the woods and stayed there for over an hour.

"Do you think they were aiming at us," I said.

"I don't think so," Irmi said. "But if they would have hit us, they wouldn't care. I think they just wanted us out of the field." Needless to say it worked, but within a few days, we were back, just a little bit smarter this time.

Omi started coming home early some days. She could no longer perform any hard work. If they assigned her to anything physically taxing, she would just come home because she knew she could not make the quota. Why waste a whole day of energy working, if there was no reward of food? She only stayed if it was a matter of sorting laundry or folding clothes. Even that was difficult for her. She was now seventy-five, and as long as I knew her, she suffered from severe arthritis. She walked slowly and found it difficult to use her hands and fingers. She never complained, though. She wanted so badly to help provide food for us, especially Irmi and me. She helped out where she could around the house and did cleaning and cooking. I think through guilt of not being able to provide food from work, she now gave almost all of her food to Irmi and me.

Once Irmi pushed the serving back to Omi and said, "*Nein*, you need to eat too."

Omi got mad and slammed the food in front of Irmi, and yelled, "You eat this and that's final!" Omi walked outside. This wasn't like her at all. Irmi put the food in her mouth reluctantly, like it tasted horribly. Clearly, Omi was giving up and sacrificing herself for Irmi and me. Her breathing got noticeably louder and she began coughing often. Her health was rapidly deteriorating and lack of nourishment didn't help.

Opa, Irmi and I took her to the hospital. They diagnosed her as having pneumonia. They said that there was nothing they could do. Pneumonia is not contagious so it was safe to take her home. They recommended that she rest and drink plenty of water. We made sure that she remained hydrated. However, rest she didn't.

Opa cried out to her, "Luise, you need to rest. We can take care of that, please lie down." Omi just ignored him and kept working. It was silly; Irmi and I could have easily done what kept her preoccupied. "If you don't stop, you won't get any better," Opa insisted.

"*Ach*, I'm fine," Omi declared. Stop worrying about *me*." She was on such a self-destructive path. She knew it; there was just no stopping her. It was painful to watch. She was noticeably thinner. Her wool skirt that used to hit mid-knee, no longer fit her waist and the hem now reached her upper ankle. There her knee-high socks that she used to diligently keep pulled to her knee lay pooled at her ankles. Omi's wooden sandals, hand-made by Opa, lost their clop as she walked. Her straight grey hair was always neatly combed to one side, pinned and brought to the back of her head in bun. Now the bun flopped loose and her hair was a tangled weave.

She was so weak that a few times she fell. Opa would come to her. She waved her hands at him, "I'm fine, leave me alone!"

Opa had tears in his eyes and all he could do was watch. It was only a matter of about two days after we returned from the hospital that she became incapable of getting around—she was now bedridden. Her skin was pale and clammy and her sunken cheeks were an almost bluish hue.

Opa was constantly at her side. "Luise, here take some water." She was too weak to lift her head. He held her head up and she still drank some water, but didn't speak.

She went downhill in a hurry and, as much as none of us wanted to admit, the inevitable was upon us. Opa finally broke the silence, and uttered in a soft calm voice: "Go find Pastor Jänicke, and bring him here as soon as possible." Pastor Jänicke was the pastor of our church before we were evacuated. He stayed with his flock; he was loyal to his church, even sacrificed his own safety. Someone went and got him and he rushed over that afternoon. He gave Omi communion and prayed over her. She was still conscious and responsive, but terribly weak. We sang a hymn together and she sang along, mostly only moving her lips:

> Lord, take my hand and lead me
> Upon life's way
> Direct, protect and feed me
> From day to day.
> Without your grace and favor
> I go astray;
> So take my hand, O Savior,
> And lead the way.
>
> Lord, when the tempest rages,
> I need not fear;
> For you, the Rock of Ages,
> Are always near.
> Close by your side abiding,
> I fear no foe,
> For when your hand is guiding,
> In peace I go.
>
> Lord, when the shadows lengthen
> And night has come,
> I know that you will strengthen
> My steps toward home,
> And nothing can impede me,
> O blessed Friend!
> So take my hand and lead me
> Unto the end.[4]

Omi sang along for the first two verses. During the last verse, her lips moved out of sync to the song, she closed her eyes and, amazingly, the Lord took her away before we finished. My grandfather broke down in tears. "Luise, Luise, don't leave me alone." He hung over the bed with his arms around her, hugging her and sobbing. I never saw my grandmother and grandfather argue or disagree on anything. Not only were they married for over fifty years, they were best friends.

We were all in tears. The aftermath of war had claimed yet another from our family. I couldn't help but think: if she hadn't given up her food to Irmi and me, would she still be with us? There was a guilt that I couldn't shake. I felt somewhat responsible for her death. I prayed for her soul to go to heaven and I prayed to God to take away my guilt. A vision came to me of Omi holding my baby brother Hans in heaven. I realized she was a selfless God-fearing woman and led her life the way God would want anyone to live. Omi was our matriarch; she was the level-headed thinker and provided logic and reason. She had a calming effect on us all that gave us faith. With her gone, that role became Mutti's.

The night Omi died, I reflected on her and my thoughts took me back to the days before I was old enough to attend school when Omi often took care of me. *I remember seeing her sitting in the bedroom on a wooden rocking chair draped with a grey wool blanket. She sat next to the window to enjoy the natural light. Her frail reading glasses defied gravity on her nose. The glasses were often left on her nose even when she wasn't reading. She sat studiously in her chair, feet on a small cloth-covered stool, cat on her lap, reading her Bible with what light was available. The lazy black and white cat was content to sit on her lap as long as she read. When Omi did get up and walk around, the cat was always winding between her feet.*

I would barrage Omi with lots of questions. I viewed her as a wealth of wisdom, perhaps because she always looked so studious reading her Bible, but more because she had a wonderful way of answering questions. She had tremendous patience in helping me understand things, even using parables and real-life examples. She also had a certain excitement in her voice that captivated my attention.

I recall one day when I was about four, I asked: "Omi, what do you learn reading that Bible?"

She put down her Bible. She picked me up, and just before I landed on her lap, the cat jumped out of the way. "The Bible is God's word. He teaches us how to live a good and proper life. God gives us a choice in everything that we do; the Bible gives us guidance to choose the right decisions."

"What did you read today?"

She hesitated and curled her lips together, "Well, Ilsechen, although the Bible is full of wonderful stories, it also tells of evil. Evil is unavoidable. The devil places evil in our paths to tempt us and he tries to make us lose our faith in God. If we trust in the Lord and read our Bible, God will remove our fears and ultimately destroy evil. We need to have faith in him." She paused for a moment and looked upward through the corner of her eyes. "Hitler is an evil man. He will destroy Germany. The Bible tells me that he will be defeated, and there will be horrible times to follow."

Herr Färber built yet another coffin for us. Opa actually talked the Russians into allowing Omi to be buried in the cemetery across from our old house, where Hans was buried. The old cemetery was already fenced in. They allowed only Opa and Mutti to enter to bury Omi and gave them just one hour.

Two doors down the street from us, on the same day as Omi, a young mother died of starvation. She had a two-year old son. We knew her and knew of her plight. She couldn't work because she had to care for her child. We gave her some food occasionally, but we didn't have enough, either. Like Omi, she gave her food to her son in order for him to live. But in this case, it was, unfortunately, all for naught. With the mother gone, the child had no one to care for him. He died two days later.

Death had become a too-regular occurrence. *Who was to blame for all of this?* I refused to believe that all of these Russians were bad people. *What were they supposed to do?* How could we let a child die? How could we not find just a little more food? Questions like these had no answer. There simply wasn't enough. And survival meant taking care of yourself and your family first.

6

Desperate Times

One evening Anneliese, Irmi and I were sitting outside. During nice weather, we spent most of our time outdoors to avoid our cramped quarters. A soldier entered the center quarters of our building where the Bach family stayed. "What's that all about?" Irmi questioned.

Irmi and I both looked at Anneliese. "I don't know," she said, "but he's not allowed in civilian homes."

"I've seen him around here a lot," I said.

"*Ja*, me too," Irmi said. "I was always wondering why he wandered around here ... but I never saw him go in their room."

Anneliese looked around. "We should tell Mutti and Opa. What if he comes in our room?" Before we could make our way indoors, the door to the Bachs' quarters opened and Manuela and Sigrid came out.

"They don't look scared," I said. "They must be all right." They walked over to us.

Irmi, with her head down and lower jaw hanging, looked up at Manuela and said, "There's a Russian in your house ... what's he doing in there? Should we get the military police?"

Manuela held her head down and clenched her lips together. After a long pause, she said, "My mother is a whore! Instead of working, she has sex with this soldier." Her eyes started to well with tears. "He gives her food, in return for sex." She put her hand over her mouth. "Sometimes Sigrid and I are right there in front of them—we only have one room—it's smaller than yours."

I was shocked. I could hardly catch my breath. This was difficult for me to understand. A few months ago women were calling the Russians sub-humans, perhaps having been raped by them, and now they were having sex with them. This world was upside-down.

We told our family about Frau Bach, but they didn't seem shocked. I think they already suspected it, but didn't want to tell us. A few nights later, we heard a drunken soldier knocking on her window slurring: "Lisa, Lisa." It became more frequent. One night the soldier was so drunk and disoriented that he knocked on our window. "Lisa," he yelled.

Opa was furious: "Go, get away!" he shouted through the window. The soldier didn't care. He just walked one room over continuing his call for Lisa.

I tried to refrain from judgment and be compassionate, particularly where young mothers had infants with no working family members. Did Frau Bach do this because she had to care for Sigrid, who was only five? I'm sure the woman who died the same day as Omi teetered on the fence of ethics. Did principle drive her and her two year old son to an early grave?

Prostitutes without infants took the brunt of criticism from our civilian community. Mutti often said, "These women are just too lazy to work and find food." It was a harsh criticism. Regardless of the means, the rations provided by the Russians were not enough to keep anyone alive for long; food had to be supplemented somehow. Perhaps it was easy for us to judge; we had plenty of workers in our family and we were crafty at finding food in the fields. Still, for everyone, survival was the only rule.

* * *

One early August morning, Opa did not go with the rest of the family to seek work. He gathered Irmi and me and said, "Let's go see about our potatoes. We need to go before anyone sees us." Irmi and I bolted into action and were excited about our quest. We vanished into the tree-line undetected. Once past the hump in the field, Opa started digging in the dirt and pulled up some potatoes. They had grown significantly. He picked about a dozen of the largest ones. "Here, each of you take four and put two in each side pocket. I'll take the others. We can't make this look obvious as we walk back home." We slipped back without a trace. When we got back home, Opa said, "Let's boil six potatoes—one for each of us. The others I will store for a later day." That afternoon, we boiled some of the potatoes and asparagus and had a meal ready when the rest of the family came home. We were all very happy to eat a whole potato each. It provided well-needed sustenance.

Every morning for the next few weeks, we did the same thing. There were only a few days that we had to abandon our attempt because Russians were in the area. Not only did we have potatoes for dinner every day, we were also able to stockpile some food for later. One day, the field was being prepped for harvesting and the Russians brought civilians to the field to start picking potatoes. The next morning, Opa decided to see if they would use him for picking. They took him and Irmi, while Mutti, Anneliese and Tante Friedel continued their work doing laundry. That evening Opa looked despondent. I prepared potatoes for dinner and Opa talked about the day in the field. "I was tempted to take some more potatoes, but there were too many soldiers around keeping an eye on us. I told Irmi not to take any—we have plenty at home. Good thing we didn't, because they searched every picker at the end of the day. They found a few women who stuffed some potatoes in their pockets." He looked down at the potatoes on his plate. "They took the women away to a prison camp."

We knew the women that were caught and we never heard from them again. It didn't matter that the women had children to care for: they turned into someone else's problem. It was a harsh punishment for trying to stay alive. It could have just as easily been us.

During the day, I found myself alone, now that Irmi joined the rest of the family working for the Russians. I wandered in search of food, but also found time to explore. One day, after begging for food from the soldiers, I meandered in the direction of the coast. I walked along a fence. I heard the thundering waves and could see the water, but because of the steep cliff, I couldn't see the beach. I walked in the direction of our old house. The area was remote and, from a safety standpoint, I questioned myself, but something compelled me—I had to see my beach for one last time before the Russians completely blocked it off.

I kept going even though I knew a young girl alone would be easy prey for Russian soldiers. Finally, I reached a section where the fence was not yet attached to the poles. Here was my chance to get to the beach. I slowly walked to the edge of the sand dune cliff, looked in every direction and realized the coast was clear. I sat on my bottom with my feet in front and hands in back and started a controlled slide down the cliff. I would struggle getting back up, but we used to do this every day in other summers.

A quick scan along the beach revealed that I was alone less than a kilometer from the beach near our old house. I was never allowed to be alone on the beach. Even when I was with other family members, there were always people at the beach, swimming, walking, sunbathing or searching for amber. My mind couldn't quite accept the fact that this was really our beach. The physical surroundings were all familiar, but vacant of people, the scene looked surreal, like a dream. I felt nervous and frightened, but now that I was at the water, I was compelled to say good-bye to my beloved beach. My stomach churned with nervous apprehension. I knew this beach and knew all of the paths up the cliffs. I scoped out each escape route as I walked the beach, in case I came across Russian soldiers.

Palmnicken was home to the largest amber[5] mine in the world. The amber mine was roughly three kilometers from our old house and offset from the coast by less than one kilometer. It was in operation for a long time. Even though the amber was excavated in deep pits, we managed to find pieces that washed up on the shore, especially after a large storm had agitated the beach. During my walk, it appeared that no one had been on the beach for weeks. I found a few pieces of amber and put them in my pocket. I wouldn't dare show my family because I would get in trouble for being on the beach alone.

I arrived at the section of beach that my family used. In front of me was a steep sand bank with a well-worn trail heading to the top. Above the cliff, not visible from the beach, were a small field, a gravel road, and then our house. It took only five minutes to walk to the sea. With the right conditions, from our house, we could hear the deep thunderous waves crashing onto the beach. Most of our summer life was spent at this beach. From morning to evening we played in the dunes, swam in the sea, and searched for amber. It was the most wonderful life a little girl could ask for: a loving family, a beautiful home, and a year-round paradise.

I took off my shoes, rolled up my pants and walked into the sea. I stood and looked around and realized this was where I learned to swim. My older brother Günter decided it was time for me to learn when I was roughly three. He simply carried me into water that was over my head, dropped me, and walked away. It worked! I flailed with every limb and gasped for air every time my head bobbed above the water line. I thought I would never make the shore when finally my foot scraped the sand. Out of breath and finally on solid ground, I saw Günter bent over on the beach in laughter. I walked over to him, picked up some sand and threw it at him. It wasn't fifteen minutes later that I was back in the water testing my new found skill.

Memories played in my mind as I tried to absorb everything I saw around me today. I walked toward the cliff. There ahead of me, resting upside-down, was Papa's wooden boat. I rushed over to it, only to find that someone had shot holes into its side. When I was about four, Papa bought this boat. It had four bench seats and could fit the whole family. It was very sturdy and could handle the waves on a normal day with ease. Papa named the boat *Ilse*. I was so proud. I don't know if it bothered any of my siblings that he named it after me, but they never made mention of it. I always wanted to tag along when Papa went for a boat ride. After all, I had a boat named after me! Well, I was able to go on many trips, but Papa bought the boat mainly for fishing, and I wasn't allowed to go because it would be too dangerous.

The Baltic Sea gave us sustenance. Papa and Opa would go out together with large nets. They made big circles and generally left the nets out all night. The next morning they hauled in their catch. The right time of the year would bring in herring. Salmon was more typical, although other species would find their way into the nets and end up on the dinner table. Papa built a smoke house and he would take the freshly caught fish, clean them and immediately hang them in the smoker. There the fish hung for days as he kept adding woodchips to the smoker. We ate some fish right away, but most were treated and stored for later. People from all around came when Papa smoked fish. He never sold any, but gave much of it away. The smoked flavor was mouthwatering. I was so hungry. I wished I could have one of those smoked fish right now.

Then I recalled a time when a boy swam too far from shore and couldn't make it back. He screamed for help, and his friends took our boat to save him. With help from *Ilse,* they saved his life. I walked around the boat. My name on the bow had a bullet hole through it. Why would they shoot holes through a perfectly good boat?

I decided to take in one last pleasure. I dropped my clothes on the beach and ran into the sea for a swim. As usual, the icy water took my breath away. The Baltic Sea was always extremely cold. Even at the height of summer, it felt as if icebergs were still on the North shore. But the sea was beautiful. Even on the calmest of days, waves splashed upon the shore, churning up the sand and making the shoreline murky. The lack of clarity gave it a mysterious aura. Once away from the shoreline, the water was crystal clear. The sea had a stealthy undertow that claimed many good swimmers. As children, it was fun to allow the sea to carry us out against our will. We quickly learned not to fight the tide, but let it carry us to a point down-shore and re-attempt an approach. We learned that the undertow eventually changed directions or waned. On turbulent days, parents kept a close eye on their children.

I realized that I better get back. Out of breath, I threw my clothes on and quickly back-tracked the way I came in, fortunately unnoticed. I was thrilled by this moment of freedom at my beloved beach and sea. One week later, the Russian fence was completed.

7

The Commandant's Assault

Irmi's participation in our family's workforce provided another much-needed ration of food. Once the potatoes were harvested, she mostly did laundry. The Russians didn't take her every day, but they took Irmi over Opa. Our stockpile of potatoes was quickly depleted, and we needed to find more food. There was an abundance of wild raspberry bushes along the edges of fields, and some wild grape vines as well. None of these were ripe yet. Opa and I sometimes walked for hours, looking for food in the woods. We came upon marshy areas and found some wild blueberry plants. Opa looked at them and tasted a few. "They aren't quite ripe, but we need some extra food." I didn't question him. He was right about everything so far, so we spent a few hours picking. They were tiny, so picking a liter of berries was time-consuming.

We proudly served the berries to everyone that evening and they all loved them. Unfortunately, the next morning, we were all violently sick with vomiting and diarrhea. Apparently, the unripe berries did not agree with us. Tante Friedel and Anneliese managed to go to work. The rest of us lay in bed, sick, that day. Fortunately, it looked like the symptoms only lasted one day. All of us recouped, with the exception of Mutti. She went back to work, but was still sick. A few days passed, and she was getting worse. She developed a high fever, was very weak and could no longer work. By now, thankfully, medical supplies were starting to filter in regularly. The Russians converted a house in the middle of town into a hospital. One morning, Opa and I took Mutti there. As with the previous make-shift hospitals, most of the help was from civilian women.

Frau Söhn was a nurse at the hospital. She was a family acquaintance and it was good to see someone we knew and trusted attending to Mutti. Her immediate reaction was, "I'm sure it's typhoid fever. We're seeing a lot of that now. We will keep her here at the hospital until she gets better."

Opa looked at her and questioningly said, "What do you think?"

She hesitated, "Do you really want to know?"

Opa looked at her and quietly said, "Yes, I really want to know."

"Well, typhoid has been the leading cause of death here lately, but we're starting to get some medicine now that should treat it. It's too soon to tell. But understand: typhoid is very serious. She needs to rest and she needs to get her fever down if we have any hope of helping her." My eyes welled up, and I couldn't swallow. I wished Opa hadn't asked the question. I didn't know what to think anymore. If I lost Mutti, it might be the end of the line. There couldn't be any worse news. I prayed on the way home for God to save Mutti. It was in His hands. He could save her if He chose to.

As we walked from the hospital, Opa recognized my fear. He put his arm around me and placed his hand on my shoulder. "Don't worry," he said. "She will make it through. She is in good hands." His words made me feel better, but they didn't completely remove my fears.

I visited her several times a day in the hospital; sometimes by myself. I wanted her to know, above all, that I needed her and I wanted to instill in her a will to live. Frau Söhn was always very kind and attentive and always assured me that Mutti was doing better, but to me it seemed she was getting worse. Her face was drawn and she was sweating profusely. She shivered frequently and at times was unresponsive. Worst of all, I thought she was giving up. I desperately tried to give her confidence. I sat at the edge of the bed, holding her hand. There was no strength in her grip. She didn't attempt to hold my hand or even acknowledge that I was holding hers. Frau Söhn saw me and came and sat next to me. She put her arm around me and felt my concern.

In a tearful voice, I said, "It's my fault." I sniffled, "I gave her unripe blueberries and now she's going to die."

Frau Söhn chuckled and affectionately bumped her head to mine. "Ilse, typhoid disease does not come from blueberries, it comes from unclean water. It may have triggered the symptoms, but the blueberries weren't the cause." She took her hand and brushed the tears from my cheeks and leaned her face in front of mine. "It's not your fault, Ilse." Frau Söhn gave me a big hug and slowly rocked me back and forth. I don't know if she was telling me the truth, or just wanted me to believe it was not my fault, but in either case, it worked. After a moment of silence, she calmly and confidently told me, "She needs to sweat out the fever. I know it looks bad, but it's a sign that her body is expelling the fever." I finally looked up at her with watery eyes. Her message was more uplifting than I could put into words. She inspired hope and, after all, hope was all that I could cling to. Frau Söhn was a tremendously wonderful and caring person. Every time I came to visit Mutti, she lifted my spirits.

I visited Mutti every day in the hospital for about a week. One day, when I arrived, she actually sat up in bed. Frau Söhn was trying to feed her some soup. At first, I was all excited that Mutti was sitting up and eating, but then I quickly realized that she was too weak to even feed herself. Frau Söhn cautioned, "We need to be careful what she eats; bread and bland soup is all she can tolerate. We need to slowly get her stomach used to solid food, and then she can get her strength back."

That afternoon, worried about Mutti, I sat on the steps at our door which faced a narrow back road. I heard footsteps and down the road walked a Russian officer. He was the Commandant of the area. He was in charge of Herr Färber's woodshop and I think several other workings. He was always pleasant and respectful, and almost always said hello. He lived in an apartment that was attached to other army-operated buildings down our road and just around the corner. Sometimes, he walked home via this back road. His attire was always meticulously clean and without wrinkles. As he walked, the crease in his trousers resisted the bend in his knees and the cuffs were hemmed perfectly to just bounce on top of his fastidiously polished boots. Even though it was a dirt road, his boots seemed impervious to dust. He tilted his head back slightly so that he could see under the brim of the hat that he wore low across his eyebrows. His jet-black hair had a bluish shimmer from the fading sunlight. He was tall with broad shoulders and walked with an exaggerated erect posture, conveying arrogance yet commanding authority. Mesmerizing, uncommon violet-colored eyes were set back deep behind his eyebrows. He was very handsome and was said to be a womanizer. I didn't totally believe that, because he was nothing but friendly to us and never offered any suggestion of impropriety.

He said hello as he walked by, and I responded in kind. Spontaneously, I asked in Russian, "Could you spare some bread?" Admittedly, I tried to look as cute and irresistible as I could as I spoke. I had learned this method garnered results.

He smiled and continued walking with his head pointed in the direction of travel. *He ignored me,* I thought. "Follow me to my house," he said, as he walked without turning his head. Hesitantly, I followed him at a distance— close enough to let him know I was following, but far enough to let him know that I was afraid of him. Mutti desperately needed food and this was an avenue to help her build up her strength. He periodically glanced back to see if I was following. He entered his apartment. I stopped about one house away. There was a bench in front of a neighboring house and I sat, waiting, hoping he would come out with some bread. A few seconds later, his door opened and he peeked out and searched for me, then waved for me to enter. I stood up, but didn't move. He vanished back into his apartment. Again, he opened his door, and, leaning out, he waved me in. This time, he waited to see if I would move. I walked toward his apartment and the door closed again. I got to his steps and was terribly frightened. But Mutti's well-being compelled me to go up the stairs. I stood in front of the door, it opened, and he was holding a plate with a thick slice of bread and a substantial slice of canned corned beef.

I told myself, *under no circumstances, enter his apartment.* I felt my knees start to quiver. This was really stupid! Against all good judgment, I stepped forward and said in Russian, "It's for Mutti, she is ill."

He quickly grabbed my arm, pulled me in, and shut and locked the door behind him. He said gently, "Don't worry, don't be afraid." I wanted to believe him, but by now, I was terrified. I couldn't catch my breath. I was locked in. His tiny apartment was perfectly spotless. In fact, it was cold—without character. There were few furnishings: only a table and chair in the kitchen. As an officer, he apparently had an apartment to himself, as opposed to barracks used by most soldiers. I immediately suspected he must have women clean his apartment and give him sex for food.

I didn't know what to do. *Stay calm and in control and emphasize that I need the food,* I thought to myself. I said, "Mutti is dying. She needs food."

"You will get your food, don't worry," he said again, very calmly. Then he grabbed my hand and walked me to the back room—a bedroom. There, he placed the plate on a small table and sat in a chair. He pulled me toward him and sat me on his lap, and started touching me on the inside of my thigh. He leaned over and began kissing me. I was in an awful predicament. At this point, it was obvious what his intentions were, and I was locked inside of his apartment with no escape. Instinctively, my mind shifted into an escape mode. I thought of split-second strategies of escape: *Plan A: Take the table, throw it through the window, jump on the bed and leap through the window; or plan B: Pray; or plan C: Kick, fight scream as loud as I can and pound on the door with all my might, making enough noise to attract attention from anyone outside, especially the MP.* I chose B and C simultaneously and improvised plan D: *At all cost, don't forget the food.* Adrenalin pumped through my veins. I pushed and kicked and screamed so loud, I could have awakened Omi from the dead. I grabbed the plate of food on my way to the door.

He followed me and grabbed me again and said, "Shh, don't worry, don't be afraid." I started kicking the door and nearly knocked it off of its hinges and kept screaming as loud as I could. I think I scared him; I know I scared myself. He grabbed both of my arms and tried to calm me down—no way—I was completely hysterical. I was so out of control that I don't even completely recollect everything that I did in my attempt to escape. Frustrated, he couldn't open the door fast enough to let me out. As I ran out, in a stern voice, he warned me: "You better make sure you bring that plate back!" I couldn't believe how unconcerned he seemed about the whole thing. This was one of the most traumatizing events that ever happened to me and, to him, just a casual missed opportunity. I ran as fast as I could, until I got to the door of our house. I can't believe I hung on to the food through all that commotion and didn't drop a thing.

Out of breath and emotionally drained, I entered our home and was relieved that I made it back safely. It was late afternoon and Opa was the only one home; the others had not yet arrived from work. Still out of breath, I told Opa, "I was almost raped by the Commandant. I tried to get food for Mutti and he grabbed me and dragged me into his apartment." I raised my head and cupped my throat with the palm of my hand. Why did my voice sound so funny? Then I realized that I must have shouted so loud that I hurt my throat.

He lowered his eyebrows and clenched his lip, "Come on, Ilse, what would a man like him want with a little girl like you?"

"No, Opa, it's true. It's entirely true. It happened!"

He started shouting, "*Ach*, you imagined it. Don't go telling anyone this!"

I can't believe this, I said to myself. Why would I want to make up a story like that? Opa was in denial and refused to accept the gravity of our situation. I put the plate on the table and crawled into bed, put the sheets over my head and silently cried. The fact that Opa didn't believe me almost hurt more than the actual event with the officer.

Soon, Tante Friedel, Anneliese and Irmi came home from work. Tante Friedel was the first to notice the corned beef and bread on the table. "My goodness," she said surprised. "Where did this come from?" By now, I had the sheets pulled down and I was just sitting on my bunk bed. I didn't say anything. I thought Opa would say something. "Well, is someone going to tell us where it came from, or is it a surprise?" Tante Friedel went on.

Opa just looked up at me and obviously noticed my discontent "Ilse got it," he said in a flat tone.

"Ilse, this is wonderful! This will be delicious and your mother could use this nourishment." Tante Friedel paused, "But how did you get it?"

I sheepishly answered, "I got it from the commandant, he took me in his apartment and gave me..."

"You did what?" she shouted at me. "Tell me you didn't go in his apartment!"

"Well, he grabbed me and dragged me in."

"Ilse!" She grabbed both of my arms. "Are you okay? Did he touch you?"

She saw the terror in my eyes. "He tried to rape me, but I kicked and screamed and almost broke the door down and then he let me go."

"*Ach*, come on. That didn't happen," Opa continued in his denial.

"Papa," Tante Friedel angrily replied. "That filthy *schwein* would do that. My friend Sonja got raped by him. He bit her in the lip when she refused him. Ilse, I believe you."

I felt vindicated by Tante Friedel's comments. At least someone believed me. I think ultimately, after Tante Friedel's passionate response, Opa ended up believing me also, although he never apologized.

"Tante Friedel," I asked in a tone of someone seeking help.

"Yes, Ilse."

"He wants his plate back. I don't want to go alone."

She smiled and gave me a hug. "Of course, Ilse, I will go with you to return the plate."

Tante Friedel took the food and moved it to one of our dishes and washed his plate. She held my hand as we walked to the commandant's apartment. I

The Glaus family at beach. From left: Papa, Irmi, Mutti, Günter, Ilse, Anneliese.

stayed back two steps on the stairway entrance as Tante Friedel knocked on the door. She stood back as far as she could and still be able to hand him the plate. He opened the door. Tante Friedel quickly handed him the plate, I immediately said thank you. He never looked at us, took the plate and slammed the door shut. What a relief! That was now behind us.

When we got back, Tante Friedel split up the corned beef and bread and left a healthy portion for Mutti. We ate our share and enjoyed every bit of it. This was the first taste of meat that any of us had for two months. After dinner, I quickly packed Mutti's portion and ran to the hospital. I'm sure others wanted to go with to see how Mutti was doing, but Tante Friedel silently held them back to let me go alone. I think she realized I had a rough day and deserved all the glory for getting Mutti this food.

As I walked to the hospital, I realized how much Tante Friedel meant to me. I worried that I would arrive at the hospital and find Mutti dead, and Tante Friedel would try to fill in as my new Mutti. I loved Tante Friedel with all my heart, but she still was not Mutti. *Could I call Tante Friedel Mutti?* I didn't like the way my mind wandered. I looked to the sky as I walked, trying to block out these despondent thoughts.

I reached the hospital, exhausted in thought. Reluctant, yet compelled, I entered. I walked in the direction of Mutti's bed and, to my surprise; she was sitting up. She was obviously feeling much better. "Mutti, you're well." I quickly put the plate on the table next to her and hugged her. What a wonderful sight to see Mutti's recovery. It was as if someone pumped a cleansing fluid through my veins and erased my despairing thoughts. "Mutti, I have something for you." I handed her the small dish with her portion of the bread and corned beef.

"Ilsechen, oh my, where did you get this?"

She asked me an obvious question for which I didn't think to rehearse. I quickly thought, *it's best I don't tell her the whole story right now*. I responded, "I got it from the Russians." I was proud of that answer—it was quick and accurate and wouldn't get her worrying.

"Ilsechen, this is wonderful." She was so hungry and gobbled it up in short order. "It tasted great. Thank you." She sat back and sighed and looked content. "Ilsechen," she said with a big smile. "This food will give me the strength to come home tomorrow." Her smile spread all the way to my face. I spent about an hour with her, joyful about her wellbeing. We hugged goodbye and on my way home, I was so pleased, knowing the events of the day were all worth it.

The next morning, I got up early and ran to the nearest field. It was a beautiful cloud-free day. My shoes were getting soaked from the heavy dew on the grass. It was still crisp out, but I could tell it was going to be warm. How fitting, a beautiful day for Mutti's return home. I picked some flowering weeds from the edge of the field. Once arranged in my fist, they made a beautiful bouquet. I ran back home with a smile on my face; I couldn't wait to go pick up Mutti. The others were at work already and Opa was waiting for me. We walked to the hospital, got to Mutti's bed and, to my disappointment, she was lying down, looking weak and pale again. "Mutti, I thought you were feeling better, and—and you were coming home today," I stammered.

"*Ja*," Mutti straining to speak. "I thought so too. The food that you gave me yesterday was too rich. Frau Söhn said that after typhoid, I need to eat a bland diet until I get my strength back. I'm too weak to digest solid food. The corned beef tasted great, but was too rich." I felt horrible. Everything I did to help, failed: I gave her the berries, and now the corned beef.

"Don't worry." I heard the familiar voice of Frau Söhn behind me. "It's just a short setback." I turned to see Frau Söhn with a comforting smile on her face. She put her open hand on the back of my head and pulled me toward her. "The typhoid looks like it is gone, we just need to slowly let her stomach settle and get her strength back." I took a cup that still had a little water in it and placed the flowers in it. The flowers were tall for the cup, but they still looked pretty.

"Ilsechen, you picked flowers for me?" Mutti forced a smile.

"*Ja*, Mutti, I picked them this morning. I thought they would lift you up."

"They're lovely. I appreciate that you cared about me."

Sure enough, Frau Söhn was right, the next day, she was home, and although still extremely weak, was back to work the following day. What a relief. I was so pleased to see her better. I couldn't bear the thought of losing her. I didn't know the whereabouts of my father. If I lost Mutti, I would be an orphan in a brutal environment—it couldn't be any worse. I prayed and thanked God for her recovery—oh, and asked to be done with this imprisonment under the Russians already!

As summer waned, I became more independent. I started to understand the safe paths of travel and was no longer afraid to go somewhere on my own, as long as it was in the town. I started spending more time with other children near my age. I still went on many excursions with Opa, searching for food, but it was good to have friends. I became especially close with Marion. I went to school with her before the invasion and we knew each other, but now, we bonded. She lived nearly across from us, so we spent a lot of time together. Marion and I would go exploring. She was daring and adventuresome. She reminded me of Irmi; perhaps that's why I liked her.

One day, Marion and I were wandering the streets. It was a hot and muggy day and it reflected in our attitude. We were just feeling lazy. Marion jumped at an idea, "Ilse, let's go check out the army base at the coast." It was no surprise when soldiers congregated and started erecting temporary quarters that it would soon turn into an army base.

"Oh, I don't know Marion, Mutti..."

"Come on, don't be silly. They're not going to bother us. With all the MPs around, the worst they'll do is chase us away." We arrived at the temporary base. A chain link fence about twice my height surrounded the complex. Big tents with no sides canopied rows of tables and benches. They looked like circus tents—they probably were. We leaned against the fence, our fingers in the links and our faces right up to the fence. Marion pulled her head back a little and gazed down the fence row on either side. "What's up with this fence? My God, do they think we're going to attack them?" I burst out laughing, and Marion followed. We turned around and sat on the ground with our backs against the fence. We had a great laugh. It was wonderful to have a good friend here.

It was mid-day and we noticed there was more activity under one of the tents. "Hey, maybe they're getting ready to bring in the elephants," Marion said jokingly. I burst out laughing again at her wonderfully sarcastic sense of humor. As it turned out, the Russians were actually preparing meals. More and more Russians started arriving under the tent. I got a little scared; thinking we would get in trouble. I was just getting ready to tell Marion that we should go, when she shouted through the fence, "Hey, can you give us some bread?"

"Marion," I whispered. "Are you crazy? Keep quiet." The Russians ignored us.

"Can you spare any bread?" she shouted a little louder. This time, a few Russians turned their heads and looked at us. They muttered something among themselves.

Oh my God, I said to myself. *We're doomed.* To my amazement, one of the Russians got up and threw a whole piece of bread over the fence. It landed on the ground behind us. I immediately ran to pick it up.

Marion didn't even turn around. She was still facing the Russian. "Thank you very much," she said with a big smile. Then she turned and walked toward me, and wearing a gleeful grin, she tilted her head from side to side with a, "see, I told you so," attitude. I broke the bread in half and we stuffed it into our pockets and ran home, thrilled to provide an extra piece of bread for our families.

$$8$$

The Statue

Irmi came home early one afternoon. She was an efficient worker and often finished her quota before others. I loved when she came home early because, more often than not, she and I would explore abandoned buildings. This afternoon was no exception.

"Ilse, have you gone into the old school yet?"

"No." I looked at her, puzzled. "What do you expect to find there? There won't be any food in a school."

"Well, you never know. That's where we're going today." She led the way and I was her faithful follower. As we walked, I wondered why I hadn't thought of going into the school before. It was at the edge of the forbidden fence. The two-story solid brick building was only a farm field and street crossing away from our original house. I recalled that from our house, we could see the school. I wondered if I would be able to see our old house once we were inside the school.

The Palmnicken school was a transformed house of a former owner of the amber mine. It was a beautiful building and, at that time, was probably already fifty years old. All ages were taught at this school, but there weren't enough teachers to teach each age group individually, so some age groups overlapped.

The amber mine provided school free of charge for all of the children in the village, regardless of whether the parents worked at the mine. The school taught geology and used the mine for many studies and field trips. In those days, it was assumed that folk stayed near where they were born their whole life and worked in the same factory their parents did. So the mine was investing in its own future by educating children in the neighborhood.

We arrived at the front of the still-intact beautiful school. "Irmi, what if there are soldiers inside?" I inquired.

"*Ach was!* If there were soldiers in here, where are all of their trucks ... and did they just walk here?" She gave me her usual, "what are you, stupid?" look. She opened the door and fearlessly entered, and I followed cautiously behind. Inside, it was eerily dark and desolate, save for late afternoon sunlight penetrating through dirty windows. Months of dust rested on every surface.

"Look." Irmi stopped, hunched down in the limited light, pointing in front of her. "Footprints—there's probably nothing left in here—and these are recent." Even so, she kept walking: Irmi, the eternal optimist.

I felt uncomfortable being here. Strict rules used to govern this place and I still had a great deal of respect for the institution. I felt as if our principal, Frau Schmidt, was going to walk out of her office and demand to know what we were doing and why we missed school for over a year.

"Do you remember all of those refugees?" Irmi said. "My God, they were crammed in here."

"*Ja*," I replied. "And they pretty much took over our school—that was the end of our teachings." I loved going to school, and education was a pinnacle of our society and one of Hitler's promises; the school closing was a clear sign that things were not going well for Germany in the war.

Last October (1944) was the beginning of the end. The "wheels were coming off the cart" for the Nazi Party, and for that matter, Germany. Refugees arrived daily from the East. They were pushed our way from advancing Russian forces. Refugees were from Estonia, Lithuania, Latvia, Poland, and yes, Germany—East Prussia. However, there were some Finns and even Russians: *why would their own countrymen flee?* This should have been a sign to get out at all cost. Russia needed to go through Poland, or Latvia, then, Lithuania to get to Germany. Well, they just ran through all of the Baltic countries!

A late mandate was adopted by the Nazi Party: any household with more than two bedrooms must take in refugees; a good idea, since they were chased out of their own homes and had nowhere to go. The refugees also knew of this mandate and as they approached villages, they started looking for places to stay.

"Do you remember the first refugees coming to our house?" said Irmi.

"You mean Tante Friedel, Omi and Opa."

"*Ach*, come on, they were not refugees," Irmi barked. "That's family. I mean real refugees. I think you and I were outside doing chores when a family stopped in front of our house. An older couple, a young lady and two children."

"*Ja*, what country were they from?"

"Latvia, I think. They just stood in front of our house, pointing upstairs and nodding. The young lady peeked around to the side and saw that we were home. Mutti went to talk to them."

"I think Mutti was excited for her first refugees."

Irmi smiled, "*Ja*, I think so too. Mutti—do you remember her talking to them so slow and deliberate like they were stupid, 'Do—you—need—a—place—to—stay?"

I laughed. "And then, in almost perfect German, the lady responded with, 'Yes, please, do you have room?'"

The boat named *Ilse*.

"We sat and watched them like they were fish in a bowl. I don't think we made them very comfortable. Hey, do you remember, they were headed to Pillau. I still remember her saying, 'We heard that ships are still leaving from there and taking refugees to Western Germany or Denmark. It is safer there. I urge you to go as well." Irmi and I just looked at each other like a revelation occurred. "I wonder if they made it. They may have been killed when the *Gustloff* sank."[6]

"I guess we may have been lucky, in a way ... if we listened to them, we may have been at the bottom of the Frisches Haff also," I said.[7]

"Well, the refugees were right. Do you remember Papa's shortwave radio: that next day it talked about the Russians occupying Riga, Latvia?" Irmi paused and a look of frustration came over her, and her voice became louder, "Why didn't Mutti listen to Papa and all of the refugees? All the signs were there—why?"

"Well, now wait," I said. "You just talked about the *Gustloff* and who knows how many people died trying to escape. How do you—."

"—I'm talking about the plane ride!" Irmi shouted. There was nothing more to say.

We walked through several classrooms on the first floor. "There's nothing left in here," I said.

"Even the furniture is gone ... probably used it for firewood or for their headquarters. Hey, what about the upper floor where some of the teachers lived?"

"Yeah, but how do we get up there?" I remembered the office room. "I bet there's a stairway from the office."

Irmi, reassured, looked at me. "Yes, of course." We entered the office and, sure enough, there was a door in the back of the office. Through the doorway was a narrow stairway heading up to a hallway. There were four living quarters and a shared bathroom at the end of the hall. We entered the first room. It was pretty barren except for some things, mainly wood carvings, left on a book shelf.

Opposite the entrance was a window with a bench seat under it. I immediately approached and sat on the bench and looked out the window. *Our house! I could see it!* It looked like Russian soldiers took it over, because there were army vehicles near it. Proudly, I thought, *they must have searched and picked the best built house for themselves.*

Irmi was holding one of the wood carvings, when I called for her. "Irmi, I can see our old house." She quickly came over and we both kneeled on the bench and had our noses to the window.

"*Ach*, I wish we could go back," Irmi groaned. "What a wonderful place to grow up, huh, Ilse?"

"*Ja*, do you think we'll ever be able to go back home?" Dead silence that offered the opportunity for a second question. "Do you think we'll ever see Papa again?"

I think Irmi sensed my fear and confusion. I'd asked her these questions numerous times. She remained quiet for a while, then looked at me and responded, "Papa's coming back ... he's alive, and after this is all over, we can get our house back." I wanted to believe her, but I could sense doubt in her voice.

Irmi turned around, sat on the bench and looked down at the carving in her hand. She twirled it in her hands, examining it. "You know what? We must be in Frauline Neumann's quarters." I thought she just wanted to change the subject. "Do you remember when she was trying to sell carvings for *Winter-Hilfe*?[8] She was a real Nazi supporter." Frauline Neumann always had a few statues for sale.

"I wonder what happened with her." I questioned. "She must have taken off in a hurry, and couldn't carry everything."

Irmi looked at me with a half-grin. "Well, she couldn't carry much with that *Humpel-Bein!*" She snorted, and I burst out laughing.

"That's right! My goodness, do you remember how she lost her leg?"

"I think it was from a farming accident when she was a child. I remember we could tell when she was coming from way down the hall: *Clump ... Clump ... Clump.*" Irmi made me laugh. It was fun to reminisce.

"This carving sure looks real." Irmi held it up closer to the window. The carving, only about thirty centimeters tall, was of a young woman who wore an ankle-length skirt covered with a light-colored apron. Her loose-fitting blouse with sleeves to mid-forearm was dark. To complete her outfit were wooden clogs and a babushka. The artist brought out the struggle in the young girl explicitly. She was walking, somewhat uphill, with her back hunched over. Her right elbow pointed straight up signifying her difficulty with holding a large tied bundle of straw that draped across her back. Her left arm wrapped around her lower back to steady the heavy load, while her head hung low to balance the weight.

Irmi was captivated by the statue. "Let's take this and give it to Mutti. It's Mother's Day next week." I agreed, and we were pleased to provide Mutti with a gift this year. The Russians had no use for Mother's Day, but we still celebrated it. We usually presented Mutti some hand-picked wild flowers. This year would be different.

Irmi kept searching through the school as I sat on the window seat, captivated by the view of our old house. I slipped into a melancholy reflection of school days past. *I attended this school beginning in pre-school which was only half-days. In the mornings, I walked the ten minute path with my siblings. Mutti came and picked me up at noon. I was spoiled. Weekday afternoons, I was queen. When I was with Mutti, I had her undivided attention. She would sing as she sewed in the afternoons, often waiting until late dusk before turning on the lights. I loved this time of the day. It was quiet and surreal. I would watch the sun, through our front room window, slowly disappear into the horizon. I think she knew that I was fascinated with the sunsets.*

Other days, Omi would come and pick me up if Mutti had things to do. On rare occasions, no one picked me up and I walked home alone. Back then, four or five year old children walked around freely without anyone worrying. Everyone knew everyone else in the village, and people watched out for other families. As a child, I never felt unsafe. Similarly though, other adults had no problem reprimanding others' children either; so, as children, we had a respect for elders, even if they weren't family.

I looked up and wished we still had school. Unlike my sisters, I loved the classroom. Then my memory of school turned a little sour. *I remembered one of my teachers touting the greatness of Hitler and the Nazi party. He was a true Nazi. He even went on to tell us how the Jews were evil and needed to be destroyed. None of the children said anything. I think they were all coached by their parents to stay silent. This hatred coming from one of my teachers, who I respected, bothered me. It just seemed wrong to think of people with such disdain and to advocate eradication. Somehow I thought that I had to respect my teacher and believe what he taught, but I found myself doubting him. It felt wrong, but I knew that Papa would not agree with him either, so I found comfort in my discontent.*

Irmi suddenly reappeared in the room after searching through the rest of the quarters. "Nothing else worth taking, but this carving is a great find." She looked at me, still at the window. "You're still looking at our old house?" I nodded. Irmi came over and sat down on the bench next to me again.

"Irmi, do you remember my first day at school—even before kinder-garten?" I asked.

Irmi stared out the window, then at me, puzzled, "Your first day ... No, no, I don't remember."

"I was so excited about going to school with other children. Irmi, you were in kindergarten, and you dropped me off in the pre-school room, since it was right next to your room." I looked at Irmi to see if she was remembering, but she still had a blank stare. "Suddenly, I became scared and lonely, and started to cry. The crying got louder, and then two young teacher's aids came and tried to comfort me. 'What is wrong, sweetheart? Don't be afraid. We are here for you,' I remember them saying. It didn't help. I slobbered, 'I want my Irmi. I want my Irmi.' 'Your Omi is not here right now,'" they replied.

"Yes," Irmi acknowledged, clapping her hands together and laughing. "They thought you said Omi."

"Yes, so even louder, I cried, 'I want my Irmi.' They still didn't understand me because of my crying and blathering, how could they even understand me?" I paused and looked at Irmi questioningly. "Now, I don't remember, how did you end up coming to my room? Did you hear me?"

Laughing and talking at the same time, Irmi replied, "No, one of the teacher's aids came to me, not knowing what to do with you, saying you wanted Omi. I then listened and you were crying for me." She paused to catch her breath. "*Ach was!* I said to her, 'She's looking for me—Irmi—not her Omi.'"

"*Ja*, and then you came into my room, grabbed my hand and hauled me into your classroom, and there I sat, with you, for the rest of the morning." We had fun, recalling our good time. I looked around, and then commented, "I don't think I learned anything in school that day ... other than how to get my way." Irmi and I walked home that day, satisfied with our find and our fond memories.

On Mother's Day, we got up early and placed the carving in a bowl on the center of our table. The day before, we had picked wild flowers and kept them in water. The flowers were then placed in the bowl around the carving. Irmi and I waited for Mutti to get up and see the gift.

Mutti was moved by our thoughtfulness. She loved the statue. "This carving is unbelievably realistic." She closely analyzed it. "She carries a heavy load and struggles with it. The artist really accented that. I will carry this with me and keep it as a reminder." Her voice cracked. "This lady's struggle, carrying her difficult burden, reminds me of my own."

9

Attempted Kidnap

One summer day, we were greeted by thunder and lightning. It was raining quite hard. Opa was supposed to take Marion and me to pick berries, but today looked out of the question. Still, Marion came to our house in the morning. Opa answered the door and told her, "Marion, we're not going picking today unless it gets better outside."

"Yes, I figured, but Ilse—" she looked into our room, "maybe we can find something in town."

"All right," I responded.

"You girls are going to get soaked and catch a cold," Opa warned.

"We'll bring an umbrella," I said as I dug it out. We had found a worn out umbrella one day when we were rummaging through some abandoned homes. It happened to be raining that day and we used it on the way home, and kept it.

"Well," Opa acquiesced, "if you get too wet make sure you get back here to dry off."

We both agreed and off we went into the muddy streets, sharing the umbrella. It had a few tears, so it didn't completely protect us. The moisture enriched the smell of the musty canvas. The rain was coming down with such force that Marion and I shouted at each other to overcome the rumble of the rain hitting the umbrella. We could barely see across the street. "What are we going to do today?" I shouted.

"I have an..."

"What?"

In a louder voice, Marion replied, "Let's go to the Russian women's base."

"What will we do there?"

"Maybe we can help and they can give us some food for our efforts." I had to hand it to Marion, she was always thinking. It was about a fifteen minute walk to town. By the time we arrived, the rain subsided to a rhythmic splatter on the canvas. We jumped up onto porches that had overhangs to escape the rain, and then ran to the next ones.

It dawned on me that my little town had become an eyesore. The yards and gardens were all overgrown with weeds. Little farmettes were without animals, and weeds camouflaged sheds and chicken coops. No one was maintaining the homes and properties. We stopped on one of the porches to rest. Sadly, I said, "Our little town is starting to look so sloppy." Marion didn't say anything, but looked at me. I don't know if she didn't care or just didn't notice. "Look." I pointed to a huge pile of rubble down the street. "That house was hit by a bomb during the war." I looked at Marion. "No one touched it since." The house was adjacent to the railroad track. The rail system was a target of the Russians during the war. They never had managed to hit a rail, but had damaged many homes in our village.

"Yeah, it does look ugly," she acknowledged.

There was a gap of silence as we just stood on the porch. "I remember when our house almost blew up," I said.

"What are you talking about?"

"The bombings at the end of the war." I think Marion finally got it. I continued. "Sirens went off and we ran for the cellar. *Kaboom*! A bomb hit so hard, I thought our house was gone... Then *kaboom* again."

"I don't remember your house blowing up."

"Well, it didn't get hit, but it was close. It was eerie, broken glass and shrapnel was flying well after the explosions. As scary as it was, it was amazing. You can just imagine our fear. We ran out of the cellar expecting a leveled house." I caught my breath and went on. "The cloud of smoke and dust was unbelievable. A few seconds later, we realized our house was not hit A bomb landed in the cemetery across the street ... a second one just missed the railroad. Opa thought, the Russians were trying to hit the tracks, but missed."

"So, your house was all right?"

"Only damaged on the side where the cemetery bomb went off. Mostly broken windows and some clay tiles slid off the roof."

"Wow, you were lucky."

"*Ja*, that was pretty amazing. God held his hand over us that day."

We decided to continue on and finally arrived at the base. We were able to walk right up to the entrance of the building. The Russians converted the old Palmnicken courthouse to an all-women army quarter. It seemed odd to me that there was a women army. Did they fight, and shoot guns, or just help with supplies, cook and clean?

We simply walked into the building. It was good to get out of the rain. The entrance had huge thick walnut doors with long vertical beveled glass panes. Inside, it was dark and quiet. The lofty entrance room had a broad circular stairway going to the second floor. The main floor, including the stairs, was pale marble. The grain of the marble gave it a dirty look. I couldn't help but wonder what the hand-picked Nazis, who used to run this building, would think of it now. In a way, I was glad to see us rid of them, but which was worse?

We walked into one of the first rooms and there were a few women sitting at the desks; presumably, all of the desks and furniture were still from the former German government. We walked up to the first desk and Marion said, "Can we get work?" The lady looked at us, not understanding.

In my limited Russian, I asked, "*Rabota* (work). Can we get work?"

She raised her finger and said in Russian, "*Podozhdat*," wait, and she walked away.

A few minutes later, she came back with another lady who said in Russian, "You want work?"

"*Da*," I said, because I didn't think Marian understood.

"Come with *myenya*." She walked us out the door from which we entered, down the hall and took us to another room. The hallway smelled like a kitchen, and I thought, *good, we're working in the kitchen, maybe we can steal a few bites while we work*. Apparently, the Russians converted this courthouse to the cook station for their soldiers. As we neared, it became warmer and more humid and the smell of chlorine cleared my nostrils. She opened the door and a cloud of humidity consumed us. We were in the kitchen, but in the dishwashing section. She pointed to a lady who was sorting dishes and said, "See her," and walked out. I thought, *they are as rude as the Russian men*. I wondered how all of these Russian women came to live in our town so quickly.

This lady didn't speak any German either. I thought she was probably in her late forties. She was slightly overweight with an extra chin and a constant frown. She said in Russian, "Are you German?"

"*Da*," I replied. "We are looking for work."

"*Da*, here's what you two can do. Take this pile of dishes and sort it by item. Here go the spoons, here the knives, here the forks..." She went on pointing out where everything went and how it should look. "Once you're done with that, you can each have *pitaniye*."

I translated what I could to Marion. The lady spoke too fast to understand everything, but excitedly, I said to Marion, "Once we're done, they'll give us food!" We dove into our work. Wow, this was my first real job. "Marion, this isn't so hard, it's actually kind of fun."

"*Ja*, and we should be done with this by noon." We worked as hard as we could and pushed ourselves. People were walking around inside the kitchen. A young male soldier walked in. All of a sudden, I got scared. I thought there would only be women in here. What did Marion get me into? He stood right next to me, looked across the room at the lady who oversaw us, and, with his hands waved toward me and shouted "What's this?" in Russian. She responded and I made out, "German, work, and little,"—perhaps meaning us, or the amount of work. I thought we were in trouble. *What was he going to do with us?* He asked me in Russian, "What's your *imya*?"

"Ilse," I replied reluctantly.

"Ilse, hmm." Then he looked and pointed at Marion: "And *vy*?"

"I'm Marion," she said confidently.

In half-Russian, half-German, he said, "I saw you girls at the fence yesterday." He looked at me again and waited for a reply of which he got none. "Bring a canteen tomorrow and I will fill it for you."

"I will," I replied timidly. Off he went. From what I could gather, he worked at the kitchen; maybe ordering supplies or managing activities. He had his hat off in the kitchen. That's why I didn't recognize him from the previous day. Rarely did we see any soldiers without a hat; I always thought it was forbidden for the soldiers to be without one. In any event, I was glad he left and I didn't expect that he would remember us tomorrow. I recalled what Opa said regarding the Russian officer who almost raped me: "What would a man like him want with you?" These soldiers wouldn't remember someone like me. But then again, he had remembered Marion and me from the day before, hadn't he?

We continued with our chores and, sure enough, we finished by noon. We walked over to the lady that oversaw us.

"We're *zavyershyena*," finished, I said, with a big grin across my face.

"You finished all of that. I have to go see." She took a look and said, 'You really did work hard. Good. Follow me." At least, that's what I gathered she said. She took us to the cooking section of the kitchen. She had us wait in the hall. She then came out with two slices of bread. We were so excited. We worked for food! We put the bread in our pockets, grabbed our umbrella and started walking home.

"Our first day at work—we did it," Marian gloated.

"*Ja*, that wasn't so bad. I could get used to that." I felt proud. No longer did I feel like a liability. It was only a slice of bread, but it was symbolic that I was "part of the system." I was a worker and not just a berry picker.

"Hey, we're a block away from the army base, let's go back today and see if they'll give us any food, too," Marion suggested. We went and stood at the same spot.

This time, I said, "Marion, let's just wait a while before we ask them for food. Let's see if they come give us something." We clung to the fence and waited. Some of the Russians under the tent finished their meal and got up and just walked away. They saw us standing at the fence with our umbrella but ignored us. Then from under the tent appeared the same soldier who questioned us in the kitchen. He walked over to us even though it was raining. This time, he had his hat on.

"Hey, Lisa." He pointed to me.

"No ... Ilse," I corrected him.

"*Nyet*, you are Lisa. You are a Jew."

"No." I was starting to get perturbed. "And I am Ilse."

He reached through the fence and handed me the piece of bread. "Lisa, you bring canteen tomorrow," and he turned around and ran back under the

The whole family, Christmas, 1944, from left: Mutti, Papa, Irmi, Günter, Onkel Ernst, Tante Friedel, Ilse, Anneliese, Opa Ilian, Omi Ilian.

tent away from the rain. His German wasn't all that bad. I was able to understand him. "*Spasibo*," I responded in Russian as he ran back. I started splitting the bread in half. I figured it was a good gesture to thank him in his language, since he was trying out his German.

We ran home in the rain, less worried about getting wet. One-and-a-half pieces of bread! Not bad for one morning. That evening, I shared the bread and the story about working for the Russian women. "Ilse," Mutti warned, "I don't like the idea of you working for the soldiers."

"Mutti, it's working for women." I didn't dare tell her about the man who was in the kitchen. "Besides, it's only for a few hours and they may not have work every day."

Mutti looked at me and grinned, "Thank you for wanting to help—be careful, and if it gets too..."

"Mutti, we'll be fine. I like it." She grinned again and continued with her food.

"Ilse," Opa changed the subject, "today was bad weather, but tomorrow, weather permitting; we should go hunting for berries."

"*Ja*, Opa," I replied enthusiastically. "I look forward to it, but if I can work in the morning, I can get some more food and then I will be home by noon. Can we go in the afternoon?"

Opa could tell my excitement concerning my new job and replied, "Sure,

sure, we can go in the afternoon." I no longer felt like a drain on the rest of the family—I was thrilled to be a real contributor.

The next morning, Marion and I walked to the army base. I brought my canteen, just in case the soldier was telling us the truth about the soup, although I didn't dare tell Mutti. I was getting used to the fact that in this environment, hunger trumped fear. There was a slight wind coming off the sea, so it was fairly humid and slightly overcast. The dirt streets had two ruts from the army trucks. Yesterday's rain turned these ruts into skinny water puddles for stretches, so we walked in the center and made a game of balancing in the center ridge with our hands out, trying not to get wet. The streets smelled of mud and oil. The Russians apparently weren't that good at building trucks; there was plenty of oil that leaked from them onto the roads. I slipped on an oil slick and my shoe submerged into a puddle. Marion started laughing. At first I was upset, but then laughed along with her. We laughed even harder as I started walking: *squish, step, squish, step.* "Oh well, it'll dry up," I said to Marion, laughing as I walked.

We reached the women's base, and we lucked out; they once again had work for us. We washed the dishes and finished, again, by mid-day. This time, my soldier friend didn't show up. We got our piece of bread and proceeded to the tent. Today, there were some other children at the fence, two girls and a little boy.

"Hello," said one girl. Marion and I remembered Petra from when we all used to go to school together.

"Hello," I replied. "Hello, Petra."

"I haven't seen you in a while, so your family didn't get out before the Russians either, huh?" Petra asked.

"No ... I wish we did. Unbelievable—just lost Omi and my baby brother a few months ago. And almost lost Mutti to typhoid... How about you?"

"We lost my baby brother as well. Opa got shot when the Russians came. He tried to protect Mutti—three soldiers came into our house—he tried to stop them." She became silent and looked to the ground.

We went on sharing sad events, when, from over the fence, we heard, "Lisa, Lisa."

Petra's older sister said, "Who's Lisa?"

I leaned over and whispered to them, "He calls me Lisa, for some reason. I told him that I am Ilse."

"Lisa, you have canteen?"

"*Da,*" and I handed it to him.

"*Vy?*" he pointed to the others. They didn't have anything. He turned around and left with my canteen. Petra and her sisters were astounded that I befriended a Russian soldier. I admit that I felt a little proud.

Petra's oldest sister stuttered, "You ... What; how did..."

He quickly returned before she finished her sentence and handed some bread to the girls and gave me back my canteen—full. "Lisa, I take you back to Moscow with me."

I shook my head and backed off a little bit. I looked down at my canteen so as to ignore him. I didn't want to say thank you, but Mutti always taught me to be polite, so I did an obligatory, "*Spasibo.*"

"Come back tomorrow," he replied. He made me nervous. Was he kidding about wanting to take me with him? He was very pleasant, so maybe it was just small talk and he was just being nice.

Petra turned to me and whispered in a girlish, sassy tone, "I think he likes you."

"Oh, he's just being nice."

Petra's oldest sister clenched her lips together, then cautioned, "Ilse, be careful. Soldiers have been known to rape girls your age and don't think for a minute that he's not allowed to take you with him. Who's going to stop him if he wants to take you?"

Those were some sobering comments and I didn't want to think about it too much. "I have to go back to pick berries with Opa. Marion, are you coming with?"

"No, I will stay here this afternoon. I'll come by in the morning."

We shared goodbyes and off I went by myself. I opened the canteen on the way to see what he gave me. It smelled great and was still warm. It looked like Kasha mixed in with some vegetable soup. Wow, my family will love this!

I got home and showed Opa. He couldn't believe that I got such a serving. I didn't tell him everything about how I got the food, only that we worked and some of the soldiers gave us food. We saved it for dinner, when we could share it with the family. We grabbed our pails and off we went. The sky cleared since the morning, so we had the sun beating down on us. It was warm that day. We walked along potato fields and managed to find an abundance of ripe raspberries. We didn't have to go too far. However, we had company; there were a lot of other people with the same idea. No matter, there was a bumper crop and plenty for everyone.

We picked for several hours. My biggest complaint was not the other people; it was the bees and horse flies. Once, a big horse fly bit me in the arm and it stung terribly. I swatted it with my other arm. I missed the fly, but dropped my pail. I muttered some nonsense to the flies as I managed to get most of the berries back into my pail. These bugs were frustrating! As the sun verged on the horizon, the bugs finally got the best of us and we left. Between the two of us, we had about three liters of berries in our pails and perhaps a liter in our bellies.

When we got home, we quickly started preparing the food for the others. I washed enough berries for after dinner—the Russians finally got the electricity fixed in the town, so we now had running water—filled a bowl of berries for each of us and split the soup six ways. When our workers came home, they split up the bread, stored the potatoes for another day and we had a feast. Since the potato harvest, each worker now received a potato for a day's work, along with some lard and sugar.

"This soup is good. It's very filling," Tante Friedel said. The soup was a nice departure from the usual potato. I served the berries; dessert was a rarity.

"These raspberries really taste wonderful," Anneliese said.

"We have more," I said eagerly.

"We should try to preserve them," Opa commented. "This supply won't last forever. We need to prepare for the winter. We don't have canning supplies, but we have plenty of sugar, I can make marmalade." That night, we went to bed with full bellies.

The next week, Marion and I worked, hit-or-miss, at the women's base. We weren't always successful at the tent, either. One day, soldiers with guns chased us away, although twice, my Russian friend was there and gave us food. I had been warned to be wary of him. But hunger drew me to him and I ignored the threat, telling myself he was just being nice.

One evening, our family, along with the Bachs and the Färbers, walked into town. We often did this in summer rather than spend time in our cramped quarters which were made unbearably warm by the woodstove we used for cooking. At the center of town was a square where all the main streets converged. The small park in the square used to be meticulously kept, but now it was overgrown with grass and weeds and was a dumping ground for spent building materials and other junk.

There were about a dozen young girls among all of the families. We all stood at a street corner and started singing folk songs. A group of Russian soldiers walked down the street and stopped to listen to us. I noticed one of them was my friend from the tent. He struck up a conversation with Tante Friedel. He seemed to take a liking toward her. He again was very pleasant and respectful.

He stayed until we were done singing. He raised his hand and looked at me, saying, "Lisa, remember, I will take you with me," and they all walked away. We started walking home.

Tante Friedel said to me on the way back, "Did that soldier call you Lisa?"

I was afraid to answer, but responded: "*Ja*, I don't know why he calls me Lisa, but he's the one that gives me the soup. He is very friendly."

Tante Friedel warned me, "Don't get too close to him. Don't trust him."

"Oh, he was a friendly guy, he was just being cute," Mutti countered. I was surprised she would say that and stick up for him.

"Hanna," Tante Friedel shouted, scolding Mutti, "He did seem nice, but come on! You never know with atthese Russians. Don't trust them."

Mutti looked ashamed. "I didn't mean it that way... You're right. Ilse, listen to Tante Friedel. Be careful with this guy." Mutti really didn't appear all that worried, it sounded more like she was just placating Tante Friedel.

The next few days brought much of the same, including a few rain-outs. My Russian friend seemed to be everywhere. He was always walking around. I think he was a helper to the commandant, because I often saw them walking together. He even walked by our house sometimes, waving to me, calling me Lisa. It was a little scary, that he knew where I lived.

Friday came and Marion and I were at the fence again. My friend came and filled our canteens. By now, Marion brought hers every day as well. "Lisa," he said, "Tomorrow, our troop is heading back to Moscow. I take you with. Mother say I bring home little German girl. I take you. Be ready mid-day." He sounded serious. I was terrified. I ran home and told my family.

Mutti said, "Don't worry; he's not going to take you. He's not going to take a little girl back to Moscow." Tante Friedel once again, the voice of reason, cautioned: "You better be careful, don't trust him." I couldn't sleep that night. I dreamed that he took me away from my family and I ended up as a slave in Moscow. The next morning, I woke up in a sweat. It was Saturday, so there was no work. I had a nervous stomach all morning. I started to strategize where I would hide in case he came. A rumbling sound of army trucks came from down our road. It was unusual that trucks would drive down our back road.

In a panic, Tante Friedel, shouted, "Ilse, hide, the soldiers are coming!" I was terribly frightened. There was no time to hide outside. My only option was to hide under Opa's bed. I grabbed a sheet, covered myself and crawled under the bed. Tante Friedel sat on the bed to make it look inconspicuous, in case they came in. She quickly shouted, "Hanna, tell them Ilse is not here. Say she went berry-picking." Two army trucks stopped right in front of our doorway. My friend came out with two others. I could tell it was him by his voice. "Where's Lisa?"

Mutti, quivering, responded, "She's not here now." I heard him arguing and yelling. He was clearly upset and wasn't his usual friendly self. A few of the soldiers searched the area, but fortunately, they didn't come inside. They could be court-martialed for entering a civilian house, and, in the town center, they didn't dare try it.

"Lisa," he yelled. My hands were shaking. I prayed for God to protect me. They wandered around and he kept yelling for me. I heard him yelling and threatening someone; I think it was Mutti. Time seemed to stretch out and my rapid heartbeats rang loudly in my ears. Finally, I heard the truck doors slam and then a quick grinding of gears before they drove away. Mutti came into the house, got me out from under the bed and hugged me. I was so relieved, I cried and cried.

10

The White Horse

Late summer offered additional sources of food. Raspberries grew wild at many field edges. Strawberries and blueberries were found in meadows and forest edges. Mushrooms flourished in the woods. But the Russians were our only steady source of food. We knew that we could only last a few weeks without them. Although we hated being under their rule, there was no way we could leave. How could we possibly make it through winter on our own?

Some days our whole family didn't go to work—at this time it wasn't mandatory—because it was more worthwhile to tap nature's resources. Searching for mushrooms was especially fun for me. This, Opa and I usually did alone, while the others sought berries or other food that was more abundant, always being mindful of the need to offset their rations forgone from not being at work. Mushrooms were more of a treasure hunt. They were generally found in the thicket of forests, but could be anywhere, as long as it was a shaded, cool and moist setting. The problem was that there were several species of mushrooms that were deadly poisonous. The challenge was to know the difference; that's where Opa taught me well. He didn't trust me at first; he wanted to make sure that I was able to identify them on the ground myself. If I made a mistake, I could have killed us all.

After a few days of coaching, I was on my own. One thing that Opa instilled into my mind was: if I couldn't identify it, let it be, it was not worth it. Smooth bottomed mushrooms with bright colors and speckled tops were a sign of poison. Also, other than my favorite, *pfifferlinge*, ridged bottoms were better left alone. I only picked *pfifferlinge* and *stein pilz*. They were easy to identify. My confidence in mushroom hunting grew and I ended up teaching my friends. An afternoon of mushroom hunting usually only yielded half a basket full, but it was very rewarding seeing my family's pleasure at dinner when this fresh taste was added to our bland meals.

Opa made marmalade from the berries and fruit, dried the mushrooms in the sun, and made concentrated syrups from beets and fruits, all to help sustain us through the coming winter. I eagerly watched him to learn the art of preserving. We used whatever jars, cans or bottles we could find. And Opa melted the wax from candles in order to seal the preserves. It was clever and worked well.

When Opa cooked the preserves, the aroma that filled our room created a happy feeling inside of me. As though it were Christmas' past when Mutti was baking and we children couldn't wait until the oven opened and we could sink our teeth into the warm flaky goodness of *lebkuchen* cookies.

We tried to store dry goods, such as flour, sugar, or wheat that the Russians provided and eat perishables instead. We didn't have any storage room and certainly no locked hiding place, so our food supply was packed under the beds. There was no assurance that someone wasn't going to steal it, but generally Germans didn't steal from Germans. Opa kept warning: "With the food we're getting from the Russians, we will never make it through winter. We need to store what we can now or we won't see spring."

Work changed as well. Tante Friedel still cleaned rooms for officers and Mutti still did laundry, but Anneliese and Irmi no longer worked on the farm as there was nothing left to do. The Russians started a small factory, and Irmi and Anneliese began to work there. They were bone tired when they got home. It was hard labor and long hours.

As the summer faded and autumn took over, the berries were gone, mushrooms became scarce and most fruits and vegetables were picked. We started tapping into our reserves. At this pace, we were going to run out of food before winter's close.

One day Opa decided that he and I should go visit Sorgenau, which was only a half-hour walk south. There, Tante Minna, Mutti's sister, lived before her and her daughter, Ingrid, fled in January. They left their home and boarded a ship in Pillau that headed to Denmark before the Russians invaded.

There were some villages that were simply left uninhabited. Those without Russian occupancy were also without civilians, who couldn't subsist without the Russian rations. We knew that many of these abandoned homes had gardens with vegetables, fruit and berries. Opa remembered Tante Minna had some late harvest fruit trees and he thought there might be a chance that no one found them.

Opa and I walked on the dirt roads toward Sorgenau. Opa stopped, "*Shh* ... listen!" We heard the rumbling of a truck in the distance. He frantically looked back and forth down the road. He looked at me with fear in his eyes and pointed to a tree line between two fields. "Quickly, run to the trees for cover. I can't run so fast. I'll never make it, but they won't bother me." I took off in the direction he pointed. "Faster" he said, "they're coming."

I ran full speed to the trees. The sound of the truck became louder. I couldn't look back. I was too afraid and it would slow me down. I figured they were close enough to see me on the road and I wasn't to the tree line yet. I dipped into the ditch on the side of the road and started running hunched over. The truck slowed down and came to a stop in time for me to make it to cover.

Out of breath, I leaned against a large tree that concealed me from the road. I heard voices and one of them was Opa's. The truck started moving again and was driving toward me. I lay down behind the tree and the truck simply drove by. I didn't move until I heard Opa calling for me from the road. I got up and ran to him. He hugged me. "That was close," he said. "I saw that you were not at the trees yet and I flagged down the truck and pretended to need directions to Sorgenau. It was just enough time for you to reach safety."

Like it, or not, this was the life we lived—constant fear. We had to be alert and cunning to survive in this environment.

Finally, we arrived safely in Sorgenau, but sadly Tante Minna's fruit trees were barren. Fortunately, searching through the abandoned town, we managed to find some carrots and beets, as well as a few pears clinging to a stunted tree, enough to make the trip worthwhile.

We headed back home. We walked along the fence line that was erected near our old house. The fence was on the south side of town, within what we considered the safety zone. On a side street there were about six soldiers standing around a horse lying on the side of the road. One of the soldiers waved us over. We apprehensively approached and I saw it was a beautiful white horse lying motionless. His back legs were black up to the first joint and he had a small black patch on his forehead; the rest of him was pure white. None of these soldiers knew much German, but one soldier pointed to a fallen electrical wire, indicating that the horse died of electrocution. The wire was apparently no longer live because another soldier was holding the end in his hand.

"*Kozha,*" he said. "You cut?" He pulled on the horse's skin and did a cutting motion with his other hand. "You cut for me."

"*Da,* I know how," Opa agreed. He also knew a little Russian. Opa grew up on a farm and did plenty of butchering in his time. He was very good at it, and did most of the butchering of our pigs at home. The soldiers handed him a nice sharp knife and they all stood watching with big smiles. Opa made precise cuts and carefully peeled the hide from the carcass. Once one side was done, six soldiers grunted and struggled until they manhandled the horse to its other side. It didn't take Opa long to complete the task. He handed the knife back to the soldier. They all ran their hands over the fur. Then one soldier shook Opa's hand. They carefully folded up the hide and started walking away.

"Meat ... we keep?" Opa inquired in his broken Russian.

They stopped, turned around and some of the soldiers gave him an odd look. "*Da,*" one said, glancing at the others for acknowledgement. He shook his head and waved his hand just above his waist. "Not for me."

The soldiers walked away with two of them carrying the hide. I remember Tante Friedel had a coat made of horse hide. It was beautiful, and she wore it often. However, the Russians stole that long ago. Opa whispered to me, "Russians don't like horse meat. Many people won't eat it. Horse meat is delicious though. This will be excellent. We hit a gold mine." I was puzzled that they didn't want the meat. It was difficult to believe anyone in this environment wasn't feeling the hunger pains I did. Even if the soldiers had more than we, wouldn't they want some fresh meat?

Opa got out his pocket knife. His knife was always very sharp, but it was a little short for the job of butchering. Opa cut along the belly of the horse and started pulling out its organs. With knife in hand, he reached deep into the body cavity. He grunted as he pulled out all kinds of things and struggled to talk as he pulled. "We need ... to remove ... the organs ... and as much blood ... as possible, so we don't ... ruin the meat." It was a disgusting arrangement of slippery tubes and round things and smelled foul. Yet strangely, it didn't bother me too much. I remember watching Opa and Papa butchering farm animals; this one was just a lot bigger.

He then started cutting at the neck and back. "The loin is the best part. Let's cut these out, carry them home, and come back for the rest with others." I held the loin as he cut along the horse's back. The meat was slippery and hard to grip. Even with this abundance of meat, hunger drove us to hang onto what we already had. We emptied our pails, stuffed the fruits and vegetables in our pockets, then rolled up the loins and put them in the pails.

We rushed home carrying our pails full of meat and our pockets full of fruits and vegetables. It was a good ten minute walk. On the way, Opa was so excited; he couldn't stop talking about our little gold mine. Once at home, we unloaded our precious cargo. I was tired, but this trip was well worth the struggle. We grabbed some more containers and Opa brought a larger knife. Out of breath, Opa said, "Go to the Bachs and find Herr Färber in his shop. Let them know about the meat and have them tell anyone else, I'll go back to the horse and start cutting." After I told the others, they split up to tell more people and soon we had about twenty hungry souls marching to the horse, armed with any container they could find.

Back at the horse, Opa already started cutting; no one else had discovered it yet. A few pieces of meat were ready for someone to take. As quickly as he was able to cut a piece loose, it was snatched up. Some even carried it by hand. It was like a horde of ants. It was wonderful to witness. People were so excited; an opportunity to get meat and enough to feed their families for several days.

Opa was the only one cutting, but others helped by lifting and turning the carcass. In short order, only bones and bowels were left. The carcass looked as if wolves and buzzards pecked away at it. Some of the soldiers who had taken the hide came back. Even they looked amazed at the activity and excitement surrounding the horse. While Opa was still butchering, the soldiers started digging a hole to bury the remains. Watching the Russians help us was an unusual sight. I didn't know what to make of this. I started to feel less afraid of them. Once we were satisfied there was nothing left, the soldiers dragged and pushed the carcass into the hole they dug.

Opa managed to keep a couple more steaks for us. It was already late afternoon. "Let's surprise them when they come home," I said to Opa.

"Good idea. I'll start cooking steaks and you set the table nicely." I found an old bed sheet and used it as a tablecloth. Wildflowers were placed in a vase and added to our elegant setting. The table was set as formally as was possible using our mismatched collection of dishes and silverware. Opa was preparing the steaks and the smell of fire-seared steak was irresistible. My mouth watered as we waited for our family to arrive.

The door burst open. Mutti exclaimed as soon as she entered, "We smelled your cooking ten minutes away. It smells amazing!"

Opa had a big grin on his face. "You probably smelled half the neighborhood cooking the same thing."

"What is it," asked Anneliese.

"Horse. A horse got electrocuted by the Russians, and they let us butcher it. We probably got at least a dozen families meat for a week."

We went on explaining what happened, but everyone just wanted to dig in to the steak and enjoy the feast. Mutti at first didn't want to eat it, but tried it and liked it. It was a pleasure to see them pop a piece of steak in their mouths, lean back with their eyes closed and slowly chew, enjoying the morsel. It was the first time in over half a year that we could all eat until there was no more room in our bellies. After dinner, we all sat or laid down rubbing our stomachs.

Even prior to the Russian invasion, meat was scarce, and this was my first time with horse meat. It was really quite tasty and tender. It sounded strange to eat a horse because it was a working farm animal, but given the circumstances, we couldn't pass it up. We had enough meat to last several days. There was no ice, so we kept the meat wrapped in the corner of the room, next to buckets of cold water that we changed several times a day. Blankets covered our makeshift ice box. We kept other perishables like this to extend their shelf life.

Since we couldn't eat all of the fresh meat before it spoiled, Opa cut much of it into very thin strips. We had a good supply of salt, so he liberally sprinkled the strips with salt to marinade for a few days. Then the strips were hung over the wood burning stove all day, until the meat was hard and dry. In this state, the jerky would last for months, enough to make it through the winter.

11

The First Winter

A brigadier transferred his family to Palmnicken. He was in charge of the whole operation in Palmnicken. Since he had to stay, while battalions came and went, he was able to move his family to stay with him. Once in a while, Irmi cleaned for the brigadier's office and also sometimes cleaned his house. She became friends with his daughter, Erika, who was the same age as Irmi. They often played together and got along well. Irmi even was invited to dinner with them one time.

One day, Irmi came home all out of breath extremely excited: "The brigadier wants someone to teach his daughter German and since we get along so well, he picked me."

"That's incredible," Mutti acknowledged. "That will be great for you. You deserve it." Having an offer like this meant that Irmi, and our family, could perhaps benefit politically and through charity. At this time, who you knew and who you were connected to made a big difference; the brigadier was king, judge and jury.

"I really like this family. They're very kind to me." Irmi's voice became louder, "He said that he would pay me with food ... I would even do it just for the fun of it."

Herr Reisenkowski was a teacher at our school before the Russians came and was an alleged communist, even under the Nazis. Communism was a strong force in Germany, especially after the Russian Revolution and subsequent formation of the communist Soviet Union in 1917. Herr Reisenkowski didn't teach anymore, no one did, but he was politically savvy, and maneuvered his way into favorable situations, and would say and do anything that could potentially benefit him. Somehow he caught wind that the brigadier wanted Irmi to teach his daughter German. Herr Reisenkowski also had a daughter the same age, and recognized the potential benefits of having ties to the brigadier.

He managed to talk the brigadier into allowing his daughter, instead of Irmi, to teach German to the brigadier's daughter. Irmi came home in tears and explained what happened. "That *schwein*," she said. I hated him as a teacher too ... that communist!" I've never seen Irmi this angry. I felt bad for her as did the rest of us. It was very disappointing for all of us. Having ties to him could have made our life less difficult. Just having someone in power who would listen was often enough. Unfortunately, adversity often brought out the worst in people. It was disgusting to see someone stoop to this level. When life hung in the balance, slimy characters like Herr Reisenkowski were predictable—they would push anyone aside for their own gain.

After that, we often saw Herr Reisenkowski chumming with the brigadier. He was cloaked in a phony smile and our ears rang with his obsequious laughter.

* * *

Now that the Russians were settling in to their newly occupied territory, regardless of age and nationality, everyone needed to carry Russian-issued identification papers at all times. One evening after dinner, Tante Friedel said, "They're trying to make us Soviet citizens. This new paper states our nationality, the town we live in, all kinds of things. Does this mean we will never be able to leave?"

Opa half-heartedly agreed. "I'm sure if we stay, we will become citizens of Russia or whatever the Soviet Union decides to do with this portion of land." He tilted his head and grimaced, "We really can't leave, so I guess we're stuck."

"What if we did leave?" Tante Friedel boldly asked.

"Friedel," Opa scorned. "Are you crazy? Where can we go?"

"Well ... to the west ... I guess."

"Ha, ha, well, let's just pack our things and start walking."

"Papa, don't make fun of me. Isn't there a way?"

"That's what I'm trying to tell you—no! We'd run out of food, and it would take us forever to get there, and we'd be put in prison if we got caught ... what do you think the chances are of us getting caught?" Opa looked at Friedel, waiting for a response. "See, there's no way out."

After this sobering news it was quiet for a while. Then Anneliese softly said, "Maybe they'll send us to western Germany someday."

Opa looked at her and smiled. Trying to sound encouraging, he replied, "*Ja*, maybe ... we can always hope."

December arrived and the work had changed to cutting trees. There were still the jobs of cooking, cleaning and laundry, but overall there was less work to go around. So, there was no more work for Marion and me, but we managed to get scraps here and there from the soldiers. We started slowly tapping into our reserves of food.

Snow began accumulating outside. As was typical of Palmnicken, once December arrived, snow would stay on the ground until March or early April. We cut a few pine branches and hung them over our door and window. We also arranged some branches on our table with candles. I loved the smell of pine. It made our house smell like Christmas. We had no tree, so we decorated our pine branches with small metal objects. This was the extent of our Christmas decorations. It was a modest holiday with no gifts. Christmas used to be such a festive and joyous time. Now it was just another letdown. The Russians didn't celebrate any holiday, so Christmas Eve and Day were both work days, further adding to the somber atmosphere.

"Some Christmas," Irmi said as she and I were cutting more pine branches.

"It just doesn't seem like Christmas," I replied.

"No *lebkuchen*, or *marzipan* ... and no presents. How depressing." We just trudged along at a slow place, with our heads hung low.

"I almost wish we didn't celebrate Christmas," I said. "It makes our lives feel even that much more pathetic." No one in our family was cheerful. I think the adults felt awful that we children didn't get so much as a cookie for Christmas.

Our same devoted pastor from Palmnicken had Christmas service in the church. Electricity was never turned on in the church and it was cold. The Russians removed the benches and used them for the feeding centers under the tents, so we all stood through the service. It felt good to be back in church. We huddled close together to conserve heat. Each of us held a candle; our only source of heat. We could see our breath as we sang hymns in the cold air, our hearts and voices joined in a joyful noise that warmed our hearts and transported us to happier times.

In winter, I spent a lot of time with friends like Marion, Petra and her sister. There really wasn't much to do, so we walked the streets together, sang songs and begged for food. On very cold days I didn't go out at all, although I didn't like to be cooped up all day with nothing to do when I could be gathering food for my family. Opa was home most of the time. He was used for work by the Russians when logs needed to be transported, but he was home more often than not. I loved Opa and enjoyed being with him, but to be held up in one room with him all day was admittedly kind of boring. He was in his mid-seventies and I was only an eleven-year-old. It was different when we were outside and he was showing me things, but inside all day, I became restless. I tried to occupy my time constructively. I darned socks and mended clothing. The extra fabric we brought from our old home came in handy. My childish patchwork was not of the best quality, but it was earnestly done and protection from the elements was really all that mattered.

Together Opa and I did manage to maintain the supply of wood we needed for cooking and to keep our room warm. The Russians provided some wood, but it was barely enough to cook with, so Opa and I cut and split wood from anything we could find. We gathered much of our wood from branches leftover from the logging being done.

The land was being decimated. One evening Irmi and Anneliese were despondently talking about their lumberjacking experience that day.

"I can't believe they made us cut those trees down at the Schloss Hotel," Anneliese lamented.

Prior to the war, many tourists visited this magnificent hotel. It was well-known among the wealthy. It was a palatial and decadent setting. We children were not allowed anywhere near the hotel in the summer, but I remember in the fall, there were few clients, and we used to play on the hotel grounds. There were gigantic oak and chestnut trees that bordered the long, graceful entrance. The trees littered the lawn with leaves—an open invitation to play. We moved leaves into piles taller than I was. We took running leaps into the leaf piles and became completely engulfed in the debris. We collected chestnuts and opened them, looking for twins. One oak tree was so massive that a hollow in its trunk was large enough for one of us to hide in. Amazingly, the tree was still alive. I remember the cool, crisp air, along with the smell of dried leaves. I think this hotel and park was one of the reasons that I, ever since, have found autumn my favorite season of the year.

"Is the hollow oak tree still there?" I feared to ask.

Irmi replied with watery eyes. "No, we were told to cut them all down." My heart sunk. I never thought I would be in love with a tree before, but now that it was gone, I felt deep sorrow.

"They just don't care," Anneliese said. "They have no appreciation for nature. I begged them to leave at least some of the gigantic old trees. They looked at me like I was crazy or something. They're clueless."

Trees were just a resource to them. Eventually all of the giant trees at the Schloss Hotel, roadsides, patches of woods, and atop the cliffs along the sea vanished. It looked barren. Our land was taken away, and already it was unrecognizable. Arbitrary fences and haphazard walls were constructed, adding to the unsightly landscape. For some reason, perhaps a lack of supplies, the Russians would use existing buildings as a part of their walls. Sometimes they would tear down buildings wall by wall and use an entire house wall section as a segment in the barrier wall. This ugly collage of building materials stretched from the train depot all the way to the sea. I guess they didn't care what things looked like and just did what they were told. *Build a wall and use whatever materials are available.*

Winter was wearing on all of us. The entire month of January, the thermometer remained stubbornly below freezing. One day, at the end of January, Opa frantically searched under the beds. "I know we had more food," he said. "We must have used more than I thought."

"What do we do now," Mutti said.

Opa shrugged his shoulders, "There's nothing we can do, our surplus of food is gone." Every day was a struggle. We all shared hunger pains and were visibly losing weight. Somehow I was still growing: taller, but not heavier. We used strings to keep our pants on. I stopped looking in the mirror, because I didn't like what I saw. My eyes seemed to sink deeper behind my eyebrows.

My rib cage stuck out from my sunken stomach and showed every rib. I only had one pair of trousers, and a one-piece jump suit. I loved my jumpsuit. It wasn't much to look at but it was thick cotton and comfortable and in the winter it helped retain body heat. I kept meticulous care of this suit, mending and patching. As I grew, I removed the hems and patched in some fabric because my ankles and wrists were exposed. The fabric didn't match, but somehow it added to the affection I had for it. Clothing in the winter became almost as important as food for us. As people died, clothing became available; Mutti was warmed by Omi's winter coat, and we all benefited from her cast-off stockings and sweaters.

In January and February, it seemed like it snowed every day. The weather usually came from the Northwest, carrying moisture from the open Baltic Sea, and then dumping it in the form of snow on our village. Even in extremely cold winters the saline waters never completely froze over—including the winter of 1943, when the sea only froze a kilometer or two from shore despite record cold.[9]

Although autumn was my favorite time of the year, winter was an easy second. Here, winter was such a dramatic departure from summer that it almost seemed like we moved to another part of the world after the snow fell. Everything was so different. The landscape was unrecognizable. It was not uncommon to have a meter of snow on the ground during the entire winter.

Winter lent freshness to the air—it was crisp. Walking outside, I would hear trees in the distance cracking from the wind flexing their frozen trunks. The cold invigorated me. Before the invasion, we children loved to play outside in the snow. Mutti made sure we dressed warmly and didn't stay out too long and get frost-bite. I would have been outside all day if Mutti let me.

That same winter of 1943, large icebergs were created from the breaking waves. Us children had strap-on ice skates and skated on the floating icebergs. My parents would have been terribly angry with us, of course, but they never found out. We enjoyed ice skating as children. There were small inland lakes that made for excellent skating rinks. Also, the Frisches Haff always froze in winter and sometimes was like a sheet of glass.

In January, our town experienced a baby boom. Women, who became pregnant by rape nine months ago, were giving birth at a very inopportune time. Many of the women were malnourished and the babies were stillborn; others only lived for days. It is sad to say, but for some it may have been a blessing their babies died. Most mothers cared for other children and having a baby would have forced them to stop working. Without food from work, their entire family would starve to death.

Some babies survived; mainly where there were enough family members who worked and helped provide food. Of the babies that remained, I often wondered what the mothers thought. Would they feel cursed by the baby because of its conception or would they welcome the new life?

Spring arrived and the warm weather melted the months of snow cover. We were still at least a month away from harvesting wild plants for food, but just the break in the weather and thought of new beginnings offered us promise. The Russians announced that they needed families to work in what they called a *kolkhoze*.[10] Moscow established where these work camps were to be, and how many inhabitants each would hold. The *kolkhozes* were supposed to be a model of the communist self-sufficiency system—making use of fertile farm environments. Moscow asked the officials from Palmnicken for a list of twenty premier workers, people who had shown that they could work hard and were healthy. The people on the list had four weeks' notice to prepare for their move. Our family was not on the list and we were very glad. We did not want to go to some unknown place. None of the families selected wanted to leave, but they had no choice. Somehow as the departure deadline for the first *kolkhoze* group neared, a family managed to get their name removed from the list and our family was put in their place. The announcement came a day or two before the scheduled departure. This reeked of corruption. Who knows what favors were done to get names changed at the last minute. Our whole family went to the commandant. Mutti, in tears, said to him, "We don't want to go. Can't you do something to keep us here!"

The commandant, calmly said, "*Nein*, Frau Glaus, there is nothing I can do; you will need to prepare for your trip."

Mutti clenched her hands together and they were shaking. "After all that we have been through, can't you have mercy on us?"

"I'm sorry."

"But somehow our name was not on the list originally, and then it was changed. Can't you change it back?"

"Leave now, there's nothing we can do. We will collect your family when it's time."

March 5th arrived and Opa was sick in bed. Soldiers with machine guns arrived and forced us out of our home. "*Raus, raus*," they shouted.

"Please, please," Mutti cried. "My papa is ill, he can't get up." They didn't understand her. It didn't matter to them anyway.

"*Raus, Raus, schnell.*"

"Papa," Mutti said sniffling in tears. "You have to get up. We have to leave!"

Opa, moved slowly and listlessly. Mutti quickly helped him dress and wrapped him in a thick coat and warm hat. She said to the rest of us, "pack all our things—hurry ... I'll get Opa ready." We had a half-hour to gather our belongings and go. Mutti held Opa arm-in-arm and we slowly walked all the way to the army base.

12

Off to Goldbach

Ten A.M., March 5, 1946 we made it to the main army base in Palmnicken. Oh, how I wished we could avoid this forced evacuation, but as Opa said a few days before, if we didn't show up, they would send us to a work *prison* and not just a work camp. Five or six army transporters took us out of Palmnicken; still, no one told us where we were going. In a vacuum of information, my mind filled in the gap. I was convinced that we were headed toward Russia, perhaps Siberia, to be slaves. We were provided no food, and with our personal rations depleted, a long trip could prove fatal. I prayed for a short trip.

The beds of the trucks had bench seats around the edges and were topped with canvas. Opa needed help to get in. Mutti directed him. "Papa, sit here, behind the cab. There will be less wind here." He was hunched over, rocking back and forth. Mutti sat next to him with her arms around him. The rest of us piled in, along with another family. The caravan took us south. It was still cold in early March and the canvas top was little shelter. We all started huddling together to keep warm. They drove alongside the fence line near our old home. We couldn't see our house from the road, but reality struck me that my memories of Palmnicken would be just that—memories. Tante Friedel said, "Take one last look. It may the last time we see our homeland." My Palmnicken had already ceased to exist; the Russians took that away after the invasion. We probably would never be able to come back, and if we ever did, it would not be the same. Inside the truck, I looked around and noticed that I wasn't the only one crying. I don't know who started, but we all chimed in and sang songs native to Palmnicken as we passed through our beloved homeland—perhaps for the last time.

The trucks drove slowly. Our family was in one of the last trucks of the caravan and the thick fumes of diesel exhaust and burnt oil made my eyes burn. The fumes sucked backward into the canopy where we sat and gave me a headache. I felt a hollowness inside of me similar to when Omi and Hans died; a death not physical, but emotional. There was no going back, the page had turned, and I was on to a new chapter in my life. From where I sat, I could see the church steeple get smaller and smaller until it finally faded from view.

The caravan stopped in Königsberg, and all of the soldiers got out and went into town. Each truck full of refugees was left alone. We didn't know what to do.

"Mutti, what do we do now?" Irmi inquired.

After a moment of silence, she said, "We can't leave, we just have to wait. We would get in trouble if the caravan took off and we weren't in." She paused again as she looked at a confused Irmi. "Plus all of our belongings are strapped on top of the trucks."

I knew Mutti was responding rationally, but I wished we could just take our things and run. Here was our chance, but I knew we couldn't risk it: we had no food, didn't know where to go, and risked being killed when caught. We sat in the truck like sheep going to slaughter.

After several hours, the soldiers came back, laughing and carrying on. They staggered, and one fell as he entered the truck. The rest of them burst out laughing at his expense. They must have stopped for their fill of vodka. Off we went. This went on for a few more stops before we reached our destination late at night.

"*Raus, raus,*" the soldiers shouted.

We crawled out of the truck. "Where are we?" said Mutti.

"Goldbach," said one of the soldiers.

"Goldbach," Tante Friedel said. "It took us all day to get to Goldbach?"

"That's only 80km. It should have been less than two hours," Mutti added. "Now how are we going to find a place at this time of night?"

One soldier on top of the truck threw a few bags to the ground and off went our truck bellowing black smoke.

"Hey, they didn't give us all of our stuff," Irmi yelled.

"*Ja,* we're missing some bags," Opa confirmed. "Hey, wait," even though he was still sick he shouted, flailing his arms as he ran after the trucks. His pace quickly deteriorated and his arms fell by his sides as he just stood and watched the trucks drive away. He slowly turned and walked back toward us. "I can't believe this."

"They stole my bag," Irmi cried. "Everything I had." She sniffed. I felt so bad for her. On top of everything that they already did to us, to rob us blind was the ultimate insult. In one of those bags had been Opa's amber clock that he received for his 50 years of service working for the amber mine. Other families had befallen the same fate. There we stood twenty families in the dark, with no direction. The soldiers just dropped us off, and no one was there to receive us, or tell us where to go.

One of the families came up with a plan and started walking in the direction of a large building that we had passed on the way. Like lemmings, not having a plan of our own, we all followed. Fortunately, it was a fairly clear sky and the moon gave enough light so that we could find our way there. Perhaps this would provide a place to stay for the night. It was too cold to sleep outside.

We cautiously entered the building, surprised it was not locked. I was afraid. It reminded me of the hotel in Gross Kuhren where the drunken Russian killed the little boy. It was too dark to make out what was inside. Someone lit a candle that shed enough light for us to see a series of desks, most of which were piled with papers, but the room was unoccupied.

"This must be a Russian office building," said Mutti.

Someone from one of the other families said, "We should sleep in here tonight. At least we'll be out of the cold."

We arranged our bedding on the floor. A voice in the room yelled out, "We need to get out of this building very early in the morning, before they come in here and find us."

The night was quiet and we were up and out of the building before any of the Russians arrived. They didn't even consider how we got there or where we slept for the night. They might have even thought that we arrived there that morning. No one asked and we didn't bother telling. A couple of soldiers came toward our group and shouted, "Identification, I need to see identification." They took all of our documents. "Come meet here tomorrow morning for work," one of the soldiers announced. Apparently, the building was their headquarters. We were lucky we didn't get caught sleeping inside.

Mutti asked one of the soldiers, "Where shall we stay?" He gave the same vacant look that we had grown accustomed to over the last year. He shrugged and walked away. Just like in Palmnicken, here we again went searching for a place to stay, competing with the other families. There really wasn't much of a town to Goldbach; it was a rural farm community carved out of a hilly forest. The downtown was only two or three blocks made up of store fronts, now used by the Russians, and mostly single family homes. It was a beautiful setting and the town was surprisingly still in good condition, despite the fact that it had been under Russian rule for a year now. The majority of houses were wood frame and painted white. Even the barns were white. We knocked on every door in the town center.

In most cases a young child, or a very elderly person answered, and the answer was always, "Sorry, we have no room." Now we had to start searching the farm houses. We had nothing to eat yesterday and nothing today. Our family stopped at several hand water pumps in town so we drank plenty of water and filled our canteens. We walked from farm to farm and finally came to a quaint farmstead. It was a small old farmhouse set back from the road, with a large barn behind it. The yard between the house and road had a few majestic oak trees that cast a shadow over the path to the house. There were farm implements and wagons next to the barn, and everything was neat and orderly. Before we could knock on the door, a man walked out onto the porch. Opa asked, "Do you have room to spare for us? The Russians just sent us here to work. We are from Palmnicken."

"Palmnicken, hmm." The man rubbed his chin. "We have a room in the barn that was converted to living quarters. I had workers living there when I ran this farm before the Russians took it away ... It's not much, and you'll be cramped in there, but if you want to stay, you're welcome."

"*Wunderbar*, we'll take it," Opa eagerly replied.

He called for his family to come and meet us. "I am Alvin Routenberg. This is my family." He introduced us to his wife and four children, aged four to twelve. Herr Routenberg walked us back to the barn and, on the way, told us of similar tragedies that happened to them when the Russians invaded. Apparently, the atrocities were widespread. He looked like he was in his mid-forties. I wondered why he wasn't in the war. Maybe the Nazis needed him on his farm instead to help grow food for soldiers. "They took my land and my farm away from me and now I have to work the farm as a slave to them." His words were sharp and bitter toward the Russians.

We walked into a large barn full of hay. He had three horses. He pointed toward the horses and said, "Even the horses, they took from me. I have to feed them, but they take them whenever they need them." We walked through a small door in the barn and into the living quarters. "It's small, but this should work for you. You will have to get water from the hand pump and use the outhouse." We thanked him for his hospitality and got our room situated. "I'll get you some wood for the stove. It will get cold tonight." This was kind of fun for me. I liked the idea of living in a barn; the smell of fresh hay and horses. Somehow their manure never really stunk: not like cows or pigs.

Our living quarters was one room, perfectly square, the size of a horse stall. It probably was a horse stall that was converted to a "people stall." The walls were barn boards nailed horizontally. On the dirt floor rested a small wood burning stove. In the middle of the room was a table, too small for all of us to sit around. It didn't matter, there were no chairs anyway. Three beds lined the walls, so all of us had to double up.

The next morning, we woke to a very cold room. "I felt wind blow right through the boards," said Mutti.

"We'll need a lot more wood to stay warm," Opa said. "Good thing it's springtime."

"We need to go check in for work. The soldier said to go back to the base this morning," Mutti said. "Ilsechen, you stay here until we determine it is safe for you to wander around." I spent most of my day exploring the barn. Herr Routenberg came and got his horses, hitched a wagon and took off in the direction of town. That day, Mutti and Tante Friedel worked doing laundry, and Anneliese, Irmi and Opa worked on a farm, preparing for the upcoming plantings. Each of them received a small cup of sugar, a spoonful of salt and a few small salted fish. The fish was welcome and we were all extremely hungry, but it was so salty it wasn't palatable.

Mutti complained, "What are we supposed to do with all this salt and sugar, salt the over-salty fish ... and then dip them in sugar?" My task was to soak the fish in water for about two days, replacing the water regularly to reduce the saltiness to a bearable state. We found some pots and pans and the Routenbergs were kind enough to give us a little bit of ground wheat. I made a type of grits and we ate that for dinner. It wasn't much, and it was very bland, until we added some of the sugar, but at least we had something to put in our empty bellies.

Mutti said that there were plenty of MP's, so it was safe for me to roam around, as long as I stayed within the confines of the town. The next day, I searched for and found my friend Brigitte. I knew that her family was on the list to go to Goldbach. She and I searched out the entire town and did a lot of watching. More and more trucks were arriving with supplies, along with more soldiers. It looked like the Russians were not quite prepared for their *kolkhoze* experiment. They hadn't arranged any place for storage, so within a few days of our arrival, they took over the Routenberg's home and made it a storage building. I felt bad for the Routenbergs. We offered to give up our quarters in the barn, but he was so disgusted that he just wanted to get out of sight of the Russians, so he and his family moved in with his brother's widow and remaining family.

Brigitte and I spent a lot of time in our barn, surveying the truck traffic from a hayloft window, and we noticed that grain trucks arrived at the Routenberg's house and the Russians carried the grain into the house. Oil tankers were also parked alongside the building. We saw that the tankers were full of cooking oil; most likely sunflower oil. We spent a lot of time just observing; wondering how we could get our hands on some of that food. To our amazement, we saw that other battalions stole supplies. Trucks would show up, the soldiers would look to see if anyone was there; and if not, they would quickly hook up to trailers or tankers and just take off with them. Clearly, there was a black market and an underground network that the soldiers exploited. The sad thing was that much of this food was most likely slated for us refugees.

One afternoon, after our family arrived home from work, Brigitte and I told them about the grain in the Routenberg's house. This day, Frau Söhn, the nurse who had been so helpful to Mutti when she had typhoid, was visiting us. Frau Söhn said, "How can we get our hands on the grain?"

"We have to be able to get inside," I said. "The Russians leave in the afternoon, but it's within view of many buildings and there are Russians in the streets at times."

"Hanna," Frau Söhn said, after a moment of contemplation. "You and I can distract anyone on the street, Friedel, Anneliese, and Irmi can stand in the driveway and whistle if anything goes wrong. Brigitte and Ilse can go inside and see if they can get any of the grain. They never suspect kids. They think they're just playing around."

Mutti lowered her eyebrows, tilted her head back, and half-closed her eyes, weighing the risk.

"Mutti, let's do it," I said, excited at our little plan. "We won't get caught." Mutti formed a smile and simply nodded. I was actually amazed myself that she agreed. We waited until the last truck left that afternoon. Team one headed to the road to distract anyone walking by. Team two took their place in the middle of the driveway and had a good view in either direction to warn of danger. "Come on, Ilse, now's our chance," Brigitte said in her spy voice. We ran to the house. There was a porch on the back that led to the kitchen. We silently walked up the steps and onto the porch, crouched down and peered through the bottom part of the door window. From this angle, it was clear.

"Are you sure they're gone?" I asked.

"Let's check the front." We ran around the house in a crouch and scanned the terrain to make sure no one was coming from the road. "Here, I'll boost you up to this window and you take a look." Brigitte cupped her hands and locked her fingers and I put my foot in her hands. "Hurry!" I stepped up and was able to reach the window.

"No one here!"

"*Gut*, let's go inside." To stay out of sight, we ran to the back of the house again; it had a restricted view from the road. The door was unlocked. This was too easy. We scanned our surroundings and noticed all of the kitchen cabinets had locks attached so we couldn't open them. They must have filled the cabinets from the top and locked them shut. We tried every door, but couldn't get any open.

"Hey, what's this?" I questioned as I pointed to a small accumulation of grain. "This must be leaking from the bottom of the cabinet."

Our eyes followed the path to the cabinet. "Look," Brigitte exclaimed, "there's a small gap at the bottom of the door. I need a stick. Ilse, go outside and find a stick—a thin one—I'll try to keep prying this door up a little." She was pushing and prying at the door as I ran out to look for a stick. I searched the ground and found a few good candidates while making sure no one saw me. I ran back in and handed my best choice to Brigitte. "Oh, that's perfect!" she said as she slid the stick under the door and a little more grain drained out. "What do we catch it in? Is there a bucket or pan in here?" I searched around as Brigitte stayed busy, prying her stick in under the door.

"Nothing—but what if we used our boots?"

Brigitte burst out laughing, "Our boots?" Then her expression turned serious as she looked down at our boots. "Why not?" she replied with a big grin on her face. We quickly took our boots off and I held them one at a time under the cabinet while Brigitte jabbed the stick under the door and pulled outward. We filled the boots in short order.

"We're done, let's get out of here," Brigitte giggled as we grabbed our boots and ran out the door. We ran right to the barn and into our room, dropped off the boots and ran out to get the others. *Wow*, I thought. *That was exciting*.

A few days later, we made another foray with similar results, but after that the Russians added wooden strips on the inside of the door that stopped the grain from spilling out and blocked our tool from getting in. I doubt that they ever missed the grain we took, but for us it was a godsend.

I was the main cook for our family. I made sure dinner was prepared for our workers when they came home. Sometimes, Opa cooked, but I did most of it; I enjoyed it. From the grain we stole, I made grits, using the meager rations of sugar, oil, and salt the Russians gave to us. I also ground the fish into a paste and mixed it with the grain to form patties and fried them in a pan. It wasn't the tastiest, but it was filling, and what else could we make with the fish—it wasn't very good.

March 15th arrived and it was my twelfth birthday. There were no festive celebrations, but we all tried to honor each other's birthdays with favors and friendship, and a special pastry made from ingredients saved for special occasions. That day, Mutti made me a pastry. In the summer or fall, these pastries would have included blueberries or strawberries, but in March, no berries were in season, so the pastry was plain but with an extra helping of sugar. This birthday, I had a special prize. Tante Friedel gave me a diary. It was a small book, about 15 × 15cm, with a thin black leather cover.

"Ilse," she explained, "you really need to write down the events that are happening now. Someday, when you explain this to your children, you can reflect on your diary." I was extremely grateful. I don't know where she got it; she may have carried it with her this whole time. Tante Friedel was a wonderful and generous woman. It was like I had two mothers. She treated us children as if we were her own. So, from here on out, I chronicled the daily events of our seizure under the Russians.

Brigitte and I kept our eye on the Routenberg house. As grain trucks delivered, they often spilled grain in the driveway and never bothered to pick it up. Once the trucks left, Brigitte and I would go with a bed sheet, pick the grain from the ground and place it on the sheet so that we could transport it home. They wasted more than we could eat in a day. For the most part, our collecting scraps didn't bother the Russians too much and we weren't afraid of them. One day, though, we picked up rye while some of the Russians were working outside and I think we annoyed them. One soldier started shouting at us in Russian, waving his hands at us. We got the message and quickly grabbed our sheet, folded it so that none of the grain escaped and ran off. Nevertheless, we managed to get about a half-kilo of rye.

Even in our little world, it was evident that communism, although architected with good intention, was fraught with corruption, and was destined for failure. The black market and underground thrived. Supplies intended for regions or towns rarely made it but were stolen, misdirected, sold or bartered before they could be delivered. To complicate matters: Moscow made all supply decisions. It didn't matter what the needs actually were, Moscow decided what everybody should have. As a result, if the intended supplies actually arrived, there was often too much of one thing, and not enough of the other. Many times workers labored all day, only to be told that the supplies ran out and they got nothing.

Similar to the Routenberg's home, other houses were established as supply stations by the Russians. These stations were designated as HO.[11] From these buildings, food and supplies were distributed to the soldiers and civilians.

One afternoon, as Brigitte and I were watching the Russians at the Routenberg's house, they moved a tanker trailer to the back of the property. Brigitte exclaimed, "Look, there may be some oil left in it and now it's where they can't see it!" This was a three-person mission, so we waited for Irmi to come home from work. The three of us strategized our plan of attack and then set into motion. Armed with rope, buckets and a soup ladle, we carefully and quietly climbed up onto the tanker; there was a ladder welded to the side of the tank to reach the opening. We opened the latch. "Ilse, you are the smallest and lightest," whispered Irmi. "Gitti and I will hold your feet. Let us know if you can reach the bottom. If not, we'll need the rope."

It seemed like I barely fit in the opening as I hung into the tank from the waist up. "All right, we got your feet and we're going to lower you down into the tanker," explained Brigitte.

The next thing I knew, I was upside down in the tank, a bucket in one hand and a ladle in the other. "Don't let go," I shouted.

"Quiet!" Irmi whispered back. "They'll hear us." I didn't realize my voice would resonate inside the tank as it did.

"Sorry," I softly replied. "I can reach the bottom. No need for the rope. I'm starting to scoop the oil." It was too dark to see anything. The open door didn't let in enough light. I went by feel. The smell of sunflower oil was overwhelming. I felt my heart in my forehead and temples as the blood rushed to my head. I worked quickly because I wanted to get out of there as soon as possible. I was afraid that I would fall and be stuck inside. With my fingers, I determined that there was still a few millimeters of oil left in the bottom of the tank. I dragged the bucket along the bottom of the tanker to get as much oil in the bucket without scooping. Then I used the soup ladle and filled the rest of the bucket one ladle at a time. Everything was slippery and I held on tight, because I didn't think I'd be able to retrieve any dropped items.

"All right, I'm done with one bucket." Irmi and Brigitte pulled me up halfway, took the bucket and gave me the second one. We accomplished our goal and filled two buckets with oil. They pulled me out and we stood quietly on top of the tanker admiring our stealthy work. Then as Brigitte was lowering the tanker lid closed, her hands, soaked with oil, lost their grip. The lid slipped from her fingers and slammed shut with a thundering echo, alarming several soldiers. They came out of the house and started shouting and waving their hands. We got scared and slithered down the metal stair as quick as possible.

My hands were full of oil and I slipped off the ladder half way down. Fortunately, Irmi and Brigitte carried the buckets, but even in their panic to get off the tanker and run for safety, neither spilled a drop of oil. The soldiers just walked toward us, shouting, but didn't pursue us. I think they really didn't care. They just thought we were playing on an empty tanker. I always got the impression that the soldiers loved children. As easily as they would turn in an adult refugee to be sentenced to a prison camp, I firmly believed that, at least the ordinary soldiers would turn a blind eye to the misconduct of a child. For this reason, I was the front for many thievery missions.

In Goldbach, the Russians were slave drivers. Laborers worked seven days a week without a holiday. The Russians made sure to stagger their own schedules so they didn't work every day. April 21st arrived; Easter Sunday, and everyone had to work. Not even Easter was a holiday. It was a little windy that day, but a beautifully clear sky. The Russians let children come out and help once in a while and bring the workers something to eat or drink. Brigitte and I filled a canteen with coffee and brought it out to our families working out in the field. We called it coffee, but it was really roasted grain—barley—ground fine, and filtered through a fine-mesh sheet with boiling water. They greatly appreciated our effort. Later that day, Brigitte and I picked some early blooming flowers; violets, lilacs and the like.

There wasn't much to eat on Easter. I fried some flour-water patties to resemble a cake and added a little oil and topped them with sugar. Our workers came home with their usual stipend: sugar, salt, oil and salted fish. Early spring, just like in Palmnicken's camp, was the worst time of the year for us. We were out of surplus food, and there was nothing we could pick in the wild. The work rations provided in Goldbach were even worse than in Palmnicken, especially because of the frequent shortage of supplies here. If we didn't steal and beg for food, we would have already starved to death.

There was plenty of work in the fields in spring. Fields were plowed using horses. Herr Routenberg did much of the plowing with the now-Russian owned horses on the now-public land. Other men with horses did plowing as well. Opa was too old to plow, but worked planting along with the rest. Tomatoes, cucumbers, beets, potatoes and many other vegetables were planted by hand, and later, rows were thinned and weeded by hand as well. In addition to the vegetables, grains such as wheat, rye, and barley were grown. Most of the output of our farms was shipped out; perhaps to showcase the quality and variety of produce the communist government provided. We often wondered how much of it really found its destination, due to the thriving corruption.

Brigitte and I often helped in the fields; mostly picking weeds. It was strenuous work. My back was always sore from bending over all day. I felt sorry for the adults, especially the elders. Back pain was one of the more frequent complaints.

Russian civilians started to arrive in Goldbach. Mutti thought that the

Russians wanted to create work for their own and displace us. I liked the idea of displacing us, but when and where? The interesting thing was that soldiers didn't treat Russian civilians any better than us. As much as communism was supposed to create an equal system for their people, it sure wasn't apparent here. The Russian civilians were as much slaves to the soldiers as we were, and their rations were no different. From what we could gather in communicating with them, they were peasants from remote parts of Russia. Many were forcibly transferred, others were promised a opportunity. In either case, they, too, now struggled to survive.

Late spring arrived and there was still plenty to do in the fields, but not enough for Brigitte and me. Our job now was to find additional food. We did our usual begging at the supply centers, but had only moderate success. We changed our tactics to concentrate on the feeding centers where the soldiers ate. There wasn't much success there either. My suspicion was that supplies were low even for the soldiers now. However, a Russian civilian lady, who was the cook at one of the feeding centers, noticed us begging every day and said that we could work for her cleaning dishes and serving the soldiers. We eagerly accepted. She didn't speak any German, but I was able to understand what she wanted. At first, I was afraid of the soldiers, but in time, I realized that they wouldn't bother us. In fact, they pretty much ignored us as we served them. The Russian lady usually gave us a slice of bread or half a potato for helping. I was glad to, once again, work and be a contributor.

13

Then, Five Women

May 1st was one of the few holidays celebrated by the Russians; their form of Labor Day. Workers had the day off, but, of course, didn't get any stipend. The soldiers had a big celebration this day and even a dance. A few days earlier they were soliciting refugee women to join them in their celebration. They offered alcohol and cigarettes as enticements. Even Irmi, at fifteen, was asked by a soldier to join him. Naturally, Irmi declined, and none of our close acquaintances went either.

The "owned" women, the ones claimed exclusively by a Russian soldier, attended with their escorts. We all knew who they were by now. The higher the rank of the soldier, the prettier the woman he owned. It was no secret, from anyone, who was with whom. Soldiers often asked even us children if their woman was with another soldier. Fights broke out between soldiers if they found out another soldier was on their turf. We quickly learned to keep our mouths shut.

Brigitte and I helped clean up after the celebration and were given leftovers for our efforts: herring, potatoes, sauerkraut, bread crust—and I even managed to get a handful of cigarette butts for Opa's pipe. A banner day. Too bad there weren't more celebrated holidays. The herring was a special treat. A far cry from the salt-laden fish we were accustomed to. That evening we had a feast, the best meal since the horse steak in Palmnicken. Opa even got to smoke his pipe after dinner.

Opa and I went fishing some days. There were several streams and rivers in the area. He found a cork and used it as a bobber. He used thread from rags and bent and sharpened his own hooks from wire he found. We dug up worms and spent many afternoons on the water's edge. We weren't too successful, but we did catch an occasional trout. The chance for a delicious fresh fish meal made the long hours spent fishing worthwhile.

Brigitte and I continued to work for the Russian lady, but our pay was steadily decreasing. She claimed that supplies were nearly gone and she had nothing for us. One day, she gave us only a half-piece of bread each. The next day, it was down to one-quarter piece of bread each—hardly worth our effort.

That same day, she asked us to clean up the dining room while she went to the HO for more supplies. In the morning, she had prepared pancakes for the soldiers, and as always, she made more than she needed. The leftovers would be used for pancake soup the next day. Pancake soup sounds strange, but it really was quite good. The soup was a sweet, fairly clear, broth that sometimes had dried fruit added. The fruit soaked up the liquid and became moist. Leftover pancakes were cut into small pieces and added for substance.

She carefully stacked all of the leftover pancakes onto a large plate and placed it on a countertop in the kitchen. She didn't quite trust us, so she closed the door and cleverly removed the doorknob. The doorknob was then placed in her purse and carried with her. There were no locks on the door, so by removing the knob, we had no way of getting in, or so she thought. As the Russian lady opened the front door, she called, "Girls, I'm off to the HO. Go ahead and set the tables so it's ready for the next meal. You can leave once you are done."

Brigitte and I looked at each other. "Forget the table setting .. let's find a way to get to those pancakes" I said.

I looked into the hole where the doorknob was removed. How could I open the latch? It was a square hole and the rod from the door knob had a square shaft, so if I could turn the square hole, I might be able to open the door. "Gitti," I said, all excited, "Get me a knife—one with a thin blade."

She ran to the dining room and grabbed the smallest knife she could find. "Here, will this work?"

I took the knife and jammed the tip into the square hole diagonally and kept pressure on the knife as I slowly turned it. *Pop*, the door opened. On our knees in the open doorway, we looked at each other in amazement. "You did it!" she screamed. We quickly ran to the plate of pancakes and took only one each, hoping the Russian lady wouldn't notice anything missing. Then we opened the cupboard and liberally poured sugar on the pancakes and downed them. We covered our tracks, shut the door and never went back.

One late afternoon in April, Russian soldiers were at our door. "*Raus, raus*," they shouted. We had about an hour to evacuate. Opa had warned us of the possibility of evacuation. Since they already used Herr Routenberg's house for storage, they might eventually take his barn as well. Now, that day had come. I think they were concerned that we, as civilians, were too close to their supplies and became worried about theft. In any case, here we were again, carrying our belongings in search of a place to stay. Fortunately, Brigitte happened to be with us that afternoon and mentioned that the house next to theirs was vacant.

We rushed over to claim the living quarters. There were a series of identical homes in a row near the edge of town. I assumed that they were housing for farm workers, prior to the Russians. The vacancy was an upper level of a two-flat. The lower level was more of a basement and was occupied by a family, so our floor was just slightly off the ground. We entered one narrow room. To one side was a tiny kitchen with a wood-burning stove. There was a sink basin, but no running water. The floor was rows of bare wood boards that creaked noisily as we walked across them. But at least it wasn't a dirt floor like the converted barn stall that we came from. Not so much as a chair furnished the room. A window on each side of the long walls gave the only natural light. The entrance was a tiny enclosed porch. Opa, being the only man, took the porch as his sleeping spot. In the small backyard was a shared outhouse for both flats. It was a modest arrangement, but shelter nonetheless. Our bedding took up most of the floor space, so, each morning, we rolled up our blankets and placed them against the wall to have more room during the day.

I hated using the outhouse; it smelled terrible. One day, as I sat in the outhouse, I reflected on our Palmnicken house. There, we had an outhouse for the first few years, until Papa completed the indoor plumbing. Papa added something into the pit to keep it from stinking. I wished we had some of that stuff now. *I remembered in Palmnicken, as a small child, being afraid to go alone at night to the outhouse, so Irmi would light two candles and go with me. It was a two-seater. Whether Irmi had to go or not, she sat with me, telling stories or singing until I was done. I think that's one of the reasons I became so attached to her. She made my little fears subside.*

In time, we scrounged our own crude furniture. Wooden crates turned upside-down were used for stools and a table; we found a few stained mattresses and laid them on the floor. Fortunately, we had some cotton sheets to cover them, but even clean sheets were incapable of masking the mattresses' musty smell. The blankets were threadbare and, in the cold weather, we slept side by side in front of a small wood-burning stove. It was our only source of warmth, and where we heated water and cooked our meager meals and soups.

On May 12th, the Russians decided that all refugees needed to get immunized against certain diseases. Another idea filled with good intentions, but executed with disastrous consequences. By now, the Russians had a record of every refugee, so we had no choice; no one was exempt. Surprisingly, they actually told us that the shots were for typhoid and other diseases, which raised a red flag in my mind because it was not typical of them to tell us anything about what was going on. Everyone twelve and older got a series of shots directly into their backs. Here was one of the problems with their plan: they didn't boil the needles between uses. They had to know that using the same needle for hundreds of people would have a far greater chance at actually spreading, rather than preventing, disease. Maybe they just didn't care, or this could have been another order from Moscow without proper instruction or supplies.

The immunizations took place mid-day, and the expectation was for all to go back to work for the afternoon. The shots were terribly painful and many workers couldn't finish the day in the fields. In fact, most workers couldn't make it back to work the next day either. I picked kindling for our stove that afternoon and couldn't bend over. I had to bend at the knees and keep my back straight. That night, I could hardly sleep from the pain and I certainly couldn't sleep on my back. The next day, Mutti checked everyone's temperature with the glass thermometer she carried in her first aid kit. Anneliese and Tante Friedel had developed a high fever of 40 degrees Celsius (104°F).

"These stupid Russians," Mutti barked. "Are they trying to poison us, or did they just overdose us?" She was furious. Her ranting went on all day, of course in the privacy of our home. A rash of deaths ensued as a result of the immunizations, mostly the elderly. A few days later, Opa started getting sick too. Frau Söhn came by to help and I overheard Mutti whispering to her. "I'm worried about Papa. He has a fever of 41 degrees Celsius (105°F). He struggles to move; everything aches. Do you think he is at risk?" He was still a healthy man prior to the immunization, but unfortunately, his diagnosis was critical.

Frau Söhn clenched her lips together and, with her head lowered, looked up at Mutti. "It doesn't look good. A fever that high at his age is extremely dangerous. The Russians did something wrong with this immunization, and the problem is we will never know, and they will never admit it." She paused and then looked down. "And they won't offer any help."

Anneliese and Tante Friedel slowly recovered and went back to work. Opa, on the other hand, became noticeably weaker and refused to eat. Mistakenly, our HO received a shipment of *wurst*, along with sauerkraut and even ketchup. It was a welcome error, even though it lasted for only one day, but even this welcome treat was refused by Opa, a clear sign things were not going well.

I felt awful about Opa's condition, so I wanted to do something to make him feel better. I combed the areas the soldiers frequented and found some cigarette butts. I was very excited when I came back home and handed him the tobacco. "*Makhorka*, Opa," I eagerly suggested.

He was pale and very weak. He struggled to raise his hand and stroked my head. In a soft and slow voice, he said, "No more *makhorka*, Ilse." He seemed to force a smile. I started to cry because I knew he wasn't going to pull through this. Mutti was at his side and feared his lungs were being affected. On May 20th, Brigitte's family came over and we all held church service in our house and prayed over Opa. We asked for medicine, but the Russians provided nothing. The next day, Mutti stayed home from work. I suspect she knew the Lord was taking Opa home that day. Mutti and I sat at his side. By noon, his eyes were closed and he struggled with each breath. His gulps of air were becoming less frequent. After one last breath, life finally escaped him. I cried that whole afternoon.

Opa was my surrogate father. I didn't even know if Papa was still alive, Opa filled the gap. His passing was not only painful, it struck fear in me. He was the only man we had, and he knew how to fix things and was creative in survival tactics. He was inspirational and encouraging. Without him, I felt more vulnerable and alone.

In this last year, I was the closest to him. He and I were the only ones who usually didn't work for the Russians. We spent the most time together, and in such a tumultuous environment, I got to know him better than I would have under normal circumstances. He taught me so many things, and while I was heartbroken by his passing, I was also determined to carry on with what he taught me and help the others live.

We buried Opa on May 23rd. Mutti asked a local pastor if he could do a service and provide help to bury him. He said that he couldn't make it, but that he would send a few men to help dig the grave. Mutti managed to get a German carpenter to build us a casket, but the pastor's helpers never arrived. We had to dig the grave ourselves—all women—a bitter beginning to our new man-less circumstances. We held a modest graveside service and then, finally, the men arrived to help—too late. They did, however, help lower the casket into the grave.

Mutti struggled to say a few words at the graveside: "Papa lived his life for his family. He had a loving relationship with Mutti..." She paused to wipe her tears and collect herself. "I never saw them fight or have an argument. He was a loving father and grandfather. We will all..." She simply couldn't finish. Tante Friedel hugged her and Mutti buried her head in Tante Friedel's chest. Soon, she was escorted away from the grave and we all followed.

He was such a kind and caring man. All his life, he worked hard, from his fifty years in the amber mine, to these last days when he contributed so much to our ability to bear the harsh conditions. He always helped where he could. Now, he was at rest, and only we women remained.

14

Three Dead Soldiers

Brigitte and I became bolder. Buildings that we once thought of as dangerous or out-of-bounds were now fair game. We combed through outbuildings in search of food, small tools or clothing, thinking perhaps we'd find something overlooked by competing scavengers. Churches were of no use to the Communists, other than as a building to store things. Brigitte and I walked into the large former-Catholic church in downtown Goldbach; it was open.[12] The items stored were of no value to us; mainly desks, large furniture, and heavy equipment or truck supplies. The church still had all of the stained-glass windows intact. The paintings on the ceiling and walls were magnificent. What a shame to see this place of worship relegated to parts-storage.

Brigitte, in front of me, had her head tilted back and she was looking at the ceiling, then she yelled, "Hey!"

I quickly looked around; there was no one inside, at least there better not have been or we were in big trouble. "What are you doing?" I said sternly in a loud whisper.

Brigitte shouted in bursts, "Hey ... can you hear the echo ... the sound really echoes ... in here." She started singing a hymn and I quickly pushed her shoulder.

"Are you crazy? We'll get caught. Stop it."

She just turned toward me and gave me a—"I didn't do anything wrong"— look and smiled. "There's nothing here to steal ... unless you want to lug a bookcase or tractor tire down the road."

I giggled and replied, "*Ja*, let's get out of here before you get us in trouble."

We left the church and scoured the property. The church was constructed on a hill and there were a few small sheds scattered about. We entered one of the sheds. It was filled with landscaping tools.

"Ilse, these sheds are still full. It doesn't look like anyone went through these."

"Hey, we can use this hammer and saw. I'll take it with."

"Look, shovels. We should come back at night so the Russians don't see us walking down the street with tools." I shut the door and we went on to the next shed. This one was at the edge of a tree line and somewhat concealed. It was fun searching through these sheds because we never knew what we would find.

Brigitte grabbed the door handle. My face was right next to hers, cheek-to-cheek. I didn't want to miss out on the initial excitement of what was inside. She slowly pulled the door as she said, "This doesn't seem like a shed. I think it's an outhouse." I felt let down, and backed off a bit as Brigitte continued to open the door. The inside was unclear until full sunlight passed through the doorway.

Brigitte let out an ear-piercing scream and let go of the door and it swung wide open. She took off running. There I was, staring at the inside of a three-seater outhouse. Three dead German soldiers, fully clothed, but unarmed, sat on the toilet bench, with their backs leaning up against the wall and their heads tilted onto their shoulders. Panic-struck, at first, I was paralyzed and couldn't breathe. I was finally able to take a breath and made the same screech, and took off after Brigitte.

My heart pounded from fear. I couldn't run fast enough to catch Brigitte. "Gitti, wait for me," I shouted out of breath as I ran full-speed. She didn't stop. It wasn't until we were a few blocks away from the church that she finally halted. When I caught up, she was bent at the waist, her elbows locked straight and her hands cupped her thighs. Her head, dangling from her shoulders, was bobbing up and down with each breath. Grabbing gulps of air between words, she muttered, "Those soldiers ... they were ... dead."

We didn't say anything for a while; we just needed to catch our breath. "What do we do, Gitti? We can't just leave them there."

"We need to tell our families." We walked back home and compared notes on the frightening experience. We waited in my home until my family arrived from work. Brigitte went and got her mother. We explained what we saw and, as a group, we headed to the church to view the soldiers. I clung onto Mutti as we approached the outhouse. The door still stood wide open.

"My God," Mutti sighed. "What do you think? These soldiers must have been dead for over a year ... and no one found them." She covered her mouth with the backside of her hand and turned her head.

"How did they die ... and why in here?" Brigitte's mother added to the line of questions.

Tante Friedel, not to be left out of the conversation, added, "I bet they hid in here, and were afraid to come out ... and eventually starved to death."

"*Ja*, but why no guns?" Brigitte's mother asked. "What if they were placed here? Maybe the Russians put them in here to add to their humiliation." The questions just kept coming. There were no answers, and it really didn't matter, but it was an interesting puzzle. Finally, Brigitte's mother said, "We need to tell the commandant. We would get in trouble if we didn't report this." Everyone agreed, Mutti shut the door and we headed to see the commandant. After explaining the story, he too wanted to see the bodies. After seeing them, he didn't really seem to care.

"Can we bury them?" Brigitte's mother asked.

The commandant looked at her, hesitated, and then said, "Sure, go ahead." He walked away, unmoved by the whole event.

"I need to remove their *Hunde-Marke* [dog tags], so we can inform relatives," said Brigitte's mother. "We can bury them here at the church cemetery."

I then remembered the other shed with tools. "Hey, there are shovels in that shed." I pointed to the one Brigitte and I rummaged through earlier. Later, we, all women again, dug a shallow grave to bury the soldiers. It was very unnerving to move the bodies. They were stiff and fragile and amazingly light. As we gently carried the soldiers from the outhouse, I feared an arm or leg would fall off by accident. Fortunately, nothing went wrong to add to the unpleasantness.

Mutti, gave a brief prayer at the grave site. Irmi and I planted a cross we made from twigs. Then, we turned and walked away.

15

A Stolen Potato

During the summer, it was busy in the fields and I helped occasionally, but my time was better served gleaning natural food. Now that Opa was no longer with us, I was the sole provider of supplemental and fresh food for my family. I now spent a lot of time with other children my age and we went as a group, usually four to eight, to gather berries, and I even showed them how to pick mushrooms safely. We became bolder and more creative in our quest for food. There was an inner network of communication where people helped one another. In one instance, our little network got word that there was an older man, native to Goldbach, who knew of a patch of wild strawberries that was only accessible by boat. He agreed to take us to the spot; his only request was that we give him some of the strawberries.

He led our little group of adolescents through the woods to the edge of a stream where we uncovered a small rowboat. It was well-hidden from the Russians; they would have no doubt stolen it, or shot holes in it like our *Ilse* boat on the coast. He rowed us across the stream, pointed us in a direction and instructed us to look for a clearing about a kilometer into the woods. He was old and not very mobile, so he waited for us to return. We marched into the woods in search of the clearing and, sure enough, it was a bumper crop. It looked to be about an acre with no trees, so the sun allowed the wild strawberries to flourish. We ate our fill and each of us gathered about two liters of berries to take home to our families. As promised, we shared our berries with the kind man who took us back across the stream. We took several trips while the berries were in season. I made marmalade from the berries, just as Opa taught me, to keep for times of scarcity.

Brigitte and I became good friends with Gerhardt and Gisela—brother and sister. Gerhardt was one or two years older than me and Gisela a year younger. I was fond of Gerhardt, not in a boyfriend way, although he was handsome. I felt safer having a young man with us; at least, I thought of him as a young man. I think the other reason I felt attached to him was that he was unique in our little society. Most any German male his age was either killed or taken to a work camp. He was soft-spoken, courteous and very kind.

I couldn't wait to meet up with Gerhardt and Gisela on days we got together and foraged for food. Mostly, we picked raspberries and blueberries. We even picked berries along fields where our families worked, when the soldiers allowed us. I liked this because I was able to see the others in my family during the day.

Gisela usually spent whole days with us, while Gerhardt helped in the afternoons, after working in the fields driving implements with horses. The Russians eagerly took Gerhardt as a worker, because he was young and full of energy. Some days, he skipped work, because the yield of natural food was better than a day's work in the field. Brigitte and I didn't know anything about their family, so one afternoon, Brigitte innocently stated, "Our families are going to be happy with this load of berries."

I responded, "*Ja*, I can't wait. This will be a welcome treat." There was no response from either Gerhardt or Gisela. Brigitte and I looked at each other, thinking they should have agreed. I then attempted to engage them in the conversation by following up with a question. "Won't your family be pleased with these berries?"

Gerhardt hesitated, not looking up, and responded timidly, "Yes .. yes, they will."

I sensed something was not quite right. "Is something the matter?"

Gerhardt looked up slowly. "Our papa died in the war and Mutti died from typhoid four months ago. We have two younger sisters, four and six, that we need to care for."

I felt awful for bringing it up. I wished I hadn't said anything. Worse yet, I didn't know what to say next.

"Don't you have any relatives?" Thankfully, Brigitte responded.

"Yes, our aunt and uncle agreed to take care of us after Mutti died.'

"Well, that's good. At least you have some family," I replied, glad that there was a silver lining to this conversation. Then, it got worse.

Gerhardt was expressionless. I could tell it was difficult for him to talk about it. "They lost their nerve. Our aunt lives in fear and won't leave the house. Our uncle won't work and has no ambition; it's like he's waiting to die. Instead of helping, they are a burden. It's terrible."

Now I really didn't know what to say. The only thing that came out was, "That *is* terrible." Somehow, I didn't think those words made anyone feel good, including myself. Determined this conversation was bound to get better, I said, "Gerhardt, you and Gisela are doing a kind thing, taking care of your sisters. You work so hard and try to do everything you can for them. I applaud you."

He looked at me and smiled. "Thank you. I pray that we do the right thing every day. Every day is a challenge." Regrettably, stories like Gerhardt's and Gisela's were not unusual. Many people snapped over the stresses of starvation and living conditions and lost their ability to reason. For the apathetic, it was only a matter of time until they starved to death and perhaps dragged their children with them.

Gerhardt was bright and diligent, and despite his young age had every intention of providing for his family. Gisela was also very ambitious. Between the two of them, they were able to gather just enough food for themselves and their two sisters—at least during the summer.

As for their aunt and uncle, Gisela and Gerhardt didn't talk about how they managed. What a tough decision: do they try and provide food for them, or let them starve to death because they refuse to care for themselves? Brigitte and I never asked.

Gerhardt knew that he wouldn't be able to provide enough for his little sisters through the winter, so he started inquiring about orphanages. There was an abundance of parentless children, so finding an opening was a challenge.

In late summer, Gerhardt decided to take his two young sisters to an orphanage in Königsberg, where he heard they were accepting orphans. Traveling as a young boy was ill-advised, because there were stories of Russians taking young boys and using them as slaves. But he had little choice. His sisters would not live through another winter. I was sad, thinking that I would never see him again, but to our amazement, he managed the trip to Königsberg safely and returned a week later.

"I am so relieved that they are in good hands," Gerhardt said to us. "I was heartbroken to let them go." His eyes started to water. "But I knew it was the right thing to do."

"How will you be able to find them again," I asked.

"Actually, it will be easier to track them than to track me. Who knows where I will be? If things settle down in a few years, I will find them."

Orphanages lacked funding and support and were not a guarantee of safety, but rather than have them face inevitable starvation, this brave boy had done his best to ensure his young sisters had a chance.

There were sad stories everywhere, and one could see why some people simply gave up. It took courage, smarts, willpower, ambition, and above all, hope to make it in this arena. I grew up fast, and knew what it meant to sacrifice and plan for the future. I could tell which families were going to survive and which ones weren't.

Another family, a mother, two girls and a boy, struggled in our unforgiving environment. One daughter, Frieda, was my age and she often came to my house to beg for food during the day. I sometimes gave her a piece of bread. I felt sympathy for her, even though it meant less for us. I would have gotten in trouble from my family if they knew I was giving Frieda our food. I often asked her to come with us to pick berries, and her response was always, "Yes, I'll go with you tomorrow," but she never showed up. It bothered me that she was an able-bodied person, but would rather beg from someone who had basically nothing to give than go and fend for herself. We worked for our food and gathered whatever we could to sustain us, and she did nothing. Her brother, Jürgen, was about twelve or thirteen and had a disability. He was mentally behind other children and had slanted, bulging eyes. We poked fun at him and called him pig-eyes. It was shameful, but kids were often cruel.

Jürgen had a connection with animals though. He especially had a way with the horses. Brigitte said that since he was simple-minded, he could relate to them. He worked the horses in the fields and took care of them. The horses listened best to his commands. He was, however, secretly cunning and stole food from the Russians. They thought he was stupid, so they didn't suspect he was clever enough to outwit them. Ironically, he was the only one in the family who worked or gathered food. I don't know if his mother was just lazy, or if she broke under the stress like Gerhardt's aunt, but she didn't do anything. I suspected Frieda was following in the mother's footsteps.

One day, the Russians caught Jürgen stealing a piglet. For his punishment, the Russians made him touch high voltage wires and he was electrocuted—a cruel retribution for trying to feed his family. With Jürgen gone, the pressure escalated for the remaining family members to work and gather food. Yet Frieda and her mother still didn't work. A few weeks after Jürgen was killed, Frieda stopped by our house during the day when I was alone. "Ilse, can you spare some food?" she asked.

She looked awful. Her body had swelled up, an obvious sign of malnutrition. She had a big belly, but it wasn't from food. I felt bad for her. That morning, I had made some flour-water patties. "Here, Frieda," I said, as I handed her one of the patties. She took it and bit into it.

She squeezed her lips together and squinted her eyes to form a sour-puss expression. She placed the patty back on the plate and said, "Don't you have any bread?"

"No, Frieda. I eat these patties. They may not taste that great, but it's food. Take it."

"No, I don't want that," and she stormed out in a huff. She reached the first step outside our entrance and noticed the salty fish that I was soaking in a bucket of water. She reached her arm into the barrel, and grabbed a fist full of fish.

"Frieda," I shouted. "You can't do that! Put it back!" I quickly grabbed her arm. In her weak state, she tripped and fell down the stairs onto the ground. "Frieda," I cried, as I ran down the stairs to her. "Are you all right?" I helped her get up. She moved slowly. "Come on, let's go inside." I held her arm. She twisted it away from me and walked off without saying a word. Three days later, I heard that she died.

I was shocked at how lazy some people were. Here, their lives, and perhaps their family's lives, lay in the balance, yet many refused to work, either for the Russians, or by gathering food themselves. Why? I didn't understand it.

People stared starvation in the face and simply accepted it. For them, it was curtains.

Gerhardt, Gisela, Brigitte and I were a little band of thieves. Wherever an opportunity to steal from the Russians presented itself, we took it. We were smart about our course of action, though. We knew the consequences of getting caught were severe, like what happened to Jürgen. So we had to be safe, plan ahead, and always have a lookout person who would signal an alarm, like whistling or singing, that Russians were coming. The Russians were wise to us refugees and locked doors and windows to the homes that were used as silos for food storage. We rose to the challenge.

In one such home, the Russians built a pulley system to carry food to the upper level, similar to a hay loft system. Fortunately for us, they left the rope attached to the pulley. I was the lightest, so I got the task of being hoisted up to the window. Gisela was our lookout and Gerhardt and Brigitte provided the muscle. Up I went. The upper window was open and I crawled in. The room was filled with red cabbages. I started tossing them out, and the others caught them. We only took what we could carry. We couldn't risk being noticed carrying cabbages, so we walked along behind bushes, trees and whatever cover we could find.

In early fall, much of the labor force transitioned from the fields to the woods to begin logging. Workers would cut wheat stalks and let them dry for several days while they cut trees along the edge of the fields. Logging was dangerous and difficult work, especially for women, so I wasn't allowed to help. Although, being the smallest, I became the main character in a clandestine operation to confiscate wheat.

We had a carefully laid-out plan to make it look like I was simply part of the team felling trees. After the trees were cut down, they had to be debranched, and these branches were piled at the field's edge to be eventually burned. We carefully stacked one pile so that I could fit inside, completely concealed from passers-by. Mutti and Tante Friedel used a two-man saw to cut down trees, Anneliese cut off the branches and Irmi carried the branches away. One soldier oversaw several logging operations, so when his attention was on another group, Irmi would carry branches to my pile that carefully concealed stolen wheat stalks; these she fed to me through a small hole in my branch pile. I removed the wheat from the stalks and handed them back to Irmi to hide in the woods, so that the Russians wouldn't find empty stalks and discover our theft. I laid out a few cloths on the ground, de-chaffed the wheat, tied the ends of the cloth together to form a ball and tied a string to each bundle. I then tied the other end of the string to my belt and let the wheat bundle hang inside my pants. I walked back to the house, unloaded my wheat, and went back for more. There were only two or three days to do this while the wheat was drying, but it was enough to get a substantial supply of grain.

In September, Anneliese contracted typhoid disease. We thought that the vaccinations would prevent this, but who knows what the Russians gave us? Some suspected that they were experimental drugs and we were their lab rats. Although Anneliese was terribly sick and had to go to the hospital, they made her return to work the next day. Miraculously, she did manage to work through it and recovered.

We lived under extremely unsanitary conditions. It was no wonder that people contracted typhoid. Tante Friedel, Irmi and I had large boils develop on our arms. Anneliese had one on her leg. These boils were painful and lasted for weeks. We suspected that these were either a result of the mysterious vaccinations they pumped into us, or simply our unsanitary conditions.

Logging debilitated our family. To reach their quota, they had to spend all day in the woods, sun-up to sun-down, sawing, chopping, dragging and hauling. In the midst of this, was the danger associated with trees falling. One day Irmi got hit by a large birch tree. Luckily, it was a side branch and not the main trunk; otherwise, she would have been our fourth casualty. Even so, her back was injured to the point that she couldn't work for a week; she could hardly even get out of bed.

As work slowed down in the fields, there was a rumor that less efficient workers were going to be fired. Without work, where were we going to get food? Then Tante Friedel also hurt her back and was off work for a day. The brigadier saw her at home, walking to the wood pile with me to gather wood for our fire. The next day, when she reported to work, the brigadier fired her because he claimed if she was healthy enough to haul wood at home, she was healthy enough to haul wood at work.

The brigadier was a giant man, head and shoulders taller than anyone else around him. His eyebrows were furry caterpillars on his almost perfectly round head. He never smiled and gazed unblinkingly through narrowed eyes. His lips formed a natural frown that made him look constantly angry. He was merciless. Tante Friedel was distraught. She was now home alone with me. We sat at the kitchen table and commiserated.

"I can't believe I got fired," Tante Friedel howled. "That *schwein*! What does he think? We break our backs all day working, and he fires me." There was silence because I really didn't know what to say.

Selfishly, I was glad that someone was home with me. "Hey, there will still be some blackberries to pick. We can pick them together."

She ignored me. "If I just wouldn't have gone to the woodpile ... I could barely make it ... and he caught me." She wouldn't stop.

"He is purposely mean so that women will beg for sympathy and sleep with him to avoid their punishment. He can rot in hell before I beg for sympathy." I was uncomfortable. I never saw Tante Friedel this mad. "Ilse, I will need to leave here." My heart sank. I loved Tante Friedel as much as my own mother. She often offered even more support and encouragement than Mutti did.

"You can't leave us. We need you here."

"It will be worse if I stay. It will be another mouth to feed and one less person pulling the cart. I think I will go back to Königsberg. There has to be work available there."

"Will the Russians let you go?"

"I won't ask ... I'll just go."

"No, they'll send you to a prison!"

"Maybe I'll find a way to get to the west."

She was right, as much as I didn't want to admit it. The workers here were now getting paid with money instead of food. Not that the money solved our problems, it still only bought about the same amount of food that we earned before, but it did offer a way to pay for a train ticket. We were no longer as trapped as we used to be. As more and more Russian civilians arrived, the need to pay them money became more important. The Communists did, after all, want their people to be self-sufficient. As such, the Communists wanted all of their citizens to work, and firing workers was contrary to their plans. When the authorities heard that our brigadier fired workers, he got reprimanded, and, after a few days, Tante Friedel got her job back. What a relief, I couldn't bear the thought of Tante Friedel leaving us.

In between logging, some fields still needed harvesting. One evening, on a day that my family harvested potatoes, only three returned, in silence. Mutti looked exhausted, her head hanging from her shoulders. She walked over to one of the stools and crumpled onto it with her elbows on her knees and face in her hands. I recognized the all too familiar grief. I knelt down beside her, but she did not move. "Mutti," I whispered. "Where's Anneliese?" I was almost certain of the answer. Mutti slowly lifted her face. Her eyes were sunken deep behind her high cheekbones. She lowered her eyes and searched the floor for a suitable answer.

After a long pause, she whispered, "The Russians took her away."

"Why?" I asked, trembling.

"Anneliese was stopped by the brigadier on our way home. He opened her canteen and found a potato hidden inside." Tears started running down Mutti's cheeks. "They took her to a camp for stealing." She placed her face into her hands and sobbed.

Still trembling, I stuttered, "Is—is she going to be okay?" Mutti never answered. As it turned out, Mutti's friend Frau Albart was caught along with Anneliese. About an hour after my family came home with the bad news, four Russian soldiers arrived at our door. They demanded to come in and search our home. We really didn't have any choice. A quick search revealed that we stored more grain than they estimated we could have earned working. This was the wheat that we stole. They confiscated our stored winter supply, saying that it was recently stolen and this supported the fact that Anneliese was a thief.

They told us that Anneliese was going to a work prison in Tapiau. A few days later, Anneliese returned. We were excited and glad to see her back. The prison authorities told her that the punishment was too severe for only stealing a potato. But our joy was short lived. The ugly brigadier would have nothing of it and sent her back, demanding that they take her. We were helpless under the command of such an evil man. Although he was relieved of duty and sent away shortly after the Anneliese incident, for our family, the damage was already done.

A few weeks later, Mutti and Tante Friedel went to Tapiau to try to visit Anneliese. The authorities told them that Anneliese was transferred to a prison in Königsberg, but they said that they would forward any letters to her. Mutti gave them a note and also sent many subsequent letters without any response or acknowledgement. Later, Mutti also went to Königsberg searching for her, but no one gave her a straight answer. Again she tried to forward a letter.

We heard awful stories about what they did to women in these prisons. All we had was hope. Our voices didn't matter. It was frustrating and discouraging. At least if she received one of our letters, she would keep faith, but the probability that she actually got them was remote. We knew the Russians didn't care. Why would they bother? She was a criminal in their eyes. We Germans didn't have any rights, especially in prison. I prayed every night that God would protect her. Time was not on our side. The longer she stayed in prison, the more odds were against her.

16

A Sparrow Falls

We were awakened by the clanging of the town bells—like clock-work every morning at 6:00 A.M. I awoke with a familiar hollowness in my stomach, the same feeling I had for the past sixteen months under Russian rule. I slowly uncoiled from the huddle of warmth under my blanket and scratched my head. I don't know if the lice I scratched were real or imagined, but they itched just the same.

Tante Friedel was the first to speak. "Ah, another day in paradise."

Her sarcasm was wearing on me, but strangely, the phrase aggravated us into action.

By this time, I was accustomed to hunger. It was a bitter hollowness I accepted from the moment I woke until I fell asleep, but now, it grew intensely worse since the Russians confiscated our surplus of food. With Anneliese gone, there was one less stipend and I became a bigger drain on our family.

Now that autumn was upon us, Mutti, Tante Friedel and Irmi—armed with only a two-man hand-saw and axe—cut trees from dusk to dawn, while I stayed home to cook and clean. Mutti would not allow me to do the heavy labor of a lumberjack.

Cutting trees was exhausting work. The meager rations provided did not offset the energy it took for the workers to drive saws and swing axes hour after hour. And it wasn't merely a matter of showing up to work; they had to fulfill a quota by the end of the day. If that quota was not met, they received nothing, not even a prorated portion. We all knew it was only a matter of time until we starved to death.

We sat around the table, our only light a make-shift oil lamp made of a glass jar half-full with oil and a piece of rope for a wick. The Russians never turned the electricity back on to our homes. A half-loaf of stale bread lay resting on a piece of tin I found in the field. Our weary eyes were all gazing at the bread, hoping that maybe today a slice would actually satisfy the burning hole in our stomachs. Tante Friedel grabbed the loaf of bread with her dried and callused hand. She was a young lady, but her hands looked like those of someone forty years her senior. The wrinkles and creases were accented by

126

earth and oil. Her yellowed, unhealthy fingernails were chipped and scratched. With her other hand, she reached for an old butter knife that I had sharpened on a piece of granite. She carefully measured with the knife to the middle of the loaf, and cut a notch into the crust. Then she measured halfway to each end and cut another notch on either side, making four equal segments.

Before she cut through the loaf, she looked at Mutti and said, "Does that look even?"

Mutti nodded and said, "Looks good. Make sure Ilsechen gets the end piece." I didn't care for the end piece of bread, but Mutti, for some reason, thought there was more nutrition in the crust. I didn't bother to argue.

I was amazed how accurately Tante Friedel cut the loaf every day with those trembling worn hands. There was never a question or a squabble over our fair share of the bread. We all carefully held one of our hands open under the bread as we bit into it to make sure we captured every crumb. Once the bread was eaten, Tante Friedel pointed to the bread crumbs on the tin and said, "Put these in the soup for tonight."

She groaned as she slowly got up from the table and said, "Okay, it's off to the woods." The three of them put on their boots, which took a while because every pair was ragged and held together with string and old leather belts. I helped in the ritual tying of knots and placing of extra pieces of leather or cloth in the boots so their feet would be as warm and protected as possible.

I felt awful that they had to go out and work all day while I was allowed to stay home. I knew I was a burden to them. Impulsively, I blurted out, "Mutti, can I come with? I can help, I know I can."

Immediately, Mutti shouted, "*Nein*! You can't come with us." Her voice softened as she continued, "Ilsechen, I told you before. You're too young to help. Besides, we need you here to cook and clean for us. Now, be a good girl, get some rest and have dinner ready for us when we get back." I couldn't say anything, as I watched them vanish into the darkness of the pre-dawn. I put another log into the stove, blew out the oil lamp, and went back to sleep.

The sun cast a stream of light through one of the two windows and awakened me. I had no clock or watch, so the sun was my time-keeper; I guessed it was around ten o'clock. *My goodness, I slept late today.* I put another log in the stove, grabbed the cooking pot, put on my coat and boots and ran out the door, headed for the water pump at the end of the street. Fortunately, we had no shortage of good water.

My mind took me away from the evil that surrounded us and back to the sanctuary of Palmnicken. *I remembered the clean autumn air and the unmistakable smell of the Baltic Sea. I heard Anneliese and Irmi in high-pitched laughter as we covered each other up in leaves.* How I wished we could be back home, carefree and happy, and not hungry.

I approached the well, placed the pot on a bed of rocks, reached up and pulled down the pump handle. Its familiar squeak prompted a response from a neighboring bird. After a few pumps, the bird lost interest, and soon, the cold water started filling the pot. I stopped to cup my hands in the stream of water and gathered a drink. I only filled the pot halfway; experience taught me that if I filled it full, half would splash out anyway. I walked back to our home bowlegged, the pot between my legs, stopping every few steps to rest.

As I waited for the water to heat so I could wash clothes, I pulled up a crate and started darning socks and mending clothing. I became pretty good at sewing. Over a period of several weeks, I made a green and white dress. The fabric came from old bed sheets and the thread, as usual, came from pulling old fabric apart down to the strand. I loved that dress and wore it often, proud to show off my handiwork and feeling beautiful in something new made just for me.

I took a break from my sewing and stared out the hazy glass into the backyard. Five sparrows were picking through the dormant grass, looking for food. I wondered if their stomachs were as empty as mine. They apparently were finding something, which was more than I could say. Diligent in their pursuit, they worked the ground feverishly for the tiniest scraps. Their persistence fascinated me. My head dipped down and I noticed the crate on which I was sitting. Suddenly, I whipped my head in the direction of the tin of bread crumbs. I jumped to my feet, flushed from head to foot with excitement.

I ran to my boots and quickly pulled off the shoelaces, then collected all the string pieces I could find and tied them end-to-end. My heart was pounding. I grabbed the crate and string, threw on my boots and ran out the door. Two steps later, I slipped out of my boots, and landed on my stomach. I turned and looked at the boots—no laces—that was stupid! It didn't matter. As quickly as I fell, I was up again, bare-footed, running to the back yard where the sparrows were. All the commotion scared them away. *They'll come back*, I thought. I placed the crate, open-end-down, where I had last seen the sparrows and frantically searched for a good stick. I remembered a sturdy forked stick I used for poking the logs in the stove, so I ran in the house and grabbed it as well as the tin of bread crumbs. This time, though, I ran outside carefully so I wouldn't spill the crumbs.

I tilted one end of the crate and wedged the forked end of the stick under the open end of the crate, and put the other end on the ground. *A perfect fit.* I tied one end of my shoelaces-and-string to the bottom of the stick, right near the ground. But I could see already it was too short for what I had in mind. I found some long straight branches, untied my knots and added the branches in between my little pieces of string. *Now* my string was long enough to make it to the edge of the house, where I could hide behind a large shrub. I placed the tin of crumbs under the tilted crate and scurried behind the shrub.

Then, I patiently waited. I sat back and rested my head against the side of the house and closed my eyes. After a while, I heard birds chirping. The five sparrows were back, and were pecking at the ground around the crate. My heart started thudding furiously, but I didn't dare move. A few seconds later, one brave sparrow hopped onto the tin, then another. I pulled the string and *frump*, the crate captured the sparrows.

I jumped and ran around the yard, screaming in joy. After my victory dance, I ran to the crate and realized that I was confronted with a dilemma. How could I get the birds out without letting them get away? I peeked under the crate, and saw the sparrows fluttering. I ran inside, grabbed a blanket, went back out and laid the blanket around the crate. I laid on my stomach, reached under the blanket, tilted one end of the crate up and reached my hand into the crate. One sparrow flew out! I was upset, but thoroughly determined to get the last one. I slid my arm under the crate and used my other hand to push the blanket tight under the crate to leave no space for the sparrow to escape. I waved my arm inside the crate, occasionally hitting him, but I couldn't get a grip. Finally, I had him cornered. I grabbed him, and pulled him out from under the crate.

He looked terribly frightened, yet calm, as if accepting the fate that awaited him. A part of me said, *let him go, he deserves to live*, but hunger drove me to continue. "I don't want to hurt you" I said to him, in a soft voice. "But my family is starving." Butchers kill animals all the time; it's a way of life. God gave me this gift, and we needed the food. I just wished Mutti were there to do what I didn't want to. With the bird held tightly in one hand, I used my other hand to grab him from the back of the head. I closed my eyes, pulled his head and twisted. It was done. The bird lay lifeless in my hand. I had never killed anything before and was relieved it was over.

The water was boiling on the stove. I moved it over so it wouldn't boil away. The laundry could wait another day. We needed *food*. I went back out and reset the ambush. In short order, another three sparrows met the same fate. I plucked the birds, and cut open their bellies. I remembered Mutti cleaning rabbits; she always threw the intestines and stomach away, and some other stuff. But I didn't want to waste anything, so I threw away what looked like the intestines, cut off the feet and threw the rest into the pot, even the bones. A few chopped potatoes, a handful of flour, some greens, and I'd made a real soup. I watched it simmer. *The room never smelled so good.* The aroma made my hunger grow—I'd eaten only one slice of bread all day.

Darkness prompted me to light the oil lamp. It was now a matter of minutes until my family's arrival. I decided not to mention anything until they ate; I wanted the meat to be a surprise. I heard leaves rustling and people talking outside. *They're here!* The door opened and Irmi was the first to enter.

"Oh, that smells good," she said.

Mutti was next, "Ilsechen, what did you make? That smells wonderful. I can't wait to eat." I just shrugged as if it was the same old potato soup. They untied their boots, took off their coats and sat at the table. I carefully scooped the soup into four bowls, making sure each serving was even as always, but especially this time. Everyone received the same amount of meat. I had my back to them, so they couldn't see what I was doing.

I placed the bowls in front of them. "Mmm," Irmi grunted before she even took a spoonful. They started eating.

"This is *wunderbar*, Ilsechen, what did you put—" Mutti's spoon revealed a piece of meat. She started to sputter: "How—where did you—?"

"It's sparrow, Mutti, I caught them in the backyard under a crate. I used a stick and a rope and trapped them." I could have gone on forever, giving them every detail in my excitement, but I noticed Mutti's spoon drop into her bowl. I looked up at her and saw that her eyes were squinted. She raised her hands over her face and burst out in tears. Soon, we were all crying.

Sobbing, catching her breath, in a voice muffled by her hands, Mutti said, "Ilsechen, I can't believe you did this! This tastes so good, and we need the meat. I am so proud of you!"

The taste of meat after months of near starvation was a feast never forgotten. Those few sparrows did not satisfy our hunger, but they supplied much needed protein. I continued to hunt and occasionally was successful, but eventually the birds either grew wise to me, or moved on to better feeding locations. I don't know if we shed tears of joy for the nourishment, or tears of sorrow because of our pathetic jubilance over a few ounces of sparrow. But there was no doubt that a bowl of soup had given us hope.

17

An End in Sight

January 1947 was the most difficult time during the twenty-one months we had been under Russian rule. Now ten months in Goldbach, the hard work my family did lumberjacking was taking its toll. There simply wasn't enough food to sustain us. We were a shadow of our former selves; just skin clinging to bone. Every week, more people died of starvation. One woman who was alone with three children took her fate, and that of her children's, into her own hands. In the middle of a winter night, she opened all of the windows and the family froze to death. Tante Friedel had known of her and her plight and, although she was deeply saddened by the event, she wasn't surprised by the woman's decision.

We lived from day to day. I begged, stole and scavenged for scraps to help us through our desperate time of need. I even resorted to picking through trash that the Russians discarded. Once in a while, there were bits of food worth salvaging. One day, I found a pile of potato peels. I took them home and made potato pancakes with the peelings.

Mutti said, "Potato peel! I'm not eating that. They're dirty."

"Ach, they're good," replied Tante Friedel. "That's where all the nutrition is." Mutti was the only one who didn't eat the potato skin pancakes. The rest of us found them to be quite tasty.

Unfortunately, Mutti was right. Potato peels can be highly toxic if subjected to sunlight. We vomited for days. But we were fortunate and, after a few days, the sickness passed, although it left our already ravaged bodies even weaker.

I visited the army base on a daily basis to beg for scraps. There was one soldier who was particularly unkind to me. His name was Ivan and he was shorter than me and unusually hyperactive. Ivan was always talking and play-fighting with the soldiers. And he would say and do peculiar things. For instance, he would run after me, shouting, "I'm going to get you."

The soldiers always laughed at him. I think he was their entertainment. Whatever a soldier asked him to do, no matter how crazy, he would do it. I believe he was self-conscious about his height and felt if he was their clown, he fit in. Fortunately, Ivan couldn't run very fast and I was able to fend off his attacks. Whenever I came to the base, I would carry a fist full of stones. When Ivan started chasing me, I ran and threw stones at him. My spunk amused the soldiers a great deal. I think they looked forward to our skirmishes. And I began to, as well, because it certainly prompted charity from them. I didn't like Ivan, but I came back every day because I was rewarded with food.

One time, when I wasn't paying attention, Ivan caught me. He jumped on my back and had one arm around my throat. Adrenaline pumped through my veins. Even though the soldiers were laughing, I thought he was going to kill me. I figured they wouldn't stop him. I quickly spun around and used my elbow as a weapon. As I spun, my elbow hit him in the head and he fell off of me. I ran as fast as I could, to the cheers of the soldiers. I didn't return until I found out for sure that Ivan's regiment had left.

Mutti kept some of Opa's clothing after he died. When it came to clothing, even if it didn't fit, or was worn out, we held on to it, in case we could use it to patch other clothing or somehow make it fit. There were a few pairs of pants and shirts left over and Mutti told me to ask soldiers if they would exchange the clothes for food. Since the soldiers wore uniforms, I had my doubt that anyone would want the clothes, but I delightedly came home with sauerkraut, a loaf of bread and some grain. I don't know if the soldiers had sympathy for me, or they really had a use for the clothes. Mutti was very pleased; she expected to fetch only a loaf of bread.

So this was the great Communist system of the socialist republic, the system where everyone was equal and everyone got a fair shake. The Russian peasants who moved to Goldbach were dying off just like we were. Perhaps if they starved 75 percent of its inhabitants to death, there might be enough to go around.

Our Palmnicken pastor came to Goldbach periodically. Pastor Jänicke didn't work, he lived off charity from his former congregation. We fed him when he came to town, and gave him money toward train fares. He was not allowed to preach, but he brought us news and mail from loved ones.

The Russians had a mail system, although all communications were screened and delivery was very slow. Often, mail never arrived at its intended location. And because refugees didn't have an address, mail was simply sent to villages. It was up to someone in the village to determine if the addressee lived there. If the person sorting didn't know the family, the mail was returned or quite often simply discarded. Our mail was still being delivered to Palmnicken, but the pastor knew where his flock was scattered. He kept us and many families throughout the region connected through his efforts.

Our pastor told us that those in Palmnicken were just as bad off as we were in Goldbach. Palmnicken was not immune to starvation. He delivered a letter sadly telling us of the fate of Uncle Ernst. Uncle Ernst was Mutti's brother—Tante Friedel's husband. A comrade of Ernst knew that Ernst came from Palmnicken. He wrote to tell us that near the end of the war, at the straits of Pillau, Ernst and another man ran into a bunker for safety. On April 17, 1945, which was within days of the Russians invading our home in Palmnicken, a bomb landed in that exact bunker and the men died. The battle at Pillau was one of the last conquests of the Russians as they surrounded the Germans in East Prussia. If Ernst and the other man had lasted a few more weeks, the war would have been over. The soldier who sent the message told us they were buried in a remote forest about six to seven kilometers away. Tante Friedel cried miserably. I think she suspected Uncle Ernst was dead, but didn't want to believe it. Now the truth was known.

The pastor also informed us of what he had heard regarding national and political events. Nothing could be verified and he indicated as much, but it was more than the Russians would tell us—which was nothing.

"How can I find anything out about Hans or Günter?" Mutti asked.

The pastor took a breath and cautioned, "I've not heard anything specific about them, but ... I have to tell you ... there are rumors that former Nazis are being tried for war crimes. Mainly officials, but the SS, too."[13]

Mutti's face turned ashen, her eyes widened, "Günter was ... or trained to be an SS. Pastor ... could he be in trouble?"

"From what I've been told, a member of the SS received the *Blutgruppentätowierungtattoo* when they completed SS requirements."[14]

"I think our Günter never finished his SS training before the end of the war ... I hope." Mutti had a, look of desperation, wanting to believe her own opinion.

I just couldn't believe that my brother Günter would be in trouble. He was just a young man following orders. Perhaps I was following Mutti's lead and trying to convince myself that everything was going to be all right.

Mutti tried every avenue available to get information about Anneliese, but her status was simply not known. Prisoner records were practically nonexistent, and Russian officials had little interest in responding to our inquiries. She was originally supposed to serve one year, meaning she would be released in the fall of 1947. But we could not even determine where she was, much less when she might be freed. It was miserable not knowing anything about her and having no means of finding out.

Winter plodded along. Every sunrise brought with it the challenge of survival. We barely managed to make it through each day. We existed on just the rations earned through my family's lumberjacking, and sometimes not even those, because the HO would sometimes run out of supplies. Christmas was even bleaker than last year. We had a small worship service in our home, but there was no celebration or special treat.

Goldbach didn't receive as much snow as Palmnicken, because it was far enough inland to avoid the evaporative effect of the Baltic Sea. However, Goldbach didn't benefit from the warming effect of the sea, either. Many January and February days dipped below -30°C (−22°F). Our meager clothing was no match for these extremely dangerous temperatures. Even the soldiers refused to work on these days.

March of 1947 arrived and through God's grace, we had made it through the winter. It was my thirteenth birthday. Last year, I received a plate of waffles for my special day. This year, I didn't even get a piece of bread. Tante Friedel came through with a special gift, though. Months ago, pilfering through abandoned homes, we had come across raw wool yarn. Tante Friedel fashioned some knitting needles from nails and used that wool to knit me the most beautiful sweater. It was purple with white stripes. I loved the sweater and wore it almost every day. In a time where patched-together, worn-out clothing was all anyone had to wear, a warm, bright and new purple sweater made a flamboyant fashion statement. I proudly sported this sweater and was the envy of my friends. Purple became my favorite color. It was the greatest gift anyone could have given me. I showered Tante Friedel with hugs and gratitude.

During a visit, the pastor delivered a smuggled letter from Frau Albart who had been sent to prison with Anneliese. At least we now knew they were in a prison in Königsberg. Conditions were miserable, Frau Albart wrote, but they were both still alive. It was great to hear from them and it gave us encouragement.

People continued to die of starvation and illness at an astounding rate. Finally, in May, we were able to once again cut dandelion and other greens just like Opa taught me. This year, there was a market in Tapiau, which was the largest city near Goldbach, approximately ten kilometers south. Civilians from the surrounding villages were allowed to buy and sell a variety of food and goods, including dairy and eggs. Irmi and I picked violets and wildflowers and sold them at the market for one ruble per bouquet. One egg cost five rubles, and we were elated that we were able to sell enough flowers to buy two eggs.

It was our first egg meal in two years. The eggs were fried in a pan just as I liked them: soft yokes and crispy edges on the whites. We split two eggs four ways. They were just as I remembered, with a soft creamy yolk, and a chewy white. Sheer heaven! I always loved eggs; they were one of my favorites. The taste of eggs jogged my memory of our home in Palmnicken, when we owned about a dozen chickens. *I recalled searching for fresh eggs every morning. The hens were smart and tried to conceal their eggs from us. One hen went missing for several weeks; we thought she was taken by an owl or fox. But one day, she returned to the flock, with a clutch of adorable little chicks following close behind her.*

Later in the summer, Irmi and I also sold berries and mushrooms that we picked in the wild. Finally, we were making some progress. Between supplementing our food supply and selling some of the food that we picked, we were no longer on the brink of starvation. Our situation left us by no means content, but it wasn't critical. It was hard work. We still clawed for every piece of food and every ruble.

At his next visit, the pastor arrived with new mail. Papa had sent a letter to Palmnicken, addressed to us. Irmi and I were all excited and huddled around Mutti as she opened the letter. Mutti's hand trembled slightly as she unfolded the paper, and looking over her shoulder, I could see the strong lines of Papa's beautiful penmanship. She read the letter out loud to us. Her voice crackled in the beginning. Papa said that he was captured by the Russians and spent time in a prisoner of war camp. He was released and sent to the West and was now living in Hamburg with his brother Fritz's family. Günter was captured in Normandy, France, during the war, and was now also released, but there was no word on his whereabouts. Papa said that he loved us and eagerly awaited our reunion. I missed

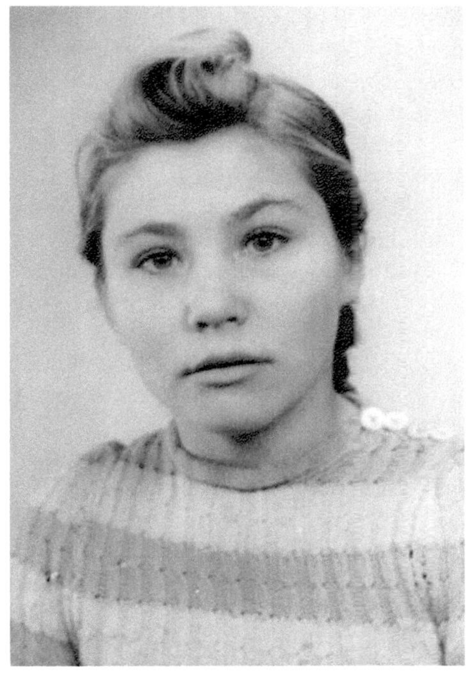

Ilse wearing the sweater Tante Friedel knitted (photographed in Berlin in 1947).

Papa severely and was so glad to hear that he was safe. In Hamburg, he was certainly in a better position than we were. I hadn't seen him for two years. Would he even recognize me?

"When will we see him, Mutti?" I said. "Is he coming to get us?"

"No ... I mean yes, we will see him soon ... but he's not coming here."

"Can we go visit him?"

"Ilsechen, please, in time."

Now more than ever, I thought an end might be near. "Mutti, why can't we leave?"

"Ilsechen, we have no money, and we have no papers to let us go.. You know. We're stuck here until the Russians let us go."

Mutti returned a letter to Papa through the pastor. She never shared what she had written with us, even though we asked.

As time marched on, Russian army squadrons remained in Goldbach for longer periods of time before being replaced. We started to know the soldiers and commanders better than previous regiments. In some cases, friendships developed. One of the Commandants was abruptly relieved of duty and sent away; perhaps because he lived with a German woman who spoke fluent Russian. It was strictly forbidden for any Russian soldier, especially a Commandant, to live with a German refugee. It was a shame to see him go as he was one of the nicer leaders and had compassion for our plight. His woman stayed behind in Goldbach.

Tante Friedel was friends with her and she came to our house one day soon after the Commandant left.

"Friedel," she said. "It's just not fair ... what difference does it make if I'm German and he is Russian?"

Tante Friedel looked confused and slowly shook her head. "I don't know."

"He was a good man. He wasn't a *schwein* like those Russians in the beginning."

"What are you going to do?" Tante Friedel asked.

"We are so in love, I need to get out of here and then we can find each other again."

I listened as she went on about how she was already looking to go to the west and find a way to reunite with her Commandant. This talk of Russian-German relationships further confused me. Some German women refugees despised the Russian soldiers, some had sex with them to feed their families, and others just simply loved them. This was difficult for a thirteen year old to comprehend.

One day, Mutti's cousin, Gertrude, came and visited us. She worked as a cook for a Russian dairy farm that was a two hour walk from us. She stayed that afternoon and we shared our struggles.

"Hanna," she said uncomfortably, trying not to be viewed as patronizing. "The pastor told me that you were here, and that people were starving to death. I don't have much, but I brought some eggs and some bread."

"Thank you, Gertrude." Mutti smiled broadly and continued, "It's not as bad as it was in the winter, but yes, it is terrible." My eyes opened wide: more eggs!

"I am pretty fortunate. I am a cook for the soldiers and get the food from dairy and egg farms in the area. There is no abundance, but I have enough and I can help. I didn't bring any milk, but perhaps you and your family can come to me one day and I can give you a nice meal."

Mutti looked at the rest of us and replied, "*Ach*, that would be wonderful. We will definitely do that." The conversation went on for some time, and while they talked, my mind wandered. I could taste the milk and cheese that she described, though the funny thing was, I couldn't exactly remember what it tasted like. I hadn't had milk in over two years. All I recalled was that it was good, so I couldn't wait until we visited. A week or so later, we set out to visit Gertrude. It was a long walk, but the reward was worth the trip. She served milk soup, bread, and cheese. It was fantastic. I ravenously devoured everything. It was even better than I remembered. Small cups of milk were our treat just before we left. The fresh milk was the high point that polished off the best meal in a long time. As we walked back home, we talked about how excellent the meal was, how kind Gertrude was to us, and how this nourishment would help us build our strength. Suddenly, my stomach began to growl and I had an unpleasant feeling deep in my intestines. I began to vomit violently. Everything that I ate came right back out again.

"Oh no," Mutti groaned. "All that good food." She put her arm around my back to comfort me as I hunched over. After a few more heaves, my stomach was completely emptied.

"It must have been a shock to your system," Mutti suggested. "Maybe it was too rich and your stomach wasn't used to it."

"Do you think the milk was spoiled?" Tante Friedel asked. She quickly answered her own question. "No one else got sick, it *was* probably just too rich." Mutti almost cried that I could not hold it in.

In the late summer, I was involved with a group of children my age that got together every few days to go berry picking. We started getting bolder and moving further away from town to find new and more abundant patches. We were still careful to take side roads and pay attention if any trucks drove by. Just two weeks ago, Helena, an eleven-year old girl we knew from Palmnicken, was raped when she and her family ventured too far from the safety of the village. Her mother and sister had to helplessly watch her being attacked by a truck full of soldiers.

We were wrapped up singing and picking berries and weren't paying attention. We got too close to the road and lost sight of our cover when someone shouted, "*Lastwagen*—hide!" We scattered toward the tall grass. It wasn't much cover, but it was better than standing in the middle of the field. The truck slowed down and then stopped at an embankment that overlooked the field. I heard doors open and some conversation that I couldn't quite make out. The soldiers stood at the edge of the road and were looking in our direction. Perhaps they saw us as they drove up. It was quiet except for the pounding of my heart deep within my chest. They stayed for what seemed like several minutes. None of us dared to move. Finally, they gave up their search. The sound of doors slammed shut and the diesel engine fading off in the distance, confirmed that the group had left. I was finally able to take a breath. I prayed and thanked God for concealing us.

In October, the Russians told us that they would provide transportation for all German refugees to reach the western portion of Germany.[15] November 17 was the scheduled day. Naturally, we were thrilled by the prospect of reaching "free" Germany and reuniting with family and friends, but we also were realists; by this time, we didn't have much faith in what they said.

18

The Expulsion

November 1947 arrived; we were now thirty-one months under Russian rule, and still no sign or word from Anneliese even though her year of punishment was already complete. This was especially worrisome if we were to actually travel to the West on the seventeenth; we didn't want to leave Anneliese behind. If she didn't come with us, she might never get out.

We continued to live our lives as if we were going to be in Goldbach through winter. I spent hours picking berries and mushrooms, and we stored all the food we could.

November 16th, we packed all of our belongings. I was excited, but reticent. I wanted so much to believe that we were leaving, but Mutti cautioned us not to get overly optimistic. Still, early morning of the seventeenth, we made our way to the army base to find preparations underway for our departure. We were not told where we were going, only that we must quickly load onto horse-drawn wagons. At that, hundreds of refugees started scrambling for space on too few wagons. Fortunately, our family found a place to sit. Although we were packed tight with many others, I breathed a sigh of relief that we were leaving. I couldn't believe it! We were actually going to be transported from this hell-hole. I felt sorry for the people who didn't get on, since it looked as if they were going to be left behind for good.

"Mutti," I said. "Are they taking us the whole way in this wagon?"

"No ... I hope not!" she replied. "We're heading south. I think they will take us to Tapiau, then we'll see."

I felt a mixed bag of emotions. I was ecstatic that we were leaving, yet worried about where we were going. I wondered how we would ever meet up with Anneliese again. I feared that we were going to a work camp in Siberia. We were still under Russian rule, and no one would stop them from sending us wherever they wanted. I figured that no one knew we still existed.

We arrived in Tapiau as Mutti anticipated; it was still morning. They let us off at the train depot. Here we waited, and waited. Other refugees arrived from other villages. Trains came and went, but the soldiers made us wait. More waves of horse drawn wagons from Goldbach arrived. I felt relieved when it appeared no one was left behind. We all had to show our papers to receive food for our journey. Each person was given three-and-a half loaves of bread, one cup of sugar, one cup of a margarine-type spread, oatmeal and some canned meat. Either they were especially generous, or we were in for a very long journey. Finally at dusk, a train hauling flatbed cars arrived. The soldiers directed us onto the cars. Mid-November saw nights dip below freezing, and here we were on an open-bed train car. We put on every piece of clothing that we could, and wrapped ourselves with blankets. There were no seats and no railings to prevent anyone from falling off. No one wanted to sit near the edge. They would have treated their cattle better than this. There were hundreds of people, so it took over an hour to get us all onto the train.

The train finally departed and fortunately it moved slowly, otherwise we would have frozen to death. However, it was heading east—the wrong direction. The train stopped in Insterburg for a few hours, then continued on to Birkenfelde. We debarked and were directed to stay at the station and wait. Here we had a little shelter and were able to get some sleep. The next morning, a new train arrived, pulling a long trail of enclosed freight cars. The soldiers directed all the refugees to get on board; 40 people to a car. We filled our water canteens, and the soldiers counted as we climbed into the cars. This was amusing to watch, because some of them clearly didn't know how to count Refugees were pulled in and out of cars as occupants were counted and then recounted. In the end, each car ended up with 40 people—more or less. The big sliding door rolled on its track and slammed shut. We heard the metallic screech of the locking mechanism that was operated from outside the car—sealing our only way out.

It was dark inside save for some weak beams of sunlight that passed through a few small holes and a narrow gap in the door. It took a while for my eyes to adjust to the darkness. In the middle of the car was a wood burning stove with a large pot on top of it and a small pile of sticks that would only last us a few hours. In a corner was a pile of hay along with two buckets, one with water in it.

Now I became more frightened. Being locked inside a dark freight car, with no information about where we were going, made me fearful of what they had in mind for us. I prayed that this trip would soon be over and we would arrive safely in the West. I heard the loud sequential clunking of the freight cars engaging ahead of us, then the big clunk from our car as my head jerked back—we were moving. This time, at least, we were heading in the right direction; west. Someone started a fire in the stove with hay and sticks. Another filled the pot with water. The train stopped often, sometimes for hours. We were apparently the lowest priority, always shuttled to a sidetrack in order for other trains to pass by. Sometimes, we stopped all day in the middle of nowhere. At least then they opened the cars and let us walk around.

During daytime stops, when soldiers slid open the doors, we all squinted and held our hands over our eyes to shield the light until our eyes adjusted. The stops gave us a chance to gather wood for the stove, and if we were near a train station or a town, we were able to refill our water. We were never told why we stopped or for how long, so we couldn't wander too far away, for fear that the train would leave us behind.

One benefit of the frequent stops was that we could relieve ourselves outside instead of over a bucket. After a few days, the cars had a horrible odor of human waste. As much as we tried to cap the smell with straw, it didn't prevent the odor. Many people were sick with diarrhea, making it even worse. Straw was our only means of wiping. We couldn't wait to dump the bucket. Women leaned against the door and urinated on the floor with a goal of finding the crack in the door. At least the men could use a bottle. We couldn't wash ourselves and wore the same clothes the whole trip.

The environment was very unsanitary and many people got sick because of the conditions. This compounded the problem and sickness spread. We were also loaded with lice. Inside the car, it was too dark to delouse each other. When the train stopped and we were outside during daylight, we tried to pick each other's lice, but they were hearty and inexhaustible. As soon as we got back in the cars, they were back as well.

It was miserable, but Irmi and I, out of boredom, started singing songs. The people enjoyed it, and some sang along with us. The songs took our minds away from our troubles, and made us think of more pleasant settings. When we stopped singing, many told us to continue; apparently, we were their entertainment. To pass time, people shared tragic stories of their past two and a half years. I wasn't aware that just a week or two ago, Herr Routenberg, the farmer who gave us his room in the barn, was sent to a prison camp because he stole a bag of grain to help feed his four children. What a shame; within weeks of being free he was now to spend ten years in a Russian prison.

People began to run out of food. Fortunately, my family had jam and other preserved food to carry us through. Mutti very quietly handed us our portions as she whispered in our ears, "*Shh.*" It was too dark for anyone to see us eating. I felt terrible that we had to sneak food and try to eat without letting anyone know. I tried to tell myself that everyone had the opportunity to bring food, but it still didn't erase the guilt. There were several old people who were getting weaker day by day. They died before we arrived at our destination. It was awful having the corpses inside the car with us and their families crying over them. At stops, the soldiers went from car to car and pulled the dead out and dropped them right on the side of the tracks and just left them there. It was a shame to know that these people clung to life all that time under the thumb of the Russians and couldn't make it a few days more to reach freedom.

During the seeming endless hours we traveled, my mind sometimes strayed to thoughts of poor Anneliese. She was a great older sister to us. She had polio when she was young and walked with metal braces on her legs for most of her childhood. She was able to give up her braces as a teenager, but still had an awkward gait. She was such a sweet and kind girl, yet children can be cruel, and she was often ridiculed. As a consequence, she didn't have many friends, so she spent much of her time with Irmi and me.

I often wondered how different she would have been if she didn't have polio. The rest of our family was very outgoing and had many friends. I'm sure her handicap was a heavy burden to her. Nevertheless, she never complained or even spoke about it, and she kept up with us swimming and running along the beach every day.

Still, she wasn't as strong as others and, in prison; the Russians would show no sympathy for her handicap. I hated the fact that we left without her. But I wasn't about to lose faith. Perhaps she would soon be released and we would be reunited.

It was a miserably slow trip. Sometimes we stayed in place for two days. At one stop, Irmi and I counted all of the freight cars; there were fifty in all. I spent daylight time catching up on my diary entries.

All in all, it took fifteen days to make it to what was still considered Germany. We probably could have walked the distance quicker, but thankfully, the train finally arrived in Thüringen. We were let out and greeted by Red Cross agents. This was it—we made it—we were free! The emotion that I experienced could only be described and understood by someone who experienced a horror like we did. I was overjoyed, relieved and overwhelmed as I took the first step out of the train. The Red Cross workers gathered us together and led us to what looked like an old school. I don't believe I ever turned around to give the train and soldiers one last look.

The Red Cross was very organized and the workers were extremely friendly. Once inside the old school house, they separated the men from the women and the first order was for us to remove all of our clothes and get washed up. The inside of the building was very clean and rooms were equipped with hospital beds and general hospital equipment. They were to delouse and wash all of our clothes while we took a shower. My God, that shower was heaven; warm water, soap, and even shampoo that made my scalp tingle. I washed my hair several times and stayed in the shower until my skin wrinkled. I never knew a shower could feel so good. They handed us nice clean cotton towels to dry off. While we waited for our clothes, doctors inspected us and nurses applied treatment to our hair to kill the lice. When our clothes arrived they were still warm from the dryers. All my life, clothes were dried on a clothes line. Putting on these warm clean clothes was just another subtle reminder that things were going to get better.

After the medical examination, we were given healthy portions of food. We were told that we had to be careful not to overindulge because our systems weren't used to fats or rich food. They started us off with soup that contained some meat and vegetables, so different from the bland and watery soup that we were accustomed to. We were also given orange juice. I never had an orange, even before the war. The tangy, thick juice bounced on my tongue. I couldn't get enough of this sweet new flavor. For a blissful moment, the two and a half years we spent under Russian tyranny were overshadowed by these new simple pleasures.

Once we were clean and fed, we were each interviewed independently, perhaps to corroborate stories. First, we had to show our papers and fill out forms verifying our identity. Secondly, during an interview, we were asked questions, such as:

- Who is your next of kin? Are they still alive? Do you know their whereabouts?
- Where were you taken during the time after the war? How were you treated?
- How many Germans did you witness dying as a result of the Russians? Do you know their names?

I told them about Anneliese, and that she was left behind in a work prison. Their questioning gave me the expectation that they would find her and bring her to us. The questions went on and on. Initially, I actually thought there would be retribution for what the Russians did to us. Then, I realized that some of these questions were simply meant to placate us. However, in terms of the names and numbers of the deceased, I could understand that our witness would lead to valuable information for others inquiring about loved ones.

As close as we were to freedom, we were once again detained. For fear of the spread of disease, we were quarantined for about two weeks, until the doctors could verify that we were disease-free and properly cared for. During this time, no one was allowed to visit us and we were not allowed to leave; we were only allowed to write. We stayed in cramped quarters, perhaps twenty to a room, but what bliss, the beds and sheets were clean and they fed us three full meals per day.

The Red Cross encouraged us to send letters to loved ones, so that we could arrange a place to stay. Mutti had Papa's address in Hamburg, from the letter he sent us. She wrote a letter to Papa and the Red Cross paid for the postage. Every day, Irmi and I waited for the mail delivery person in anticipation of Papa's reply. Finally, a letter arrived. Irmi and I sat next to Mutti as she read it. Papa had found Günter and both of them would come pick us up in East Berlin (Berlin was now split, with the East being Communist). Once we were released, we should board a train to the city, and they would be waiting. We were so excited about our reunion. In the meantime, we started regaining our strength from the food and medicine provided. Then, to our dismay, Mutti developed a deep cough. We didn't want to alarm any of the nurses, for fear they would keep us longer, perhaps assuming typhoid.

I wanted desperately to share Christmas as a family again. Christmas was only a week away. But Mutti started a fever, and took a turn for the worse. I found a nurse on duty and shyly looked at her and showed her some Russian Chai tea that I still had from our trip. "Can I trade you this tea for some aspirin?" I was afraid to just ask for the aspirin, because I figured it would trigger an alarm that someone was sick.

"Sure," she agreed. "But why do you need aspirin?"

I quickly fumbled for an answer. "Oh, Mutti has a headache and I want to give her something for it."

"Well, let me get you some aspirin then." She went into a cupboard and handed me four aspirin. "Thank you for the tea. What a special treat."

I thanked her and rushed to Mutti. "Mutti, here is some aspirin for you." She was very grateful. I prayed that her illness would subside and we could enjoy Christmas with my father and brother, but to no avail. Mutti's fever worsened. Our family was held for an additional ten days. In the meantime, Papa and Günter must have eagerly waited for news of our release. We were downcast; here it was a few days until Christmas and we were kept in quarantine.

To make matters worse, Tante Friedel was released and went to go live with her sister in Lauenburg. I was distraught to see her leave, partly because we remained, but mostly because I would miss her. She was a pivotal part of our survival under the Russians. It was her drive and positive attitude that helped foster hope for all of us. Our family hugged and cried at her departure. It was at least some consolation to know that we would remain in contact once we all got settled in.

On Christmas Eve, children from the nearby neighborhood dressed up and offered to entertain us with a Christmas play, but they were turned away at the gate. The Red Cross wouldn't let them enter for fear of spreading illness. I wanted so desperately to celebrate Christmas. One of the ladies who had been on our train and remained in the camp along with us, suggested, "Irmi and Ilse, you sang beautiful songs on the train; sing us some Christmas songs." Irmi and I were delighted that they thought of us, and naturally, we went through our entire repertoire of favorite Christmas songs, some more than once! Everything was so hard to take in. Just weeks before, we scrabbled for a cast-off piece of bread, and now we were gobbling up thick slices of warm, spicy gingerbread and my favorite stollen—a special Christmas cake filled with nuts and fruits and marzipan. Then, we learned that volunteers provided small presents for all of us children: clothes, shoes and even dolls. I was overwhelmed; the kindness and protection these people provided was such a stark contrast to what we had endured. But the best gift of all, that night Mutti's fever subsided and we knew she would be well, and we would soon be released and reunited with our beloved Papa and Günter.

19

In Germany

Finally, a few days after Christmas 1947, we received our release papers. How exhilarating to be free! I rushed outside, hoping against hope that Papa would actually be waiting there outside, but as he said in the note, we were to meet him in East Berlin. The Red Cross provided the train fare for all of us to go to East Berlin. This was a fun trip for me; I had never been to Berlin before. The train car was actually for commuters, with cushioned seats, lights and, for me, a window view—a stark contrast to the nightmarish freight car in which we had traveled west. Through the window I noted that even two-and-a-half years after the war, Germany was still in shambles. Ruins blemished every town and village en-route. Berlin was the worst. Portions of the city were completely leveled. It was easy to see why Germany lost the war. How could a country have any hope of victory when its capital city was virtually destroyed?

We arrived in East Berlin. As agreed to in the Potsdam Conference, Berlin was divided up between the Allies, as was Germany. Geographically, Berlin was now in East Germany, which had been allocated to the Soviets. However, the western portion of Berlin remained under German rule—a democratic island in the middle of a communist state.

Papa waited at the station for our arrival. I saw him from a distance and I started running. I screamed, "Papa, Papa, I missed you!" He didn't seem to age one bit. Irmi and I ran to him. He had a big smile on his face as he picked us up at the same time.

"Oh, I missed you," he said, wrapping us both in his warm, strong embrace. "You have both gotten so big." It was hard to imagine: bigger wouldn't be how I would have described us, but perhaps he meant taller. I could have held him all day. Immediately, I felt a sense of security. Now that Papa was back, everything was all right again!

Mutti stood back a bit. Her head leaned forward and she looked through the corner of her eyes. I could sense that she was a little afraid. Perhaps she thought that Papa would blame her for what our family went through. She stood motionless, looking at him. There was an awkward pause, I felt like pushing them together. Then Papa reached out and gave her a hug.

"Where is Hans?" Papa asked during the embrace. Mutti's grip released and she just stood motionless and Papa held her arms. "Where is Hans?" he repeated.

"I'm sorry," was all that she could force out. She covered her face and cried. "He—he died two weeks after the Russians invaded."

Papa covered his face with his hands and knelt on one knee. Through his hands, he said, "Hanna, why didn't you tell me through the letters?"

"I just couldn't ... it's terrible!" Mutti started nervously chewing on her thumbnail. I told you about Mutti and Papa ... and that Anneliese is in a prison camp ... I just ... couldn't—"

Papa stood up, took a deep breath and looked up into the sky. His eyes were sparkling from the tears that flooded his eyelids. He shook his head, "I can't believe you didn't tell me." He turned away from her and started walking. "Come on, let's go."

This wasn't the type of reunion I had wished for. Why didn't Mutti tell him about Hans? What was she thinking?

We walked without a word for some time. Finally, he said, "War is a horrible thing. I'm glad it's over." He seemed somehow to concede the loss of Hans. For her part, Mutti tried to change the subject and talked in general terms about our time under the Russians, avoiding any of the more terribly emotional subjects. In particular, prior to our reunion with Papa, Mutti had made us promise not to tell him about her being raped by the Russians. In fact, she asked Tante Friedel not to mention what happened to her, either. She was very ashamed and didn't want Papa to know anything about it.

"Papa, what happened to *you* after the Russians came?" Irmi asked

There was a long silence, and then Papa replied, "After I left all of you —" It was obvious that he did not want to elaborate. "I went back to the airport and waited there for the Russians to arrive." I looked at Irmi, not grinning, but beaming because we guessed right. "I wanted to get on the plane with Karl, but couldn't." He looked directly at Irmi, "The Russians captured me."

"Did they hurt you? What did they do to you?" Irmi inquired.

"They were rough with us." He stopped and bent over. With his hand on his head he moved his hair to one side and showed a large scar on his head. "They beat me with a club ... I almost died." I was shocked at the size of the scar. *Almost died!* I thought, *my God, he was in a rough place*, but in a way, I was proud of him. I knew my Papa was tough, and a clunk to the head wouldn't stop him. "I went to a prisoner-of-war camp just south of Siberia. They kept me for twelve months." Twelve months sounded longer than one year to me.

Irmi, eager to hear every detail, went on. "What was it like in prison?"

He simply didn't answer. We sensed he had experienced unspeakable horrors. Papa was a brave and strong man, and I'm sure he was a target for the hatred the Russians had for the Germans, especially soldiers.

Finally, Papa broke the silence. "When I was released, I was allowed to return to Germany, and I lived in Hamburg, where Uncle Fritz lived. I looked for him, but he died in the war. I found Tante Martha, and Malisse and Jürgen who made it through." Tante Martha was Fritz's wife, and Malisse and Jürgen were her children. "I stayed with them until I heard from you and then started looking for an apartment in Berlin." He looked around and lowered his voice. "The Communists control East Berlin. The West is democratic. We're on the east side and I work on the west side."

This was getting all too confusing for me. I thought we were free so why was he whispering?

Mutti gave details about what happened to Anneliese and he was heartbroken. "They haven't released her yet," Mutti sighed. "They said she had to stay in prison one year ... that's over now. She should be out already."

"There are announcements made when trains arrive with refugees—that's how I found you," Papa replied. "We'll look out for these trains and hopefully we will find her."

We arrived at Papa's meager one-room apartment. It held a plain kitchen table with four chairs and only one bed, so it was obvious Irmi and I would sleep on the floor. Oh well, we were used to that.

My brother, Günter, came a few days later to visit. It was a wonderful reunion. Günter lived in Stuttgart along with a few friends, also in a crowded apartment. At this time, many homes were demolished and refugees were arriving daily, so living quarters were scarce.

We learned that during the war, Günter had also been captured and taken as a prisoner of war.

"Günter," Mutti said. "Did you get a tattoo, for being in the SS?"

"*Nein*, Mutti. I never completed my certification ... fortunately. I was already checked several times by officials. If I had the tattoo, I'd have been hauled away. Those Nuremberg trials are a witch hunt. I still think it's best if I leave this country. They'll eventually find something." He was bitter, but we all understood.

The next few days, I shadowed Papa like he was a magnet and I was iron filings. Everywhere he went, I followed. I yearned for life to be like it was in Palmnicken, but Papa was different. He seemed cold. I used to be his darling little girl and I didn't understand his separation from me now. Was it just that I was older, or had life's circumstances hardened his heart? Regardless, I diligently plied my charms, hoping to narrow the division between us.

One day, after he and I went to the local butcher, we sat at a bench outside the shop. I asked, "Papa, why didn't you come back that day in Palmnicken?"

He looked away and pursed his lips. Finally, he replied, "For weeks, I tried to convince Mutti to leave. Karl and I had a plan to take the last plane to the West. That morning before I came home to tell everyone to get ready, Karl and I were getting planes ready for others to leave."

He looked me in the eyes. "Leaving your post meant desertion, but no one stopped us. The end was inevitable." He was getting more nervous and twitchy, his hands roaming first to tuck in his shirt, then tug at his collar, then straighten the crease on his trousers.

"Anyway, after a dozen or so flights departed, Karl walked over to me and said, 'They'll be safe. Two to three days, and the Russians will be here.' I couldn't look at him. Then he added, 'We'll leave tomorrow morning before daylight.' That's when I told him I needed to finalize some things with Omi and Opa. Then he asked, 'Did you convince Hanna?' That's when he got upset. He said, 'Hans, you haven't talked her into this yet, have you?' He started raising his voice. I tried to convince him by saying, 'We're going, don't worry.' Then I confessed: 'She hasn't agreed yet, but she will.'"

Papa was talking more freely now. "Karl shook his head and said, 'I can't believe this!' I said, 'C'mon, Karl, this isn't easy for her. It'll happen. She'll come, even if I have to drag her here by her feet.'" Papa looked down again. "Then Karl said, 'Understand something. I wish you and your family all the best, but ... the plane is leaving tomorrow morning, with you, or without you.' As he walked away, he said, 'Remember, there's only room for five!'" Papa looked at me again, and went on, "Then I came home and you saw what happened ... Mutti didn't want to go. So I left, went back to the base and waited for the Russians to capture me."

"Are you mad at Mutti for not going?"

Papa looked at me like I was from a different planet. "What do you think? Should I be mad at her?"

I raised my eyebrows, "I don't know." I didn't want to say what I thought.

"Hans would still be here with us and Anneliese wouldn't be in some, who knows what prison. You for two and a half years fighting for survival; me in a prisoner of war camp... All of that could have easily been avoided... *Ja*, I guess you could say I'm a little mad."

Papa was clearly bitter and resentful. He loved Hans dearly. I remember the pride in his eyes when Hans was born. Now he had to live with the fact that Mutti's stubbornness led to Hans's death. I could see that he wasn't going to get over this easily, and there was nothing I could do to help.

After about a month in Berlin, Irmi and I went to the train station every time the Red Cross posted information about new refugees arriving. Mutti didn't come with us; she didn't go out much because she was still weak from the time under the Russians. I think that, mentally, she was hit the hardest of us. She was very depressed.

At the train station, people held up pictures of their loved ones and asked the de-barking refugees, "Have you seen this person?" "Do you know, *so-and-so*?" Likewise, Irmi and I asked the refugees about Anneliese. One day, we saw Frau Albart walking from the train. What a stroke of luck; she was the lady who had been sent to prison along with Anneliese.

"Frau Albart," Irmi shouted. We ran to her. Excitedly, Irmi said, "Do you have news of Anneliese? Is she with you?"

She hesitated, then leaned down to us and put a hand on each of our shoulders. "Anneliese died in the prison camp. She died of typhoid about four months ago." She squatted down and sat on her heels. "Look, it was a miserable place. Most people didn't make it. Anneliese was tough, but the typhoid was too much for her and the Russians didn't care."

Irmi and I were in tears. She leaned over to us, now on her knees, and gave us a big hug. What could we really say? It was another casualty—another innocent death due to a clash of two countries. Irmi and I walked home, crying the whole way. We walked into the apartment without a plan on how we were going to break the news. Tears were still streaming from our cheeks. Mutti asked, "What's wrong? Why are you crying?" She knew that we went to the train station in search of information about Anneliese, and she looked like she knew what we were going to say, but still had to hear it.

I remained silent. I didn't want to upset Mutti any further; this news would really set her back. There was a long pause—I waited for Irmi to explain—she finally cried, "Mutti." Irmi started sobbing more and found it difficult to speak. "We—we saw Frau Albart come off of the train. She said Anneliese died of typhoid while in prison." Mutti said nothing. She turned away, flopped onto the bed and cried miserably. I think the death of Anneliese hit Mutti harder than any other of the family members we had lost. As much as we tried to console her, she didn't talk to anyone the rest of the day; she just lay in bed and cried.

Papa came home from work and Mutti was still in bed. Irmi told Papa what happened to Anneliese. Without a response, he got up and walked out of the apartment and didn't come back until late in the night.

Mutti became increasingly melancholy. She and Papa grew further apart. Papa talked about moving back to Halle, where he originally found work after the war. "I can make more money in Halle," Papa explained. "We can find a place to stay, although we may need to stay in a camp until something becomes available."

"I'm not staying in any camp, I had enough with all the camps under the Russians," Mutti barked back. I simply could not understand her stubbornness. Why did she continue to defy Papa, after all that she had been through? These conversations were frequent and never came to any conclusion. It seemed Mutti got her way, at least for a while.

One afternoon, when I came home from shopping, the windows were open in the apartment and I heard Mutti and Papa arguing. I grabbed the doorknob, but didn't turn it, when I heard Mutti cry out, "How could you live with yourself ... sleeping with another woman!"

"Hanna," Papa pleaded. "I didn't know if you were still alive. How could—"

"*Ach*, you couldn't wait to find out ... you expect me to believe that?"

"Look, she doesn't matter now that we're together. Let's just forget about it."

"*Ja*, easy for you to say."

I waited until there was silence for at least twenty seconds, and then I walked in. I made it look like I didn't hear anything. "Here are the groceries," I sang out.

As I placed the items in the cupboard, I thought of what Papa said. He was unfaithful. I never would have expected this. It shed a different light on my hero. Mutti was right, he could have waited. Perhaps this explained his distant demeanor.

My 14th birthday arrived, my first birthday in many years that would offer more than a simple pancake or pastry. Although we still didn't have much, I received some nice presents, primarily much-needed clothing, and a special cake. It was a day to reflect on how lucky we were to be among the few that survived.

I went back to school. At age 14, I was placed back at a fifth grade level. It was embarrassing to be older than my classmates, but I wasn't the only refugee, so I didn't feel completely out of place. I enjoyed going to school and I was glad that I had the opportunity to catch up. I learned quickly and in time, moved up a few levels and got back on track. At this time, there was a large demand for nurses, so Irmi signed up for nursing school. The government paid for school and board, so Irmi took advantage of the program and lived in a dormitory at a hospital in East Berlin.

It was the summer of 1949. We were together with Papa in East Berlin for a year and a half. Papa came home from work one day and gazed past me as he went to the kitchen and sat down in a chair. Mutti was washing dishes and had her back to him.

He took a deep breath and said, "I'm going to Halle." Mutti stopped her motions and lifted her head up, but refused to turn around and then continued on with her dishwashing. Papa cleared his throat, "I can make more money there ... I can have my old job back."

Mutti threw the wash cloth on the counter and turned around "*Ja*, and you already have a place to stay!"

"Look," Papa chose to ignore her last snide remark. "You can come with and stay in a temporary base, or I'll find something for us in a few weeks, and then you can move too."

"I told you, I'm not staying in any camp ... and I'm tired of moving around. I've done enough of that under the Russians ... I'm not going."

Papa got up, "All right, if that's how you want it." He walked to the bed, reached under it and pulled out a suitcase. He packed his clothes and left.

It reminded me of his departure from Palmnicken. Again, he asked Mutti to come with and she refused. I wanted to go with him this time, but he didn't offer to take me.

Papa sent money and packages to us from Halle. We had no other means of income. In his letters, he again urged us to come join him. After reading the letters, I tried to convince Mutti as well. I wanted us to be a family again. This situation was not working. I wished Mutti wasn't so stubborn. "Mutti," I said. "Why don't we just go? We may have to stay in a camp for a while, but it would be better."

"He should come and help us move," she abruptly replied. "It's about time he did something for us."

He never came back to visit us. As time went on, the frequency of packages and money diminished. Only then, did Mutti seem to reconsider and she started shipping packages to him, in anticipation of moving to Halle. One day, a package was returned, along with a letter requesting that she sign divorce papers.

20

Mutti's Breakdown

With Papa's request for a divorce, Mutti had a complete breakdown. She became incapable of making even the simplest decisions or caring for herself. One day when I got home in the afternoon, she was in bed. "Mutti, are you sick?" I worried.

"No."

"Why are you in bed?"

"I'm tired."

"Tired ... what did you do all day?"

She raised her head, "Nothing."

"Mutti, you haven't gotten out of bed in days, haven't bathed or even combed your hair, and you haven't eaten a thing. You need to pull yourself together."

She turned her head away from me, put her head back on the pillow and pulled up the sheets. This went on for days. I finally got her to eat a little, but only if I sat by her side and fed her.

I was still going to school and working nights and weekends cleaning homes. Now I had the added responsibility of taking care of Mutti. In the brief time between school and work, I came home to feed and care for her.

"Mutti, I can't do this anymore. I don't have the time to take care of you all day. You need to take care of yourself."

"There is no reason to live," she sighed. "I want to end my life."

"Mutti," I shouted at her. "Don't talk like that! That's stupid talk. I need you. We made it through two and a half years under the Russians; we can make it through this." These types of conversations went on for a few weeks. I was frightened by the lost look in her eyes. I was convinced that if she were alone, she would follow through with her threat to commit suicide. I took away all the aspirin and anything else that I thought she could use to harm herself.

What a predicament. Papa had stopped sending us money and Mutti was too troubled to work. The only source of income was my part-time cleaning. We had nothing once again. I had little to no money to buy food. I felt as if we were back under Russian rule; *how was this any better?* I had an ugly thought: *should I leave Mutti and go live with Papa?* I felt guilty as soon as I thought it. In Mutti's current state, she would surely perish if I left. Leaving was not an option.

One day, I got home and Mutti was sitting at the kitchen table, her elbows on the table and her head in her hands. "You're up!" I exclaimed. I thought this might be a good time to confront her. "Mutti, we need help... Maybe we can go to Günter. He told us that we can come to him."

She lifted her face from her hands, and looked at me with eyes like dull grey stones. Her eyebrows formed a frown as she replied, "No, I don't want anyone to know that Papa wants a divorce. Don't tell anyone."

"I didn't say anything about a divorce, I just—"

"*Nein*, he'll know if we ask him for help."

"Mutti, this is crazy!" I actually raised my voice at her, and I think I startled her. I, at fifteen, was now reprimanding Mutti like she was a little child. I softened my voice. "Mutti, you can't keep doing this to yourself. You're burying your head in the sand." I paused, wondering if I should continue. But she needed to hear this and her decisions affected me, too. I repositioned a chair and sat down next to her at the table. She again buried her face in her hands. I put an arm around her. "These problems are not going to go away. We can't just ignore them. We need to survive, just like we did under the Russians."

She started crying. I tried to console her, but I wasn't helping much. I was desperate, I simply didn't know what to say or do. After a long moment of silence, she leaned back on her chair and wiped away her tears, took in a deep breath, lowered her hands to her lap, formed her lips together into a circle, and breathed out. It was like she exhausted the demons from within. She sniffled, and then looked at me. In a soft and relaxed voice, she said, "You know... When I was a teenager, I moved to Stettin, West Prussia, with my older sister—you know, Tante Ernestina—." I tilted my head toward her wondering, where did this come from? "—Yes—well, I don't know if I ever told you about this. After the Great War, I think it was 1918, there were no jobs. Germany lost the war, and the entire world was pointing its finger at us."

I must admit that I was intrigued to hear about the past, but Mutti wasn't one to drag on about ancient history. Nevertheless, I just sat back in my chair, hoping that this story was going somewhere. "People moved to wherever they could find a job. Tante Ernestina moved to Stettin and found a good job. I worked at the amber mine since I was fourteen; Opa got me the job there. But after the war, there was no work; I was out of a job. Tante Ernestina told me to come to Stettin; she found me a job as a caretaker."

Mutti was starting to feel comfortable in this conversation. It was the most I heard her talk in weeks, and she seemed relaxed. "I took the job and moved to Stettin. Your Papa came to Stettin as well." She smiled and her eyes brightened. "He claimed he couldn't find a job either, but I know he came to follow me. See, I grew up in Germau, and Papa in Gross Hubnicken, they were right next to each other. We knew each other since we were little. He was a little older than me, but he was always after me."

Now I knew where she was going with this conversation. It was good for her to get it out into the open, and I was learning a little of their past. "He was pushy, and I was really kind of afraid of him. He was very handsome and charming, but I wasn't ready for a relationship. I kept trying to get rid of him, but *mensch* ... if he wasn't persistent." Mutti leaned over the table onto her elbows and crossed her arms. She looked down at the table and shook her head, then offered me a blank stare. "The thing is, I never completely trusted him. It's not that he was a shifty character; he was just the object of many other women's affections."

Papa was a good looking man: broad shoulders, muscular build, square jaw, high cheek bones and beautiful wavy hair. He had deep blue eyes and a perfectly formed nose. Now that Mutti confessed, I recalled that she always kept a close eye on him. Even when Tante Friedel came to live with us right before the Russian invasion, Mutti never left the two of them alone in the house. She always came up with reasons to take Tante Friedel with her when she went out, or she changed her mind about going somewhere if Tante Friedel didn't want to go.

Mutti went on, "When Papa got a job in Königsberg, I was convinced he had a mistress there."

I sat up, tilted my head back and lowered my eyebrows. "*Ach*, Mutti, how do you know that?" I didn't want to let on that I heard their conversation about Papa and the other woman.

Mutti looked at me with a creased forehead and leaned forward. "I never caught him, but I could tell ... and there were perhaps others."

I forced a smile and shook my head. Mutti was bitter; she didn't know what she was saying. Mutti could tell that I didn't believe her. "He was smooth with the ladies. He convinced *me* to fall for him, and I didn't want anything to do with him. And he got me pregnant before we were married—yes, we got married six months before Günter was born."

I felt the blood drain from my face. I must have looked like a marble statue. I never heard Mutti talk like this—and I never knew they had to get married. She must have sensed my shock. "I'm sorry—I just needed to tell you about some of this, so you understand." We sat at the table for a while. Mutti was finished talking, and I was speechless. I got up from the table and started washing dishes, while Mutti sat for a few minutes, then walked over to the couch and lay down.

As I washed the dishes, my mind raced, trying to understand what Mutti was saying. It was inconceivable to me that Papa would be unfaithful—but then again, he did just ask for a divorce. And he admitted to having a girlfriend after the war—but that was because he didn't know if we were still alive. Then again, why didn't he wait until he found out if we were still alive? And they had to get married because Mutti was pregnant with Günter—my goodness; my mind was on overload!

I was doing the math, trying to figure out when he found out that we were in Goldbach. Did he have time to have a relationship after he was released from the Russians and before he heard of our status? Did he even tell us the truth about what happened at the end of the war? These questions engulfed me.

I struggled to remember events or instances that would substantiate Mutti's claims. All that came to mind was what a wonderful father he was. Papa meant the world to me. He was one of those people that didn't need to say much to get people to listen to him. I think everyone simply respected him and was eager to please him. This same desire to please him held true for us children. The last thing we wanted to do was disappoint our father. He was kind and gentle, and rarely did he give us orders. Instead, he made a game of the chore he wanted us to do, and the next thing we knew, it was done. He was able to build or fix anything. Mutti often talked about how talented he was at building something from nothing, saying he could turn dirt into gold. The more I thought about him, the more Mutti's comments about his unfaithfulness over the years didn't hold water.

The next day, while we were eating breakfast, I decided to bring up the topic that I originally wanted to address yesterday, "Mutti, we never talked about how we are going to make ends meet."

"*Ja, ja,*" was her response. "Papa needs to send us money." I thought I might burst from frustration.

Ultimately, I was able to catch up in school and graduate from high school. I wanted to continue, but I was being pressured to join the *Freie Deutsche Jugend*, or FDJ, in order to be accepted into higher education which would include a 100 mark per month stipend.[16] A stipulation of joining the FDJ was a confirmation that I would join the communist ruling party; the Socialist Unity Party.[17] But after what I went through under the Russians, I didn't agree with Communism—I wanted nothing to do with it. So I refused.

Now that school was over, I found a full-time job cleaning. I still didn't make much money, but at least we were able to buy enough food.

Mutti continued to live in denial. She still thought that Papa was going to come back to us. One day, she said, "Ilse, we are going to Halle."

I didn't quite know what she meant. "To live?" I responded.

"Well, maybe," she replied, sounding unconvinced herself. "I need to talk to Papa. I need to convince him to take us in." So, impulsively, she dragged me to the station and we boarded a train for Halle. I think she figured it would be harder for him to say no if I were there. She had his address, because we sent packages and letters back and forth. Once we got off the train, she asked for directions. We eventually arrived at the right street and found his apartment. Mutti looked very nervous as she approached and knocked on the door. A woman opened the door—*how awkward!* "Can I help you?" She asked.

"*Ja*," Mutti answered in a broken voice. "I'm looking for Hans." Cordially, the woman let us in, without asking what we wanted. The lady was outwardly nervous, so I suspected that she knew who we were. We stood in a hallway for a while, and she didn't know what to do.

Finally, she turned and said, "I will get him." I heard some conversation in the back and soon, Papa arrived. He didn't greet us, but shrugged and looked to the floor.

"Why did you come here, Hanna?"

"I need to talk to you. I—we need you to come back." Mutti turned and motioned to me as she spoke. It was now clear why she brought me.

"Hanna, let's go outside," Papa said, as he walked out the door. Mutti followed. I was left alone with the woman who stole Papa away. I wished I had never come. *What could I say to her?* She asked me to sit in the living room and wait. She was pleasant and offered me something to drink. She made small-talk, but I didn't pay attention.

"Can you give us..." I started to cry and had difficulty talking. "Mutti and I want my Papa back?" My sobbing made her very uncomfortable. She reached out to touch me on the arm, but withdrew. I looked her in the eyes and pleaded, "Can you give him back to us?"

She narrowed the space between us and bent down in front of me. In a gentle tone, she said, "That, only your father can answer. He needs to decide which way he wants to go."

I heard shouting outside the door, so I knew it wasn't going well. After about ten minutes, they came back into the apartment. Papa walked to the back of the apartment and into the bedroom and closed the door; he never even looked at me or said goodbye.

I must admit, Mutti made a bold move, and quite frankly, I was hoping it would work; now, my spirit was dashed. He didn't say hello or good bye to me, or for that matter, even look at me. The wonderful memories of Papa were quickly fading in my mind, and were being replaced with the ugly realization that Papa no longer cared about me like he once did.

"Ilsechen, let's go," Mutti said, as she walked out the door. I looked at the woman and her eyes were swelled with tears. I didn't know what to do. Was she innocent in all of this? I thought not. She could have told Papa to come home with us. Oh, this was all too confusing for me.

I walked to the door, but felt impolite about leaving without saying any-thing, so I turned and whispered, "Goodbye." Outside, Mutti was in tears and very upset.

"Papa is not coming back," Mutti said.

I looked at her and replied, "I know."

We started walking back to the train station. After a long silence, Mutti added, "Papa left us for her... He had an affair with her while we were under the Russians."

"I know that too."

Mutti turned to me. "How did you know that?"

"I overheard you and Papa talking one day."

"I think his head injury as a prisoner of war affected his logic. He's not thinking straight. Since we've been together after the war, he's just not the same Papa." I believe that she was right, but I didn't think it was from a head injury. I think he just couldn't get over Mutti's defiance of him. And she was certainly living in denial.

It was a silent train ride home. I reflected on what had just happened and realized this chapter in my life had come to an end.

A few days later, at breakfast, I said to Mutti, "It's clear, Papa will not help us, and we can't live on my job alone."

Mutti rubbed her chin. "I will go to work. I will find a job." She had a spark in her eye that I hadn't seen in some time. Within a few days, she found a job as a house cleaner and caretaker. It was good for her to be occupied. It took her mind away from Papa, and with her income, we were able to once again make ends meet. And sure enough, she began to come out of her depression. It was great to see her back in good spirits.

Mutti continually insisted I shouldn't tell anyone that Papa wanted a divorce, but I thought it was senseless to keep it a secret. One day, I went to visit Irmi and let her know what happened. She agreed to come home with me, to try to convince Mutti to tell Günter and the rest of the family. Mutti was mad that I defied her, but eventually agreed to write letters telling our family; realistically, they would ultimately find out anyway. Günter was horrified and terribly upset. He wrote a letter to Papa, telling him to come back to Mutti or he would disown him as his father. When he received no response from Papa, my brother vowed never to speak to him again.

One day Günter came to visit. "Come to Stuttgart. I will look for an apartment large enough for all of us."

"That won't be so easy," Mutti said.

"*Nein*, but for God's sake, get out of East Berlin."

"Why?"

"Because as time goes on, it will be harder and harder to get out of there... It's run by Russians. It's communist, even though they call it socialist, or democratic, or whatever... It's communism and you need to get out before they won't let you."

Günter was very bitter toward the Russians, but he was right. Politically, I was afraid in East Berlin. It *was* getting harder and harder to leave. Paperwork, rules and armed guards became increasingly more daunting at border crossings.

Mutti's sister, Tante Minna, got word of the divorce and urged us to come to Eifel; she had room for us. It made more sense for us to go to Tante Minna than to Günter, since she had room. Mutti and I decided it was best for us to move out of East Berlin. Unfortunately, we had East German passports, so we had to concoct a plan to escape to West Berlin. Mutti remembered a family from Berlin that came to the Schloss Hotel in Palmnicken every summer. We had become good friends with them over the years. Mutti contacted them and we went to visit. They agreed to help us and arranged for us to get West German passports. At that time, West Germany liberally issued passports, hoping to keep as many Germans as possible from being trapped in the East. To our disappointment, Irmi decided to stay in East Berlin; she was almost done with nursing school. She assured us that as soon as she finished her schooling, she would cross the border.

For several days, we traveled back and forth between East and West Berlin by train, carrying our belongings over the border in briefcase size packages. The Communists would have grown suspicious if we carried large suitcases. We heard stories of people being arrested for trying to cross the border illegally. I tried to maintain a neutral expression as the train attendant checked our tickets and passports. Armed guards were on the train and kept a look out for suspicious packages. I held my breath as they passed and glanced at our bags. Already, the Communists didn't allow East German citizens to seek residence elsewhere; a reminder of what it was like being under Russian rule.

Finally, we held West German passports, and all of our belongings were waiting for us in West Berlin. We made our last border crossing. I had butterflies in my stomach and felt as if we just pulled off the greatest escape. It was 1950, and we were finally free: Democratic Germany. It was the end of Communist rule for us. A feeling of relief came over me. No longer were we restricted on where we could go; we weren't forced to sign an allegiance to a political party; there were no armed guards watching over us. Now it was onward to Tante Minna.

It was wonderful to be welcomed to Tante Minna's and her daughter, Ingrid's, home in a rural area near Köln. We celebrated Christmas 1950 with them. Günter came up to share the holiday cheer. It was a shame that Papa was not with us, but we had to accept the fact that our Christmases would no longer include him. Here, we stayed happily for three months until we received good news from Günter. He had found me a job as a live-in nanny for a family that owned a small grocery store. Off I went, alone this time, to Stuttgart.

I worked from 7 A.M. to 9 P.M. every day except Sunday, when I had one-half day free. I was just sixteen years old, and worked almost eighty hours per week; all for only forty marks a month. I had to care for the children, ages three and six, cook, clean, wash and repair clothes, and manage the household. It was a back-breaking job but I loved the children and relished the opportunity to be on my own.

After a few months, I found a job for Mutti as a housecleaner. I convinced the family that employed me to allow Mutti to live with me for a few weeks, and it wasn't long before Günter found her a place of her own. At least now, Mutti, Günter and I were in the same town.

As time passed, my employers began to have me run the store now and then. I relished the opportunity to putter around the store stocking shelves, neatening displays, and helping customers with their purchases.

Once, I was given a whole Sunday off of work, so I decided to go visit Irmi in East Berlin. I was fearful to cross the border again, and I couldn't help thinking that they would somehow detain me and make me stay in East Berlin. But I crossed with no complications. Irmi lived with three other girls in a dormitory at a hospital. It was good to see her again.

"I'm pregnant," she said.

"Wha ... You ... Irmi," I finally blurted out. "Are you crazy?"

Irmi looked at me. Her complexion turned red. "It's complicated. We were living it up here—me and my roommates. Maybe too much ... and every doctor here is a *schwein*."

"But Irmi, what are you going to do ... are you getting married to him?"

Irmi took a deep breath, "Here's where the complicated part comes. I'm getting married ... but not to the man who got me pregnant."

"My goodness ... Irmi, am I hearing this right?"

"Look, I made a mistake. One of these *schwein* doctors got me pregnant ... he's married ... and I would never marry him anyway. I met another man, a nice man. He asked me to marry him."

"Does he know about you—"

"*Ja, ja*. He's fine with it. He still wants to marry me."

I smiled at Irmi, "I'm sorry I reacted that way, but you caught me off guard. I ... I didn't know what to say. I'm happy for you."

"Thank you. I knew you would understand. I know it's crazy, but he's a good man. We're not having any fancy wedding. We're getting married in two months and it'll just be at the courthouse. Then we're getting out of here and moving to West Berlin before it's too late and we're stuck here."

I hugged her and wished her well. She was still my Irmi. I told Mutti about Irmi and at first she was angry, but finally warmed up to it and soon she went to visit Irmi as well.

I continued being nanny and storekeeper for the family for one and a half years. It was tough and I had no time for anything else. The Russians took my childhood and this job took my teenage years. I had only enough time to myself to eat and sleep; no socializing. As time went on, I spent more time working in the store and serving customers, which I always enjoyed. A regular customer came into the store one day and said that her sister had a confectionary store and needed someone to work for her. She thought that I had the right personality.

I went and met her sister and she offered me the job, at 160 marks a month! Above all it was only eight hours per day and five days per week. I told the family I worked for that I found another job and they were disappointed. I was treated very much as family, even though I worked ridiculous hours. It was sad to leave and I would miss the children, but I knew this new job was a better opportunity and would give me more time to enjoy life outside of work.

Now, I needed a place to stay. Günter arranged to convert a closet in the apartment building where he lived into living quarters, and he added a sink and toilet. Now Mutti and I could live together, in the same building as Günter. Our rent was only 35 marks per month. In the meantime, Mutti found a job doing laundry for the U.S. Army base. She made about as much money as I did. Finally, we were paid enough money to not only make ends meet but to put something away. Plus, every day Mutti came home with a handful of U.S. coins; many soldiers failed to check their pockets before sending their uniforms to be washed. These coins she always placed in a special can.

Early in 1952, Günter came home and told us, "I have an offer to manage a ranch in Argentina. A friend that I met needs someone he can trust to run his operation. It's hard to find a good job here and he's going to pay me well."

"Argentina!" Mutti exclaimed. "What ... why all the way over there?"

"Well, believe it, or not, Argentina is loaded with Germans. For some reason, ex-Nazis and SS are fleeing to Argentina to avoid war crime prosecution. Somehow the Argentina government protects them or is lenient toward them. I just think it's safer if I leave Germany... It's turning into a witch hunt."

I was crushed. We finally lived together as a family, at least the three of us, and now we were to separate again.

21

Gerd

As Mutti and I were walking the streets of Stuttgart one summer day in 1954, we were surprised to run into the Färber family, whom we had lived with in Palmnicken, after the invasion. What a coincidence! We shared our stories of how we got to Stuttgart and had a great reunion. Frau Färber mentioned that a group of East Prussians met regularly in Stuttgart; they even had a youth group. She encouraged me to join them and let me know when and where they met.

Frau Färber also informed me, that as a refugee, I was entitled to free college education, and for attending college, I'd be entitled to 150 marks living expenses.

"Do I need to join some political party?" I asked.

Frau Färber looked at my through questioning eyes, "What?"

"In East Berlin, they had a similar program, but I needed to join the Socialist Unity Party."

She started laughing, "*Ach*, those stupid communists ... no of course you don't need to join a political party."

It was great to see them and they gave me valuable advice. I was definitely interested in continuing my education. The youth group intrigued me even more. I was excited to attend my first meeting with the youth group. On my way to the hall, I realized that I haven't ever gone to an event without a family member. I've been a social hermit for too long. It would be good for me to get out with some people my own age, with a common background to mine, and with any luck enjoy leisure activities.

I arrived at the hall. It seemed to be a converted store-front used for a variety of purposes besides the youth group. About thirty young people attended and we all sat in folding chairs in a large circle. Two well-dressed young men came in a bit late. Few people, in our economy, had the money to buy nice clothing. I looked down at my well-worn clothing and immediately felt embarrassed. The two young men had an air of sophistication about them. One of the men, in particular, attracted me. I suspected they were brothers, because they had similar features, but the one I favored had a slightly stockier build. He wasn't especially muscular, but looked athletic.

I couldn't help but look at him. Our glances met, and held until that uncomfortable point, when I looked down, but not for long; I had to look again. His eyes drew me to him and seemed to radiate kindness, gentleness and trustworthiness.

The leader of the group made a few announcements and read of upcoming events. The group was to put on a few shows: plays and musicals. It all sounded interesting. Since this was my first time to the meeting, I was asked to introduce myself and tell the group where I was from. I got up and told my story. My eyes kept meeting with the kind eyes of the young man who attracted me as I talked.

After the meeting, a girl that sat next to me said, "Hello, I'm Gertrude. A few of us go to a local tavern after the meeting; would you like to join us?"

I must have shocked her with my expression as I replied, "A tavern—I don't know—and I don't go ... I mean, I don't have much money."

She chuckled and brushed off my apprehension, "Oh, it's not what you think; it's just a chance for us to get together and socialize."

Cautiously, I acknowledged, "All right, maybe for just a little while."

We walked to a quaint tavern a few blocks from the hall. It was my first time in such an establishment. I expected it to be filled with loud obnoxious drunks. On the contrary, it was more of a peaceful family atmosphere. I would have called it a restaurant. We sat at a long table. Only about a dozen people from our group attended. I sat down next to Gertrude. The two well-dressed young men then sat at my end of the table, with the one I liked right next to me.

Neither of them said anything for the first few minutes, they just observed. I was talking to Gertrude and tried to engage them in the conversation, but to no avail. Finally, I asked the one next to me, "So, what's your name?"

He looked startled. "Gerd—Gerd Stritzke—this is my brother Wolfgang." He pointed to the other man that was with him.

"Oh, brothers," I tried to sound as if it wasn't obvious. "Where are you from?"

"Bad Cannstatt."

"No, I mean when you lived in East Prussia."

Gerd blushed. I think he was embarrassed that he answered my question wrong.

"Allenstein," Gerd replied.

There was a long silence. I thought he or his brother would have elaborated. It was clear to me that both were very shy. This, somehow further attracted me to Gerd. His shyness added to my comfort with him. He was humble, even gentler than I previously thought.

"Were you captive under the Russians?" I asked.

"No," Gerd answered. "We left before they came. Refugees warned us the Russians were close and told us of some of the horrible things they had seen.

My father died in combat, so Mutti was smart and brought us—" Gerd looked at his brother "—to the West, to safety, where we had relatives. We were fortunate."

I looked down, "My family was not as lucky. We had a chance to escape before they came. Mutti didn't want to leave her parents behind ... she kept saying, it won't be so bad. For two and a half years we were under Russian rule in East Prussia." I explained what happened to my family, but left out many of the worst details. I felt uncomfortable talking about it. Time seemed to simply stand still. I could have spent the entire evening talking to Gerd. He didn't say much but showed a real interest in what I had to say. He made me feel important.

Finally, people started leaving. Wolfgang leaned over to Gerd, and smiled apologetically, "It's time to go."

We said our good-byes and they left. I watched Gerd walk out and said to myself: *I can't wait to see him again.* On my way home, I realized this group was something special. It gave me a sense of belonging.

At the next meeting, I sat down next to Gertrude. Again, the two well-dressed brothers walked in late. Gertrude leaned over to me gleaming and whispered, "There comes Gerd and Wolfgang. Their father was a teacher." I wondered if she had an interest in Gerd. His father being a teacher further intrigued me about him. After the meeting, we attended the same tavern and Gerd again sat next to me. As time passed, my weeks were preoccupied with anticipation of the youth group meetings. I became closer and closer to Gerd. The more I got to know him, the nicer he appeared. I felt safe with him. I kept giving hints that I wanted to date him and, finally, after three months, he asked if I wanted to join him at the Oktoberfest in Bad Cannstatt.

I was so excited I could hardly contain myself, my first date. Still, I was a little afraid. After what I went through under the Russians, men still scared me. And, my father's unfaithfulness added to my apprehension toward men. I just found it hard to trust them, and while I had been asked out on dates by other men, I always turned them down. Something just felt right about Gerd. So I said yes.

My first date was absolute bliss; my head was in the clouds all day. He was the perfect gentleman. We spent most of our time walking the fest and enjoying the events. In the afternoon, we found a picnic bench and just sat and talked for hours. He was so easy to talk to; it seemed as if I knew him forever.

After that, all I could think about was Gerd. I couldn't wait to see him at the youth group meetings. Now, I always sat next to him. Surprisingly, there weren't many people dating each other in our group. We were one of the few. At least, I was pretty sure we were dating, although so far we had had only one date! Finally, to my relief, after several weeks, he mustered up enough courage to ask me out for another evening, and thereafter, we were together just about every weekend.

It took three months of dating before our first kiss. His holdout for affection further added to my trust toward him. But that first kiss sent shivers through me, telling me, this is the one! I surrendered my fears. Finally, my life turned around. Gerd was the catalyst that sparked a change in my life. From here on out, everything in my life seemed to have a positive spin to it; I had real joy in my heart. Gerd took me away from my terrible past and made me feel positive about our future. From eleven years old until I met my Gerd, my life was a day-to-day trudge through a mud field. With Gerd, that barren field grew into a meadow of the most glorious flowers.

22

The Engagement

I applied for school at a local junior college, training as a secretary. The Färbers were right: as a refugee, I was entitled to free college and a monthly stipend for attending school, without swearing an allegiance to some political party. I was able to work part-time at the confectionary store to accommodate my classes. With the school stipend to offset my lost work hours, Mutti and I still managed to make ends meet. Gerd was a big part of my life now, so my weekends were dedicated to him.

Irmi did end up getting married and she invited friends and relatives, including Mutti and me, to a restaurant after they officially got married at the courthouse. My brother Günter was already in Argentina, so he didn't attend. It was odd seeing her with a big belly. She looked like she was ready to give birth. I was relieved that she followed through with moving to West Berlin, and we were able to see her once a month or so. As for Papa, Irmi sent him a letter that she was getting married, but she never heard back from him.

My life continued to revolve around Gerd, and I was pleased that Mutti and Irmi liked him. Gerd and I were together for almost a year. One day he said, "Let's go to the Oktoberfest and celebrate our one-year anniversary."

"What a great idea," I replied. I was excited about our anniversary date and told my friend Ruth, the niece of the owner of the confectionary store where I worked.

"Oh, can I come with, please, please," She begged, all excited.

Immediately, I regretted my decision to tell her. I felt Ruth was after my Gerd. "Ruthie, I don't know. Gerd wanted this to be a special—"

"I won't be a bother," Ruth pleaded. "I just really want to go to the Oktoberfest."

"Well," I said. "I guess it's all right."

When I told Gerd, he got a little upset. "Why did you ask her to come with? This was supposed to be just the two of us."

"I didn't ask her," I lamented. "She just pushed her way into coming. I couldn't say no."

The day came and Ruth joined us for the Oktoberfest. We were all having a good time. We approached the Ferris wheel and Ruth started jumping up and down, "Let's go on the big wheel. That will be fun. Let's go."

"I can't go Ruthie," I explained. "I get dizzy—especially after the half-liter beer we had at lunch. I'll get sick."

Before I could suggest something else for us to do, Ruth grabbed Gerd by the arm as she giggled, "Well, then Gerd and I will go for a ride."

There I stood with my mouth open, watching Ruth arm-in-arm with Gerd, still laughing as they headed toward the Ferris wheel. I may as well have gone on the ride, because my stomach was in knots. I agonized until the ride was over. Finally they were done and as soon as Gerd was near, I leaned into him and he put his arm around me. I immediately felt better, and we made our way through the rest of the Oktoberfest. We arrived at the arcades and Gerd wanted to try his luck at the shooting range. I was surprised at how good a shot he was. His first attempt, he won a prize. He decided to try again and won a second time. He chose roses for his prizes; one red and one yellow.

He walked over to Ruth and me, with a big smile on his face "Here, a prize for you." Gerd handed me the yellow rose and offered Ruth the red one. I was stunned.

Ruth, all excited to get the red rose, clasped her hands together and smiled widely, "Thank you, what a beautiful rose."

I was furious, but didn't say anything. Fortunately, it was toward the end of the day and we were heading home after the arcade. Once Ruth left us, I angrily asked Gerd, "Why did you give her the red rose?"

Gerd looked puzzled. "What do you mean?"

"You gave Ruth the red rose. Why?"

Gerd's face turned red with embarrassment, and then he lowered his head. He took a breath and replied, "I'm color blind—my greens and reds get mixed up."

I felt bad for getting mad at something that wasn't his fault. He gave me a long hug good night and I ended the emotional roller coaster ride on a high note.

A few weeks later, Gerd asked me to join him for dinner. This evening was different. He was unusually talkative, and somewhat nervous. I was surprised to see he had chosen an elegant restaurant. Not that Gerd was cheap; he was just a simple man. Spending a lot of money on a meal didn't make sense to him.

We sat at the table and Gerd struggled through the menu. He ordered something, but I don't think he really knew what it was. It had a French name, but the description said *beuhnchen*, his favorite, so he must have figured it can't be bad if it's chicken. I ordered a beef entree and both meals were superb. As we ate, he became silent and fidgeted. Then, he reached into his pocket and handed me a small white box.

"Ilse, this is for you."

Suddenly, it all made sense to me; the restaurant, the nervousness, *he's proposing to me!* I was in shock, this caught me totally by surprise. As slow as Gerd moved, I thought this day would never happen. As if he didn't already add a spark to me life, this was the entire firework display. My hands were shaking so badly, I struggled to open the box. Inside was a shiny gold ring. Flashes of light hindered my vision, as I tried to focus through the tears that welled in my eyes. I started sobbing uncontrollably, and made a real spectacle of myself.

Finally, I regained my composure enough for him to ask, "Will you marry me?" The whole sobbing scene started all over again.

As soon as I could catch my breath, I replied, "Gerd, of course I will." I don't even remember if I finished the meal, or much else about the evening; I was fluttering through the clouds.

I couldn't wait to tell Mutti and Irmi. The thought of marrying Gerd felt so right. My life was on the right track. Not since I was a little child on the beach of the Baltic, did I see as optimistic a future.

We set a date for October 27, 1956, and started thinking about where we would live. Because of the number of displaced German refugees vying for living space, the government instituted a program to fairly assign housing. Women with infants had priority. Since we knew there was a waiting list, the following week, I went to the housing department and explained that I was looking for an apartment. I filled out a lot of paperwork and had an interview with one of the case workers.

"Do you have any children?" the lady asked.

"No, but I am getting married in one year."

The case worker chuckled. "I'll put your name on the list, but right now it looks like a six year waiting list."

"Six years!" I cried.

"Well," she said, "Your name is on the list and who knows?"

I was very upset and told Gerd the bad news. I was surprised at his response. "Don't worry, we'll find something," he reassured me. His words comforted me and calmed my anxiety.

I was getting a taste of Gerd's positive attitude and calming effect on me.

In June, a friend of Mutti's, who we called Uncle Gustav, came to visit. He was an East Prussian refugee and had relatives in Chicago. Uncle Gustav had just returned from a visit to America. Gerd and I listened attentively as he described his journey.

"Kids," he told us. "If I were your age, there would be *no question* that I would move to America. I'm too old and I still have relatives in Poland. But you have your entire life ahead of you. The best advice I can give you on your future, is to go to America. There's nothing here for you. America is the land of opportunity."

At the same time, Gerd's mother had a friend who just returned from a visit to Arizona to see her daughter who married an American G.I. Her message was just as passionate for Gerd and me to consider immigrating to America.

After hearing this advice, Gerd said to me, "What future do we have here? Let's go to America. We could live there for a few years, make some money, and then come back."

That night I dreamed of America and what it would be like. I recalled memories of Omi Glaus, my father's mother. Her name was Rosena and she was married to Wilhelm Glaus. He was a blacksmith and in 1935, died at age 71. I was only one year old, so I had no recollection of him. My dream brought me to Omi Glaus' home.

She always had candy for me. I felt completely comfortable around her. She made me feel like her only purpose was to please me—what grandmothers do so well. She loved to sing to me. I remember one song in particular:

> *If I one time travel*
> *I'll travel to America.*
> *There I am the littlest,*
> *Of all that are there.*
> *The ladies and the gentlemen,*
> *Stand before my door.*
> *And want to get a glimpse of me,*
> *Me, the little marmot.*[18]

Did she really want to visit America? Was this a sign to lead me to America? Was she telling me to go to America?

My Omi Glaus died in 1938. I was only four, but I recall her wake. She was laid out in my family's front room. All of the adults were occupied in discussion and I walked over to her by myself, moved a foot stool next to her and stood on it to get a closer look at her. I was not afraid. I looked into the coffin, and saw her lying there peacefully. She looked very pretty in her white dress; her Sunday and special occasion dress. I don't recall any sadness. Maybe I was too young to recognize what was happening. Perhaps my parents ingrained in me that she was going to heaven, and I shouldn't worry. She was buried close by in the cemetery across the street from our home, and I visited her gravesite often.

The next week, I went to the American Consulate to inquire about immigrating to America. The lady behind the counter laughed, "Where are you coming from? In one week, the quota runs out. I doubt that you will be able to get everything filled out in time and there's no guarantee that you will be able to go."

Disappointed, I replied, "I will try anyway." Armed with piles of paperwork, I came home and Gerd and I spent the evening filling out forms and preparing photographs for identification.

The next day, I returned and handed the lady the documents. "You will hear from Munich if your application is accepted," she informed me. "Then you will get more instruction on what to do."

It all sounded very discouraging and we didn't put much faith in ever hearing from the consulate. But surprisingly, in August, we received a letter from the Munich consulate, requesting us to come for an interview. We took a day off of work and traveled to Munich. During the interview, they drilled us with all kinds of questions in an attempt to see how serious we were about immigrating. They asked questions like:

- Were you or anyone in your family, part of the Nazi party?
- Do you have relatives in America?
- What skills do you have to work in America?
- Do you think the streets in America are lined with gold?

There seemed to be no end to the questions and it was somewhat humiliating. In closing, I said that we want to immigrate as a married couple. One of the interviewees said, "Good thing you said that, because they could otherwise split you up once you arrive in America. You need to notify us when you get married."

We still weren't optimistic, but we didn't give up. I started learning English. I bought a translation book and tried my English out on anyone who would listen. I actually thought I was getting good at my new language.

One week before we were to get married, a letter arrived from Munich stating in order for us to immigrate to America as a couple, we needed to have a record of being married by October 22.

There we were one week before our scheduled wedding, what were we to do now? "Gerd, we need to get married at city hall this weekend!"

He started laughing. "Can we get married that fast?"

I raised my eyebrows, "Why not? If we want to go to America as a couple, we have no choice."

We quickly made arrangements and got married that weekend. We tried to formalize it as much as we could, but it wasn't much of a ceremony. As witnesses we only had Mutti, her friend Uncle Gustav, Gerd's mother and Wolfgang. We had a dinner afterwards to celebrate. As crazy as this was, we all laughed and had fun with it. We knew this was just a formality.

Quickly, I needed to get my passport changed with my new name, so I took Monday off work and headed to the passport authority. Anxious to get it done in time, I was the first one there as the bureau opened. I walked up and said good morning to the man behind the counter. He didn't acknowledge me and only looked at the papers I provided him.

"Sir," I began. "I have an emergency; I need to get my name changed on my passport right away so that we can immigrate to America as a couple. The immigration office needs proof of marriage tomorrow. Can—"

"No way!" the man replied in a snooty tone. "Six weeks is what it takes to get a passport change."

"Six wee ... No, you don't understand. I have all of the paperwork filled out. All you need to do is stamp it approved. There must be a way."

"No way," he carelessly responded. "A rush order would take four weeks. That's the best that we could do."

At this point, I got very angry. This lazy fool just didn't want to bother rushing it. I tilted my head and narrowed my eyes. "Sir, I need to talk to your supervisor," I demanded.

He finally looked up at me. "Fine," he said in huff. "Second door on your right." He pointed down a hallway.

I grabbed my papers and headed toward the hall. "There's nothing he can do either," he grumbled as I approached the second door, which had an impressively large polished brass nameplate attached under a frosted glass window pane. Cautiously, I knocked. "*Herein*," A voice bellowed from within the office. I opened the door and there, behind a large ornate wooden desk, cluttered with papers, sat a middle aged, distinguished looking man in a striking suit. With a comforting smile, he asked, "Well, how may I help you?"

I thought to myself, *this is starting off much better, now I need to turn on the charm, and play the poor, helpless lady.* "Sir," I said, leaning forward with my hands holding out my paperwork. "I have an emergency, and I need your help." I explained the entire dilemma, and that the man behind the counter told me there was no way to get my passport changed in time for the immigration office.

I handed him the paperwork, he quickly sifted through it and then, looked up at me with a sincere expression. "*Na, selbstverständlich*, we can help you. Everything is filled out properly." He laid the paperwork down and grinned, "Come back to my office in an hour, and everything will be ready for you." I thanked him profusely before I left him alone.

I wandered around town for an hour, and then returned. And sure enough, everything was complete and in order. "Now, all you need to do is to go back to the teller, have him stamp your passport, then pay ... you're all set," he assured me as he handed over the paperwork. "Have a wonderful trip, Frau Stritzke."

Beaming, because no one had ever called me that yet, I replied with a great big smile, "I will, *vielen dank!*"

I went back to Herr "Charming," at the counter, and slowly slid the paperwork toward him. He rubbed his chin as he analyzed the paperwork. "See, where there's a will, there's a way," I preached to him. He abruptly stamped my passport, took my money, and then looked beyond me to the next person in line.

"Next," he said.

The following day, I headed to Munich to show proof of our marriage to the immigration office. The lady at the office said that we will be contacted by mail if there is a possibility to immigrate. When I got home, I crashed on the couch exhausted. What a crazy week! All this and our church wedding this Saturday.

Ilse and Gerd's wedding photograph, 1956.

Even though we were technically married, Gerd and I didn't celebrate it as such. We wanted to wait until our church marriage. He still lived with his mother and brother in Bad Cannstatt and I lived with Mutti in Stuttgart. This arrangement wasn't going to change, even after the church wedding. We had no place to live.

So far, the whole marriage event was a lot more commotion than we had bargained for, but finally Saturday arrived and with it our long-awaited Church wedding. About twenty people attended at the Lutheran church in Stuttgart. Gerd's mother was good friends with an evangelist pastor and his wife. I got to know them well. They knew we didn't have much money, so the pastor's wife, about my size, offered to give me her wedding dress. I was delighted. It was a beautiful dress; perfect—just like I would have picked out at a fancy store, no extravagant lace or dazzling sequins, but elegant and stylish. Gerd wore a black tuxedo with a grey vest and a light colored tie.

The church service was moving. The pastor spoke of trust and commitment; the things I valued most in Gerd.

After the church service we all walked to a cozy restaurant down the street. We moved several tables together to accommodate our small group. Gerd's brother, Wolfgang, invited his girlfriend, Helga. They met years ago, when Gerd's family first came to western Germany at the end of the war. I had never met her before, but liked her immediately. To everyone's surprise, that evening Wolfgang asked for her hand in marriage and she accepted. What a joyous dinner we had, surrounded by friends and family. Before we knew it, our mothers were splitting the bill for the dinner, and Gerd and I were on our way.

One of Mutti's friends offered to give up her apartment for the weekend, so that Gerd and I could be alone. That evening, Gerd and I celebrated what each of us saved, for only us to share. The love we shared erased my harsh memories of how the Russian soldiers abused this precious gift that God granted to us.

I could have stayed in Gerd's arms forever, we had such fun having a place to ourselves that weekend, but Monday we had to give up the apartment and go back to work. Worse yet, he had to go home and so did I, unfortunately to different places. It was terrible being apart. We were married, but only saw each other on weekends and even then, we were seldom alone. But with housing being so scarce, it seemed our best option of living together was to immigrate to America.

23

The Voyage

In December, we received a letter from the immigration office stating that we were approved for entry into America and that our boat was to leave from Bremerhaven on February 23, 1957. We were so excited at the news. Our new life together, in a new world, was taking shape. There was plenty of planning and packing that needed to be done. Then in January, Gerd got a terrible case of the mumps. He had to go to the hospital where the doctors removed his tonsils. He was in an awful condition, and it couldn't be at a worse time. We worried that he might not be well enough to travel to America. Thankfully, he started to recover and by early February he was well. Now, we eagerly counted down the days until our departure.

Our mothers came with us for the send-off. We arrived in Bremerhaffen a day early. Our ship was in harbor already; The *General W.C. Langfitt*. We all walked along the dock to look at the ship.

"Look Gerd," I said. "There's our ship."

"Well, it's no luxury liner." It was an old battleship, converted to a personnel carrier.

"So what, Gerd. We'll have eight days together—alone—in our cabin. Even if it's not the prettiest ship, it's still our honeymoon." We were now married for four months and still didn't live together. Finally, our lives were to be as one. As we walked side-by-side, I grabbed his arm and leaned my head against his shoulder. How exciting, our adventure began!

It was an emotional afternoon. Mutti handed me a small cloth sack. As she placed it in my hand, I could tell from its weight and the clink it made that it was full of coins.

"Here this is for you. They're the American coins. You can use these when you get there."

"Mutti, are you sure?" She smiled and nodded. "That's so thoughtful. Look Gerd, Mutti saved these coins from doing laundry for the American soldiers. They always left change in their pants and Mutti collected it."

"*Danke*," he smiled. "Now we'll have money as soon as we arrive."

Mutti looked at Gerd's mother and said, "Well, I guess this is it ... this

172

Ilse and Gerd before departure for the U.S.A. in 1956, shown with mothers Glaus and Stritzke.

is where we leave you alone and we ladies head back." We all hugged and cried. As much as I looked forward to going to America, a part of me felt like I was abandoning Mutti. Still, deep down, I knew this was the right thing to do.

"We'll write as soon as we arrive," I promised. "And as soon as we get situated, both of you need to come and visit."

Off they went. My heart sank as Mutti walked away. I looked at Gerd with tear-filled eyes. He hugged me. I knew this was right, but it still hurt.

We decided to get all our paperwork together and sign in for the trip. The American soldiers spoke German and took our information and provided instructions. They explained that we didn't need to pay for the trip now, but that they expected to get reimbursed, in time, once we had money and were situated. We agreed. They also asked if we were interested in volunteering on the ship to make extra money. They needed help in the kitchen and serving food. My eyes lit up, "Of course we would," I said.

"We need help at breakfast, lunch and dinner," one soldier explained. "So you have to report for duty three times a day to receive six dollars for the full day—for each of you."

"Fantastic," I replied.

They directed us to living quarters for the first night; we stayed in military barracks, with separate sleeping arrangements for men and women. "Don't worry," I told Gerd. "We'll have a honeymoon suite on the ship."

Gerd gave me a hug. "Ilse, think about it, six dollars for each of us, for eight days: that's $96. We're rich!"

We hugged for what seemed to be hours. "I love you Gerd and I look so forward to our new life together."

"I love you too, we're doing the right thing... Are you scared?"

"You know what?" I paused for a moment. "Funny you should mention that; not at all ... *not at all.* I know that with you, things will work out for the best."

The next morning, we heard the announcement that all workers were to board the ship for instructions.

"Gerd," I gasped. "It's time. We can board early and pick out our honeymoon suite!"

We walked the narrow plank from the dock onto the ship. Already, not even on board, I felt a little funny, like the earth was moving under my feet. I tried to block it out of my mind and think pleasant thoughts. I envisioned our honeymoon suite; a double bed, small toilet room, and a small round porthole window. My queasiness subsided.

"All volunteers," a voice came from a soldier using a megaphone. "Go to the living quarters and drop off your things and come back to the deck within the hour for training. All women to the middle quarters and the men to the front. Soldiers will be there to assist you."

Every few minutes the message was repeated. Gerd and I looked at each other with disappointment. "We'll just tell them we're married and they'll give us a room together," I suggested.

We found a soldier helping direct passengers. "Sir, we are married," I said to him. "We want to stay together on the ship. Is there a section for married couples?"

He smiled and shrugged his shoulders and pointed to another soldier. "German," he shouted to him. We walked over to the other soldier and again explained our case to him.

"Sorry," he replied. "Men and women must be separated—it's the rules. Please follow these people." He was signaling for me to follow a line of women. "And men this way."

Gerd and I looked at each other. So much for our romantic honeymoon. Off we went in different directions. I arrived in the women's quarters. It was a long and narrow room with pipes, gauges, valves and wires lining the ceiling. Everything was dark grey, including the floor. There were no windows. The only light came from single light bulbs in the ceiling, encased in a glass jar and supported by a sturdy cage. The room smelled like old, sweaty shoes. There were about six rows of hammocks, three high, which stretched from one end of the room to the other, enough for several hundred people. Above each trio of hammocks were three small lockers. I claimed a middle hammock and placed my belongings in the middle locker. The adjacent bathroom offered no privacy. Twelve sinks lined one wall. Only three meters away, the opposing wall was lined with toilets and showers, with no doors or curtains.

I met Gerd back on deck and together we went through our training to serve the guests onboard. Soon, the rest of the passengers came on board and the first meal was served while we were still in harbor. It was fun to serve. Gerd and I occasionally crossed paths, and once dinner and chores were done, we were allowed to eat. There, Gerd and I had a chance to sit next to each other and share stories.

The ship started moving out of harbor, and I felt dizzy. "I don't know," I said apprehensively to Gerd. "Eight days of this and I'm already dizzy."

"Just try not to think about it," he suggested. "The more you think about it, the worse it will be." I managed to make it through the first day without getting sick. That night, fortunately I was very tired from all the excitement. The gentle swaying in the hammock may have just rocked me to sleep. The second day, I reported to work. My stomach didn't feel good, but I managed to finish serving breakfast. I only ate toast for breakfast, because already I was feeling nauseous. I was proud of myself: I made it through two full days of work, and didn't get sick.

The third day, we hit open seas. The windy winter ocean tossed our ship from side to side. I lasted until lunch time. I was carrying two trays of food when all of a sudden I had to drop the trays on an empty table and run to the bathroom to vomit. No longer was I able to avoid seasickness. I found Gerd and told him that I was going to lie down for a while with the expectation of getting better, in order to serve by dinnertime. Not only did I miss dinner, I missed the entire next day. I threw up every bit of food or fluid from my stomach. It was awful and I felt guilty that Gerd worked, while I was incapable of getting out of bed. I was not alone. Close to half of the women on the ship were in the same misery as I.

On the fifth day, Gerd came to my room. He brought me a drink that I was not familiar with. It came in a red can, labeled *Coca-Cola*, and was bubbly and sweet. I drank it and it tasted good and seemed to calm my stomach.

"I bought it out of an automatic machine, with those American coins from your Mutti," Gerd explained. "Here, I also brought you an apple and some bread."

"You're not supposed to be down here," I worried.

"Don't be concerned about that, there are so many people sick, they're not keeping track of who's going where. You need to get up and move around. Let's go up on the deck and get some fresh air."

"No," I whined. "I can't. I'm too weak."

Gerd forced me to sit up. He waited a while, then picked me up from the hammock and held onto me as I stood. My legs were wobbly.

"Let's go upstairs," he quietly ordered. Arm in arm we walked very slowly until we got outside. Once on the deck, the cold, crisp, fresh air did feel good. We stood on the deck for about an hour.

"Are you still able to work?" I asked.

"Yes," he laughed. "I think I'm one of the last ones serving. The good news is, that there's hardly anyone left to serve."

I laughed along. I was glad to have Gerd to comfort me. He continued to come to me and brought me *Coca-Cola* and bread. The sixth day, he too succumbed to seasickness, but still managed to get me and bring me to the ship's deck for fresh air. The sea was getting rougher. In between waves, our ship pointed almost straight down, then pointed almost straight up as it approached the next wave. Whitecaps started spilling over the bow. The conditions were dangerous. Soon, an announcement came over the intercom: *Everyone off the deck. Proceed to lower quarters.*

Gerd brought me to my quarters and the soldiers sealed the door behind us. The seas continued to get worse. That night, there was a loud clunk and water started gushing into our room. I thought this was the end. I pictured the ship with a large gash in its side and water streaming in. Ten centimeters of water collected in our room and splashed onto one side of the room, then came crashing into the other wall. Amazingly, the entire room of women was eerily silent. I would have thought everyone would have been screaming that the ship was sinking.

Then, fortunately, a few soldiers came into our room and told us not to worry, the sealed hatchway had broken open allowing some water to come in. "We're not sinking!" With buckets and mops, they started removing the water. I was amazed at their stamina, to maintain their sea legs in this turbulence.

We were told that the ship diverted south to avoid a storm and delayed our arrival by two days. Just what I wanted to hear, another two days of this. I was getting weaker and my continued retching assured there was nothing left in my stomach. I didn't see Gerd for two days. We were locked in our rooms during the storm.

Finally, it was day eight. The seas settled down. Our journey was supposed to have been done by now. Gerd came and brought me to the deck. "What happened to your hand?" I asked upon seeing his big bandage wrap.

"Oh, I fell during the turbulence. The doctor said that I broke my thumb." I felt so sorry for Gerd, but as I looked around, there were numerous people with casts and bandages. Clearly, I wasn't the only one wishing this trip was over. Outside, the sun was shining and it was unseasonably warm, we didn't need our jackets. We must have diverted south, near Florida, someone guessed.

Finally, on the tenth day, we arrived in New York. Once off the boat, I nearly kissed the ground. As soon as I was on solid ground, I immediately felt better. "Gerd," I sighed, "If someone walked up to me right now and offered me one million dollars to get back on that ship immediately and sail back to Germany, I wouldn't do it." I lost nine kilograms on this trip. All in all, we, or actually, Gerd, earned $35 for our service on the ship.

Some people were removed from the ship in stretchers. As one man in a stretcher was carried past us, Gerd whispered to me, half laughing, "That guy was groaning and complaining the entire trip. Finally, the doctor got fed up with him and shouted at him, "get up and be a man." Gerd and I laughed.

Authorities were very organized and were calling out names and directing people to various groups. Most people were greeted by friends or relatives. We were told that we were to board a train to Chicago. "Chicago?" I asked Gerd. "I thought we were to stay in New York."

"I wonder," Gerd replied. "We told the consulate about Uncle Gustoff, and that he had relatives in Chicago. Maybe that's why they're sending us there." In any event, we were to board a train in a few hours. We had some time to kill, so we walked around. We passed a street vendor with a push cart, who sold fried chicken. The smell was too much for us to resist. The chicken was incredible. The skin was crispier and spicier than what we typically had in Germany. It was good to get something solid in my stomach, and to have something solid under my feet.

24

Chicago

We boarded the train to Chicago. The trip took two days and we arrived Friday night. There people called our names and directed us to pre-paid taxis that brought us to the YMCA. Our taxi driver happened to speak German. He was very helpful and offered us newcomers a few pointers. He gave us his card and said to call him if we needed anything.

At the YMCA, they told us we would stay until Monday, and then someone would come and give us further instructions. They handed us keys and directed us to our room. Our room was clean—with a double bed—finally, our honeymoon suite. We stayed in the room for the night and didn't get up until late morning. I would have been happy there with Gerd all day, but we were hungry and it was nearing lunch time. The YMCA served lunch and it was only one dollar per person and it was good. We spent the rest of the day walking down State Street and Michigan Avenue.

We immediately fell in love with our new city. Everyone was friendly and we were amazed at the variety of things available for us to buy. We walked by an apparel shop and in the window was displayed the most beautiful blouse. It was pink with black velvet trim and collar. There was a tag on the sleeve that read $2.98. I fell in love with that blouse.

"Gerd, can I have the blouse?" I pleaded.

"If you like it, buy it," he replied.

We walked in and asked for help from one of the attendants. She spoke no German and it was quickly apparent that my English was undecipherable by everyone. I wasn't familiar with the clothing sizes in America, so I couldn't even write down my size. She guessed at my size and after a few trials we figured it out. It looked marvelous on me, even better than on the mannequin. I signaled that we wanted to buy it. She said, very well, three dollars and something. I ignored what I heard and gave her three dollars, expecting to get some change back.

She shook her head and assured me, "No, you pay $2.98 plus tax."

"No," I insisted. I brought her to the display and showed her that the tag said, $2.98, and I said, "Three dollars ... here."

"No," she repeated. "$2.98, plus tax—duty."

"Duty?" Then it dawned on me that in America there was a tax on purchases. Finally, we all laughed and settled the bill and I got my beautiful blouse.

When we arrived back at the YMCA, a man at the counter handed Gerd a piece of paper, saying, "Work—a job." Gerd thanked him. Neither of us could read it, but apparently, it was a listing for a job at a nearby company.

Monday arrived and a man came to visit us. "Do you have relatives here?" he asked.

After much sign language, I finally figured out what he was asking. "No," I replied.

He drove us to a Lutheran pastor. The pastor spoke a little German. "I will help you find a job and a place to live." Gerd showed him the job listing that he got from the YMCA. "Terrific, I will drive you there and you can fill out an application. Let's go."

The pastor drove us to the company, Scully-Jones. Gerd and I walked into the lobby and Gerd showed the receptionist the job listing. She handed him an application. I helped where I could, but there were many questions neither of us understood. I knew a few more English words than Gerd, so after many questions, and a great deal of help from the receptionist, we completed the application. She took the application and told us to wait.

A few minutes later a middle aged man came out to greet us. "Gerd?" he asked.

"Yes," Gerd stood up and shook his hand.

"Okay, can you start this afternoon?" Gerd didn't understand him and I wasn't sure I was hearing him right either. "Yes, start today. $1.50 per hour. Second shift—5:00 pm until 1:00 am—it's okay?"

He wrote a few things down on paper and held up fingers for the money and times. Now I understood and I explained, "No, we have no place to stay. We need to find an apartment."

"Well then, start tomorrow at 5:00 pm. And you," he pointed to me. "You can work in the office. Can you type?"

"No ... I mean, yes ... but no English ... not very good."

"That's okay, you can start tomorrow in the office. Be here at 8:00 am."

"Thank you sir," I replied very cordially. "First, I have to get everything organized. Then I can start."

"That's fine. Once you're settled in, come back. There will be a job waiting for you."

We laughed on the way out. "I can't believe this," Gerd remarked. "The first day here and I got a job—and $1.50 per hour."

We were all bubbly when the pastor came and picked us up. He was all excited about the news. "That's terrific—unbelievable—the first day. You must stay here at the church; you can even walk to work from here. I'll arrange to have a mattress put in the basement. You can stay here until we find you an apartment."

We stayed one more night at the YMCA, then gathered our things and moved into the church basement. The next afternoon Gerd went to work already. I waited up for him. He arrived back at about 1:30 am. Too excited about his first job, we stayed up and he described his new place.

"There are several Germans in the shop that helped me. Otherwise, I would have been lost. It's lathe work, just like I was trained. I really like it."

I hadn't seen Gerd this excited before. It was wonderful to see. We talked for at least an hour before we went to sleep. The next few days, I spent most of my time looking for an apartment, but I also enjoyed going to the new grocery stores—they had everything imaginable and all so inexpensive. I wrote plenty of letters to friends and family telling of our wonderful adventures in our new world.

One day, the pastor came over and said that he would soon need the room back. He was kindly trying to push us to find an apartment quickly. The next day, I talked to a German lady I met. Her family lived just down the street from the church. "Do you know of anyone who has an apartment available?"

"You need an apartment?" she asked.

"Yes."

"Well, we're leaving in two weeks. You can have this apartment. Rent is $35 per month."

"Fantastic," I answered. "We'll take it." We made arrangements and in two weeks we were to move in.

The pastor couldn't wait two weeks, so he asked his congregation if anyone was willing to take us in until we could move into our apartment. A young family, the Stephans, agreed. They lived a distance away, so Gerd had to take a bus to work. The first night, I waited, 1:30, then 2:00, then 3:00. What happened? He didn't know anyone and knew no English. I was horribly worried. I walked to the bus stop every time I heard a bus come by, but no Gerd. My mind went crazy thinking of all the things that could have happened; none were good. I was sure some gangsters killed him and here I was all alone in a strange country. I was in tears and didn't know what to do. I sat on the front step of the Stephans' house with my face in my hands.

Then, a little past 4:00 am, a police car stopped in front of the Stephans' house. Out walked my Gerd. Elated, I got up and ran to him and hugged him like never before. The policeman got out of his car, waved good bye and left. "Gerd, what happened to you? I was worried half to death!"

He explained how, since he had to switch buses, he forgot to walk across the street to get a bus going south. He picked up a bus going north. After a while, he realized he took the wrong bus, and tried to explain it to the bus driver, but Gerd couldn't explain it in English. So he took the bus all the way to the end, got out, then waited for a bus going the other direction. After waiting a few minutes, a bus came and it was the same bus driver! The driver recognized that something was wrong and he called the police. A short while later, a squad car came, stopped the bus and pulled Gerd out. He couldn't explain what the problem was until they located a German speaking officer. Gerd didn't even know the address of the Stephans. He only knew the Lutheran pastor, so the police called the pastor in the middle of the night. The pastor gave them the address for the Stephans and, finally, they drove Gerd home. Thank God, he was safe and sound.

After two weeks, we moved into our new apartment. What an exciting endeavor! Our first home together, and we were only in the country a month. The apartment was without any furniture. A Lithuanian lady we met took us to a furniture store that would allow us to buy on credit. With a $50 down payment, we purchased a bedroom set, a couch, two chairs and a kitchen table and chairs totaling $600. It was beautiful and well-crafted furniture and we were thrilled to no end. This America was easy to love.

Every payday, Gerd and I walked to the furniture store and paid what we could. Within a half year we paid off the entire amount. We got to know the store owners well, and because we paid everything off so early, they gave us a lamp and chair for free.

Gerd and I loved America. It truly was the land of opportunity. Finding a good paying job and being able to buy what we needed was so easy compared to Germany at the time.

Once we were situated in our new apartment, Gerd's manager at Scully-Jones kept pestering Gerd to bring me in to work in the office. Finally, I decided to take him up on his offer. I started working and typed memos. Since I was copying hand-written documents, it was pretty easy to type exactly what was written. I enjoyed the job and the people were so nice to work for.

After four weeks on the job, they decided to send me to school, for an entire week, to learn key-punching. I was overwhelmed. Why would they do this for me? I still hardly knew the language. After a week of training, there was a test. I was very nervous. I understood how to key-punch, but I had a hard time reading the questions in English. The test format was set up with a series of questions, for which I had to choose one of three possible answers. The problem was that, in some cases, the way the answers were given, all three of the answers seemed to be correct.

I struggled. I was able to answer a few, but most of them were too difficult for me to understand. After a while, I was the last one left taking the test. I felt so bad that this company paid me to take a week of training, and here I was, ready to fail them. I started crying. The test administrator came to me and asked, "What's wrong?"

I explained how I couldn't understand the questions, and that by failing this test, I was letting down the company. To my amazement, she sat down next to me and reviewed what I did so far. "Wait," she said, "You did these correctly." I'll read the others to you and help you understand what they are looking for."

She read every question and explained each possible answer in a clear and understandable manner. With her help, I passed the test. I was so grateful to her. Why did she do this for *me*? I was nobody to her, and she took the time to help me. It was another instance that showed how wonderful the American people were.

Gerd and I decided to have a picnic one Sunday. We walked hand in hand along the beautiful shores of Lake Michigan. We stopped at a picnic table to have some lunch.

"You know what, Uncle Gustav and your Mutti's friend were wrong about America," I said to Gerd.

"What?" he replied with a shocked look on his face.

"*Ja*, it's better than they described." I paused as he smiled in agreement. "There are endless opportunities here. Everyone has been so friendly and helpful. It's hard to describe." A tear started running down my cheek.

"Yes, it is unbelievable. I got a good paying job in the first few days that we were here ... we found an apartment and bought furniture. We have more than we'd have in Germany in five years."

"I never thought about it this way before, but you know, Germany lost the war to both Russia and America." I stopped to swallow. "I now lived under both Governments. The Russians left me with deep wounds ... here in America: nothing but showers of blessings and unselfish kindness." I started to cry again. "Gerd, even in Germany before the Russians came; we were oppressed. I never felt so free and safe in all my life." I looked at him smiling at me. I kissed and hugged him. "And I have you on top of it all ... what more can I ask for?"

"This is the place for us," Gerd said. "I don't think we're going back." He released me from the hug and looked me straight in the eyes. "I only have one regret."

"What's that," I asked.

"That I wasn't born here."

"God Bless America."

Appendix

Maps and a Brief History of the Region

The Prussian region was said to be inhabited in the early days by West Slavic tribes, ancestors of modern Poles in the western half and Baltic tribes, more closely related to Lithuanians, in the eastern half. Earliest history suggests that after the seventh century, the entire area was invaded by pagan Germanic tribes that made up the majority of inhabitants until after World War II.

East Prussia was the larger portion of Prussia that occupied the southeastern coast of the Baltic Sea. The crusading Teutonic Knights conquered the region during the 13th century, converting its mostly pagan inhabitants to Christianity. In the 16th century the House of Hohenzollern took over the administration of the area. In the 17th century, after an invasion from Sweden, the area became known as the Kingdom of Prussia, headed by the Hohenzollern line.

The 18th century brought about annexations by the self-proclaimed kings of Prussia (the most notable being King Friedrich II—Frederick the Great), who reattached East Prussia to the rest of the Prussian state and called it the Province of East Prussia. By the 17th or early 18th century, the old Prussian language became extinct. In the later part of the 19th century, after the defeat of France in the Franco–Prussian war, Germany became a world power. Under leadership of Prussian Prime Minister Otto von Bismarck, East and West Prussia merged as part of the unification of the German states. The German Empire was established under Prussian leadership with Bismarck as Chancellor. Wilhelm II, the last of the Hohenzollern dynasty, became emperor of Germany (Kaiser) in 1888 and ruled until Germany's defeat in World War I.

After World War I, the treaty of Versailles restored West Prussia to Poland, with the enclave of East Prussia still German, a part of Weimar Germany. The Memel Territory was detached in 1921 and became Lithuania. After the Nazi defeat in World War II, East Prussia was divided between Poland and Lithuania, and a small section became an unattached portion of Russia. East Prussia's capital was renamed from Königsberg to Kaliningrad

Palmnicken, where Ilse grew up, was in Samland, part of East Prussia, a rectangular piece of land that was about 80km wide and 30km north-south. It was a peninsula that stuck out into the Baltic Sea, and bordered both fresh water harbors (Kurisches Haff and Frisches Haff). The southern borders were Pillau to Tapiau, crossing through the capital city Königsberg, and the eastern borders were Tapiau and Labiau. Palmnicken (now called Yantarni) was a coastal village ten kilometers south of Brüsterort, the last land bend for ships before they reached Pillau. Once ships passed through Pillau, they entered the Frisches Haff—a large freshwater lake that had a thin, kilometer-wide dune barrier to the Baltic Sea that stretched for at least 50 kilometers—which led to Königsberg.

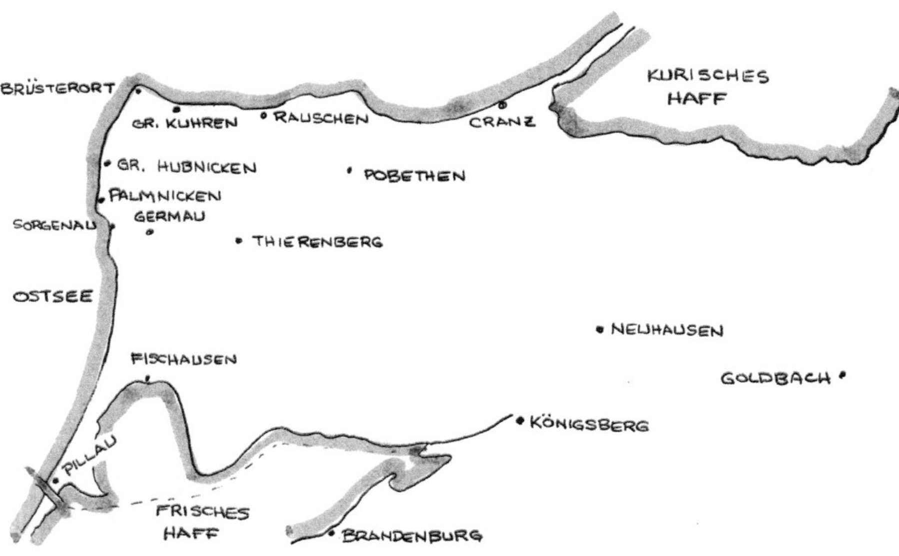

Above: Europe, 1919–1938

Opposite: The Samland portion of East Prussia.

Chapter Notes

1. In German, when the suffix –chen, or –lein is added to the end of a name, it generally juveniles the name. In this case, Ilse turns to Ilsechen. You will also notice that, depending on who is talking, Irmi turns to Irmchen, and this case the "i" is dropped. It is similar to English when Bill turns into Billy, by adding –y. In this book the "chen" is usually used by Mutti when talking to her daughters.

2. The official, unconditional, surrender of all German forces to the Allies took place on May 7, 1945, and Hitler committed suicide on April 30.

3. The Hitler Youth was actually formed back in 1922, a full eleven years before his chancellorship—a brilliant strategy to feed propaganda to a young disenchanted future electorate. In 1923 the Beer Hall Putsch found Hitler and his Nazi organization attempting to take over the government. The attempt ultimately failed, and Hitler was sentenced to five years in prison. His charisma, and crafty word-smithing at his trial, which was captured verbatim in the press, only increased his popularity and also helped shorten his sentence to only eight months. Because of Hitler's antics, the Hitler Youth was practically disbanded, but remained as an "underground" organization. In 1925 the Nazi party reorganized and a year later the Hitler Youth was once again a public organization. By 1930, the organization claimed membership of over 20,000 boys aged fourteen or older. It also created a junior division for ten-to-fourteen-year-old boys and ten-to-eighteen-year-old girls. In 1932, Chancellor Heinrich Bruning banned the organization for fear of violence and because of Hitler's escalating popularity. However, later that year, Franz Von Papen, Bruning's successor, lifted the ban to show appeasement to the ascending Hitler. The Hitler Youth were viewed as the future "Aryan Supermen" indoctrinated in anti–Semitism. The aim of this group was to train and fight faithfully for the Third Reich. The Hitler Youth was also viewed as the stepping stone for the future elite membership to the *Schutzstaffel* (SS). Members of the Hitler Youth were honored to receive a single Sig Rune symbol from the SS. The SS themselves sported a symbol that had two Sig Rune symbols; signifying the link between the two organizations.

4. Herman Brueckner, et al., based on Julie Hausmann.

5. The Baltic coast of East Prussia is said to lay claim to 90 percent of the world's entire supply of amber. Amber is derived from tree resin and that is why small insects or even small animals are often trapped inside the opaque stone. After millions of years under heat and pressure, the resin forms a fossilized rock.

6. On January 30, 1945, a German luxury cruise liner, the *Wilhelm Gustloff*, was repurposed as a hospital during the war and was commissioned for Operation Hannibal, a program to evacuate civilians and injured soldiers from the advancing Russian army. The ship, exhibiting the Red Cross flag, was to transport the passengers to German occupied Denmark in the west. The Germans knew that the U.S. and British forces protected civil-

ians and the injured soldiers, unlike the Russians. Official reports listed 6,050 passengers that day. However, many civilians clamored and pushed their way on board the ship, knowing it would take them to safety, so some estimates topped 10,000. The night the ship left, a Russian S-13 submarine fired two torpedoes into the side of the *Wilhelm Gustloff*. The ship tilted to one side, destroying most of the lifeboats. The few women and children that occupied the remaining life rafts had to fight off freezing survivors with oars to prevent them from boarding and capsizing the life rafts. The Baltic Sea at the end of January was merciless. The windy temperature was said to be -18 degrees Celsius and the salty water below zero degrees Celsius. An estimated 9,343 were claimed by the sea that night, some six times the 1,503 souls lost in the 1912 *Titanic* disaster. The captain of the Russian sub, Alexander Malenkienko, later went on to torpedo another German refugee ship, the *General von Steuben*, killing 3,000 of the 3,300 passengers. The sinking of the *Wilhelm Gustloff* demonstrated the visceral hatred that the Russians had for the Germans.

7. Direct translation: freshwater lagoon. The Frisches Haff is fed by inland rivers, most notably the Pregel, that flows through Köningsberg. The lagoon is roughly 80 km long and only 10 km wide. The northwestern border of the lagoon is a strip of land about 0.5 km wide with an opening to the Baltic Sea at Pillau. In the winter of 1945, many refugee families from Samland fled and crossed the frozen Frisches Haff to reach western Germany, to escape the advancing Russian Army. Many lost their lives when Russian warplanes shot them or by falling through the ice.

8. *Winter-Hilfe*, directly translated: winter help, was a program to help support Nazi soldiers during the brutal winter of 1944, when the Nazis stalled in their quest to take Moscow. People volunteered to carve statues and sell them, with the proceeds going toward the soldiers.

9. The winter of 1943 was the same winter that brought Germany its first major defeat as it retreated from Stalingrad during their march toward Moscow. German soldiers met an adversary more formidable than Russian soldiers—record cold temperatures.

10. Translated as collective farm, or cooperative organizations. These farms used pooled labor to create agricultural goods. Unfortunately, *kolkhozes* used persuasion by force.

11. HO was the designation for buildings that stored supplies. It's not clear what the designation meant.

12. Under the Nazis, even churches were government controlled. Hitler and Goebbels were both raised Catholic and never publically denounced their faith, but after Hitler's death, reports were found showing Hitler's idea of a National Reich Church. He viewed Christianity as a symptom of decay and an extension of the Jewish race. In 1933 Hitler appointed Ludwig Muller, a staunch Nazi supporter, as chairman of the 27 regional protestant churches that were turned into a single Protestant Reich Church. At that point, pressure was placed on the organization to accept the superiority of the Aryan race and to expel Christian Jews.

13. SS stood for *Schutzstaffel* which when translated means "protection squadron." The SS started out as a small elite group to personally protect Adolf Hitler. It became a multipurpose organization of the Nazi party when Heinrich Himmler, in 1929, became the organization's leader, and grew to 209,000 men in five years.

14. This was a tattoo given to all Waffen-SS members under their left arm near the armpit, signifying the soldier's blood type in the event the soldier was injured and needed a transfusion. Unfortunately, it also easily identified the soldier as belonging to the elite SS, a membership, at this time, that was often associated with war crimes. After the war, sporting a *Blutgruppentätowierungtattoo* was like wearing a target on one's back.

15. The end of World War II prompted the largest transportation of any population in modern history. Estimates ranged from twelve to fourteen million Germans, of which five hundred thousand to two million civilian deaths occurred during the expulsion. The

massive transportation of Germans occurred in three phases: (1) during 1944–45, when the Red Army atrocities against the civilians, publicized by the Nemmersdorf Massacre, were committed; (2) an unorganized retreat after the defeat of Germany; and (3) following the Potsdam Agreement, which proposed new borders and approved an "Orderly and Humane" expulsion of Germans (Richard Overy, *The Penguin Historical Atlas of the Third Reich* [London: Penguin, 1996]). East Prussia's population was 2.2 million in 1940, and estimated at only two hundred thousand at the end of May 1945 (Antony Beever, *Berlin and the Downfall 1945* [London: Penguin, 2002]). The Red Army created 45 forced labor camps in the former Eastern Baltics where the remaining civilians were used as slave laborers until the expulsion (Andreas Kooert, *Damals in Ostpreussen* [Munich: n.p., 2008]).

16. Translated Free German Youth, this was a socialist youth organization in East Germany for girls and boys between 14 and 25. The organization was intended to indoctrinate the youth into the ways of the German Democratic Republic, or the Socialist Unity Party of Germany. Membership was voluntary, but declining membership meant lack of funding for universities and limited access to good jobs and other benefits.

17. Formed in 1946, the Socialist Unity Party (SED—*Sozialistische Einheitspartei Deutschlands*) was the ruling Communist party in East Germany.

18. Author unknown.

Index

Allies 9, 144
amber 33, 48, 62, 63, 74, 101, 114, 152

Bach (family) 49, 50, 60, 61, 87, 92
Bad Cannstatt 161, 162, 170
Baltic Sea 17, 63, 64, 98, 127, 133
Berlin (includes East and West) 135, 142,
    144, 146, 147, 149, 156–158, 160, 164
bicycles 15, 16, 25, 29
Birkenfelde 139
Bremerhaven 172
brigadier 94, 95, 123–125
Brüsterort 44

Chicago 166, 177–179, 181
Christmas 36, 90, 96, 133, 142–144, 157
Communism 94, 95, 99, 102, 106, 108,
    109, 115, 124, 132, 142, 144, 146, 154,
    156, 157, 160

Denmark 8, 76, 90
divorce 150–153, 156

Easter 108, 183
Eifel 157
Ernestina, Tante 152

Färber, Herr 35, 36, 39, 48–50, 59, 67,
    87, 92, 160, 164
Florida 176
Freie Deutsche Jugend (FDJ) 154
Frieda 120, 121
Friedel, Tante 5, 7; coat 91; and death of
    Opa 114; desire to return to Palmnicken
    19; diary gift 106; Goldbach 101; and
    Hans' illness 33; and Hans' death 40;
    knit sweater 134–135; and Russian sol-
    diers 11–14, 19–20, 22, 87–88; second
    evacuation 47, 49–50; sickness 113;
    work 52, 61, 65, 69, 90, 103, 113, 124
Frisches Haff 76, 98

General W.C. Langfitt 172
Gerhardt 118–122
Germau 153
Giesela 118–122
Glaus, Uncle Fritz 146, 135
Glaus, Karl 7, 45, 145–147
Glaus, Rosine Wittrin (Omi Glaus) 34,
    167
Gross Hubnicken 153
Gross Kuhren 17, 24, 36, 39, 102, 153
Gustav, Uncle 168, 169, 187

Halle 149, 150, 154
Hamburg 135, 142, 146
Hitler Jugend 41, 42
hospital 31–35, 56, 65, 66, 70, 71, 123,
    131, 149, 158, 172

Ilian, Ernst 12, 25, 84, 132, 133
Ilian, Luise Plew (Omi): burial of
    Hans 40; burial of young boy 27;
    caring for Ilse 78, 79; dying 57–59, 61;
    first evacuation of Palmnicker 19, 20,
    23–25, 30; giving away food 50; and
    Omi Glaus 34, 167; orphanage 120;
    return to Palmnicken 38
Ilian, Wilhelm (Opa): burial of Hans 35,
    39, 40; butchering horse 91–93; dying
    113, 114, 118; first evacuation of Palm-
    nicken 18, 19, 21, 22, 24–26, 29–32;
    fishing 63, 110; Mutti's illness 66, 71;
    Omi's death 57, 59; potato field 61;
    rejected for labor 50; response to Ilse's
    assault 69; return to Palmnicken 38;
    running out of food 97; searching for
    food 51–53, 65, 84, 86–90; searching
    for tobacco 55; second evacuation 46;
    second evacuation of Palmnicken
    99–103; visiting Mutti in hospital 71
immunization 112, 113
Ivan 131, 132

Jänicke, Pastor 57, 132
Jürgen 121, 122

kasha 23, 24, 29, 47, 49, 86
kolkhoze 99, 104
Köln 157
Königsberg 9, 101, 120, 124, 125, 134, 153
Latvia 75, 76
Lithuania 9, 18, 75
logging (lumberjacking) 96, 122–124, 126, 131, 133

makhorka 55, 113
Minna, Tante 90, 91, 156, 157
Moscow 86, 88, 99, 106, 112
Munich 168, 169, 187
mushrooms 89, 90, 118, 134, 138

Neuman, Fräulein 77
New York 176, 177
Normandy, France 135
Nuremberg Trials 146

Omi *see* Ilian, Luise
Omi Glaus *see* Glaus, Rosine
Opa *see* Ilian, Wilhelm
orphanage 120

Palmnicken 9, 17–19, 24, 30–34, 40, 42, 62, 74, 94–96, 99, 100, 102, 108, 110, 112, 132–135, 146, 150, 157
passport 157, 168, 169
Petra 85, 86, 96
Pillau 76, 90, 133, 184, 186
plane (airplane) 7–10, 40, 44, 45, 76, 145–147
Poland (Poles) 9, 75, 166

police (military) 18, 19, 22, 26, 29–31, 39, 42, 60, 68, 72, 104
Potsdam Conference 144

rape 8, 13, 15, 20, 21, 36, 60, 68, 69, 83, 86, 98, 137, 145
Rastenburg 30
Red Cross 141–144, 147
Reisenkowski, Herr 94, 95
Routenberg (family) 104, 106–108, 111, 140

Schloss Hotel 97, 157
Schmidt, Frau 75
Scully-Jones 179, 181
short-wave radio 9, 39
Socialist Unity Party 154, 160
Söhn, Frau 65, 66, 71, 104, 113
Sorgenau 90, 91
Soviet Union 41, 55, 94, 95, 144
Stalin, Joseph 38
Stephan (family) 180, 181
Stettin 152
Stritzke, Karl 7, 45, 145–147
Stuttgart 146, 156, 157, 160, 170

Tante Friedel *see* Friedel
Tapiau 134, 138
Thüringen 141
typhoid 65, 66, 71, 85, 104, 112, 119, 122, 123, 142, 148

United States 6, 8, 21, 41, 55, 166–168, 171–173, 178, 179, 181, 182

Winter-Hilfe 77
World War I 30, 152

YMCA 178–180

www.ingramcontent.com/pod-product-compliance
Ingram Content Group UK Ltd.
Pitfield, Milton Keynes, MK11 3LW, UK
UKHW041842150726
7214IPUK00015B/112